"Clearly written, powerfully argued and thoroughly
launches a major challenge to the current speciesist pa
its reader along the exciting path of a personal transfo
but foreshadow a commitment to a larger social transfo............."

Paola Cavalieri, *Philosopher, and author of* The Great
Ape Project: Equality Beyond Humanity.

"*Making a Stand for Animals* is a powerful plea for a radical change in our attitudes to animals, and in the way we treat them. I hope it will be widely read
and that many readers will act on Oscar Horta's suggestions."

Peter Singer, *Professor of Bioethics, Princeton University,
USA, and author of* Animal Liberation.

"An inspiring and ideal book to recommend to those who are beginning to
walk the path of animal liberation, or to those who are totally unaware of it
and wish to approach the subject. Written in an agile and easy-to-understand
way, it provides simple and convincing arguments for the defense of animals,
going through all possible approaches. Definitely, a book not to be missed!"

Alexandra Navarro, *National University of La Plata,
Argentina, Director of the Latin American Institute of
Critical Animal Studies.*

"Oscar Horta's arguments are creative, inspirational, well-aimed at popular
debates, and well-formulated to catch the attention of people being awakened
to these issues, willing to learn more, and intellectually curious as well as
morally concerned."

Steve Sapontzis, *Professor Emeritus, California State
University, USA, and author of* Morals,
Reason, and Animals.

"*Making a Stand for Animals* is a powerfully written and easily read book that
highlights the most pressing issues of animal protection and the necessity
to extend the legal protection to the voiceless. The book sheds light on the
very important issue of speciesism, which is oftentimes skipped or not drawn
attention to. Both animal rights activists and experienced lawyers and profes-
sors will find the book very inspiring."

Lu Shegay, *Managing Director of the Institute of
Animal Law of Asia.*

"In his excellently argued book *Making a Stand for Animals*, Oscar Horta presents a comprehensive analysis of speciesism and outlines how we can most
effectively change the plight of animals – both domesticated and wild ones.
His accessible book is a must-read for anyone interested in the question of
what we owe to animals."

Angela Martin, *Department of Philosophy, University of
Basel, Switzerland.*

"Oscar Horta's arguments are convincingly lucid and accessible enough for enthusiasts who are either inquisitive or sceptical about the justification of making a stand for animals. An interesting and compelling read, it rejuvenates the pursuit of hope for nonhuman animals."

Adewale O. Owoseni, *Department of Philosophy,*
University of Ibadan, Nigeria.

"This well-written, accessible book makes a powerful case for ending the exploitation of domesticated animals. It's also the first book of its kind to seriously discuss the incredibly important problem of wild animal suffering. Wild animals need our help, too, and the animal rights movement needs this book."

Kyle Johannsen, *Trent University, Canada, and author of*
Wild Animal Ethics.

"Oscar Horta makes a compelling argument for expanding our moral circle to include all sentient beings. His accessible and witty book does not only outline what this implies but is itself a prime example of a growing movement in academia that is no longer content with discussing ideas but actually aims to inspire real-life change towards a better world. Highly recommended."

Jens Tuider, *Philosopher and International*
Director of ProVeg.

"*Making a Stand for Animals* is a stimulating and illuminating introduction to animal ethics. It offers a highly accessible and engaging reading for newcomers as well as an insightful approach for readers with more experience thinking about the topic."

Núria Almirón, *Universitat Pompeu Fabra, Spain and*
Co-Director, UPF-Centre for Animal Ethics.

"Though there are many introductions to animal ethics, Oscar Horta has managed to craft something new. This book offers a host of carefully constructed thought experiments, reflections on the importance of shaping the far future, a helpful frame for pursuing activism, and much more—enriching discussions about animals in or beyond the classroom."

Bob Fischer, *Texas State University, USA.*

"Horta's writing combines the logic of a professional philosopher with the engaging style of a work of fiction. His arguments are lucid and compelling; the descriptions of industrial animal harms are vivid. Not all will agree with Horta's conclusions – the vast majority of humans consume animal products. But sentience, and avoiding speciesism, demand that we should be challenged by his ideas to rethink our own practices."

Steven P. McCulloch, *Senior Lecturer in Human*
Animal Studies, University of Winchester, UK.

"*Making a Stand for Animals* explains why concern for nonhuman animals is a matter of justice, and why adopting veganism leads to a more favourable environment to help dismantle speciesist prejudice. With a clear writing style, logical structure and plenty of useful citations, this book has wide appeal. It will introduce and inspire a wide range of new readers to this important subject and motivate seasoned vegans and animal rights activists to revisit, further explore and debate issues on the scope of our moral duty to other animals."

Jeanette Rowley, *Founder of the International Vegan Rights Alliance.*

Making a Stand for Animals

Engaging and thought-provoking, this book examines how humans see and treat other animals and argues that we should extend equal consideration and respect to all beings, human and nonhuman alike.

Our world is plighted by 'isms' such as racism and sexism, but we may have overlooked a very important one: speciesism. Speciesism is a form of discrimination against those who don't belong to a certain species. It drives us to see nonhuman animals as objects, rather than individuals with their own interests and with the ability to feel and suffer. This book questions all of the assumptions speciesism is based upon. It raises many challenging questions over humans' very complicated attitudes toward other animals. Thinking about how animals are used as well as the suffering of wild animals, and what the future may be for all beings, this book calls for society to seriously take into account the interests of all animals.

For all who care about animals, or simply how to make the world a better place, this book is essential reading.

Oscar Horta is an animal activist and moral philosopher at the Department of Philosophy and Anthropology at the University of Santiago de Compostela (USC), Spain. He is one of the co-founders of the organization Animal Ethics. He is known for his work on the concept of speciesism and the moral consideration of nonhuman animals, as well as on wild animal suffering.

Making a Stand for Animals

Oscar Horta

Routledge
Taylor & Francis Group
LONDON AND NEW YORK

earthscan
from Routledge

First published 2022
by Routledge
4 Park Square, Milton Park, Abingdon, Oxon OX14 4RN

and by Routledge
605 Third Avenue, New York, NY 10158

Routledge is an imprint of the Taylor & Francis Group, an informa business

© 2017 Oscar Horta

Initially published in Spanish as *Un paso adelante en defensa de los animales* by Plaza y Valdés.

English translation © 2022 Oscar Horta

British Library Cataloguing-in-Publication Data
A catalogue record for this book is available from the British Library

Library of Congress Cataloging-in-Publication Data
A catalog record has been requested for this book

ISBN: 978-1-032-25977-2 (hbk)
ISBN: 978-1-032-25975-8 (pbk)
ISBN: 978-1-003-28592-2 (ebk)

DOI: 10.4324/9781003285922

Typeset in Bembo
by codeMantra

Contents

List of cases, definitions and featured explanations

Acknowledgments

I'm thankful to all those who have contributed to making this book better than it would otherwise be. In particular, preparing the English translation of the book was a bit of a group effort where I was helped by several people, including Leah McKelvie, Gary O'Brien, Cyndi Rook, and Ricardo Torres. I am very grateful for their help. I also want to thank Olaia Freiría and Sara Lago, as well as Paola Cavalieri, Victor Crespo, Daniel Dorado, Catia Faria, Zoë Gumm, Christian Koeder, Angela K. Martin, Eze Paez, and Steve Sapontzis, all of whom helped me to improve the book in different ways.

I am also very grateful to those who insisted that this book should be written, in particular to Marcos de Miguel, as well as to my editor Hannah Ferguson, for her patience and for believing in this book since the beginning.

Finally, I would also like to thank, more generally, those who at one time or another sent me their criticisms of other things I previously wrote on the points addressed in the book. This has allowed me to correct many mistakes that would otherwise probably still be present here.

Introduction

Teresa runs for her life

Teresa has been running for a very long time now, following the course of the River Agrò. She's in real danger. Eventually, she reaches the sea at Santa Teresa di Riva, on the Sicilian coast, more than 15 miles from the place where she had been held captive and fled from. Desperate to save herself, she jumps into the water and starts swimming across the sea toward the coast of Calabria. She continues for three hours, and manages to swim for a kilometer. However, a boat of the Italian Coast Guard is chasing her, and getting closer.

Eventually, the Coast Guard catches up to her. At this point Teresa is totally exhausted, but she keeps fighting frantically to avoid being captured. Finally, however, she's caught and brought on board. Once they land her back in Sicily she makes a final effort and tries to flee again. But she's tired and her efforts are hopeless. Teresa's attempt to escape thus comes to an end.

Teresa is a cow who escaped from a farm in a Sicilian village called Castiglione di Sicilia. Other cows on the farm have shown symptoms of brucellosis and so it's been decided that Teresa will be killed because of the risk that she has this disease too. Her prospects now are gloomy indeed.

However, Teresa's story catches the attention of the media, and soon raises much interest in Italy and abroad. The people who learn about it are amazed that this animal could fight so hard in order to survive. A big campaign is started with the aim of saving her life. They name her Teresa after the town where she jumped into the sea. Because of the pressure of public opinion it is finally announced that her life will be spared.

This sounds like fiction, but it's a true story. It took place in May 2011.[1] The year is important, as it would have been impossible for it to have occurred much earlier. Had it happened just a few decades before, Teresa would certainly have been killed, just like the rest of the cows on the farm she escaped from.

DOI: 10.4324/9781003285922-1

This story thus shows that the attitudes people have toward animals today aren't the same as they were in the past. One might think that this is a speculative claim, as this is just an anecdotal case. But there is other evidence supporting this claim. A famous Gallup Poll survey concerning attitudes toward animals carried out in the United States in 2015 revealed some remarkable results. Thirty-two percent of people responded that, in their view, animals should be given the same rights as human beings (62% said that they deserve some protection, but that it is still acceptable to use them for human benefit, while only 3% responded that they deserve no protection). By contrast, in 2008, only 25% responded that animals and humans should have the same rights.[2]

We must, however, be very careful when considering the results of surveys like this one, as they don't give us a clear picture of what people really think. It's true that many people claim they care about animals. But they make this claim without a very clear idea of what it really means. If they truly cared about animals, this concern would have to be reflected in their behavior, but in most cases, this is clearly not so. Let's think about what would happen if one in three people were really convinced that humans and other animals should have the same rights. If this were really so, the situation of animals would be very different. However, surveys such as this one do tell us something. They show that there is some concern for animals in today's societies, concern which didn't exist only one or two generations before. In fact, this can be seen without surveys. If we look around us, we can see that there are more people who care about animals and their situation. It's not unusual to meet people who actively defend animals, or that this subject is featured in the media from time to time. The organizations defending animals are getting more and more support. There are also more and more publications, books, and websites on this topic. Different people, in different occupations and situations, are taking a stand in defense of animals. This means this position is becoming more and more visible in modern societies.

What is most remarkable is that this situation is relatively new. There have always been those who defended animals, but throughout history they have usually been a minority. This change in attitudes toward animals began in the 1970s, and became widespread in a very short period of time. What was the reason for this change in attitudes? And how did it happen so fast? Why are so many people now concerned about what happens to animals?

Some people can't figure out why this change happened. They sometimes suppose that those involved in defending animals simply happen to like animals. There are even those who think this is some kind of hobby for them, just as other people may like music, sport, art, or reading. They sometimes believe therefore that this interest in animals has spread in recent years just as other hobbies sometimes do, as fashions and trends come and go.

The real explanation, however, is very different. Those who defend animals need not be people who like them. More importantly, they don't see their concern as a mere hobby. They consider our treatment of animals a very serious issue which has nothing to do with their personal interests—they see it as a matter of justice.

The following example may give a clearer idea of what this means. Consider the situation of human beings in need (people living in extreme poverty, women who are the victims of trafficking, children in wars…). No one would say that those who care for these people and actively work to change their situation do so as a hobby. That would be ridiculous. It would be just as absurd to think that they do it because they happen to like these people in need, or because they are fond of them. Their motivation is due to entirely different reasons. The people who have worked for these causes have done so because the human beings they defend are suffering and in need of solidarity and help. They would never say that their concern is merely a personal matter. Rather, they think that working to help people in such situations is a matter of justice. They want everyone to become aware of the situations of these people and to appreciate just how important it is to do something to help them.

Those who are committed to the cause of animals have the same attitude. They think that we shouldn't be indifferent to what happens to animals. They think that this question of justice is of upmost importance. Why do they think this? That is what this book is about. The following chapters will try to explain the reasons supporting this position.

The most important of those reasons is actually a very simple one. In a nutshell, animals can suffer. And suffering doesn't feel bad for humans alone. It feels bad for any being who can suffer. Pain is always pain. In the same way, living happily free from harm is good both for humans and for animals from other species. So, why should we only care about what happens to human beings? Why shouldn't we worry that other beings suffer or have their lives threatened? Most of us believe that, to the extent that we can, we should refrain from harming others, and that we should help those who need it. Why should we do so only in the case of humans, given that other beings can be harmed too?

This is a very simple idea. Chapter 1, "Speciesism: a form of discrimination," will try to clarify it in more detail. It will also explain some ways in which this idea can be criticized, as well as the responses that can be given to those objections. Chapter 2, "Feeling and suffering," will present the existing evidence that not only human beings but also many other beings can have experiences and suffer. It will also discuss the reasons why this is important. Chapter 3, "Harming animals," will describe the situation of the animals that are exploited by humans. As we will see, this is very different from what many people, possibly most of us, imagine. It is vastly worse. Given this, and in light of the reasons to respect animals, Chapter 4, "Making the connection," will explain the case for rejecting such exploitation. It will argue that the reasons to do so are much more intuitive than we may think at first. This is something that may be new to many people. For this reason, Chapter 5, "Living without exploiting animals: questions and answers," will try to clarify some doubts that may arise when we think about it. Chapter 6, "In defense of animals!" will explain why, in addition to not harming animals, we also have reasons to help them when they need it, both in the case of those who have been domesticated and of those who live in the wild. This chapter will also explain the divergences between the defense of animals and environmentalism. The chapter will also argue that it is important to be concerned not just with what is happening now but also with how the future, including the long-term future, will be for all sentient beings. Finally, Chapter 7 will briefly summarize the conclusions that follow from the previous chapters and will show how getting involved in the defense of all sentient beings can make a difference. It will claim that, by doing so, we'll have the chance of achieving a difference far more significant than initially seemed possible. For this reason, this concluding chapter will have the subtitle "making a stand for a better world."

In general, the book is intended to be as simple and clear as possible. This is somewhat complicated to do. It's often hard to say things easily, and it's complex to present them in a simple way. But, fortunately, the reasons for questioning our attitudes toward animals are pretty straightforward even though the implications of doing so are vast and sometimes unexpected. They can be easily understood if we keep an open mind.

In fact, the main obstacle to thinking about such ideas is not that they are difficult. Rather, it's the desire not to think about any new idea, and to continue to think and behave as usual, believing that we needn't learn anything beyond what we are already familiar with. This conservative attitude has traditionally been widely supported. But, in the long run, we can undermine it, even if progress is very slow, and leave it behind.

This has happened little by little with many ideas from the past, such as the belief that the Earth is the center of the universe, or the idea that human slavery is legitimate. And so it is beginning to happen now with the idea that animals are just things that do not deserve any consideration. This view has been widely prevalent traditionally, and for sure it still lives on. But it is being challenged. With each new person who rejects it, a change is taking place for the animals. Perhaps you are such a person. In the following pages, you will find a lot of arguments and information to encourage you to reflect on this. But, at the end of the day, the choice will be yours.

Notes

1 Sanna, A. (2011) "Milano: Veggie Pride, in piazza nel nome della mucca Teresa", *NewNotizie*, June 17, http://newnotizie.it/2011/06/17/milano-veggie-pride-in-piazza-mucca-teresa. The news about Teresa appeared in journals from different countries. Unfortunately, the English speaking media didn't cover it.
2 Riffkin, R. (2015) "In U.S., more say animals should have same rights as people", *Gallup Poll*, May 18, http://gallup.com/poll/183275/say-animals-rights-people.

aspx. According to the results of another poll carried out that same year by the animal organization Faunalytics, 70% of the people in the United States would be in favor of animal protection. See Faunalytics (2015) "Seven in 10 U.S. adults have a favorable impression of the animal cause", *Blog, Faunalytics*, http://faunalytics.org/seven-in-10-u-s-adults-have-a-favorable-impression-of-the-animal-cause-2. Faunalytics has continued to do similar studies in subsequent years which have yielded similar results. See Tyler, L. (2019) "Animal tracker 2019: Contradictions in public opinion", *Blog, Faunalytics*, https://faunalytics.org/animal-tracker-2019-contradictions-in-public-opinion; see also Faunalytics (2019) *Animal tracker survey, Faunalytics*, https://faunalytics.org/animaltracker.

Chapter 1

Speciesism
A form of discrimination

The Planet of the Apes

Let's start with an imaginary situation. Suppose some unexpected event alters the course of human evolution so that the descendants of current humans evolve by becoming less intelligent. After many generations, they end up as beings with cognitive capacities similar to those that most adult chimpanzees currently have. However, they still look like humans do today. For their part, the descendants of chimpanzees evolve in a way that makes them more intelligent. They end up having the capacities that most adult humans currently have.

It so happens that in this story, the future chimpanzees hunt humans down. They confine them in cages and exploit them for other purposes. That is, they treat them in ways humans currently treat chimpanzees.

As most of us know, a similar situation is presented in a series of films. What do we think about the way future chimpanzees behave in them? Do we approve of what they do to human beings? Most people who watch these films disapprove. There are some chimpanzees in the films who behave benevolently toward humans and that oppose the discrimination against them. And those who view these films think that these characters behave justly.

This situation is puzzling because many people who think this also support the current exploitation of animals. That is, they think it is acceptable to do to animals the same things that humans suffer in *The Planet of the Apes*, and this attitude seems contradictory. In this chapter, we examine whether it can be justified.

"Animals": what's in a name?

We can start by considering a small linguistic point that is revealing about our attitude toward animals. There's another curious point in *The Planet of the Apes* films. The future chimpanzees refer to the future humans, but not to

DOI: 10.4324/9781003285922-2

themselves, as "animals." This is interesting, as, today, we use that word with the opposite meaning, that is, we refer to chimpanzees, but not to human beings, as "animals."

Why is this? The reason is that the word "animals" is commonly used to name only those animals that are from a species different from ours. However, this meaning is inaccurate. Humans are not vegetables, fungi, or bacteria: like chimpanzees, we're animals (in fact, like them, we belong to what in biology is called the family of hominids, which is classified within the order of primates). This fact, which is taught in the natural sciences in schools, is fairly obvious. However, it contradicts the way we typically use the word "animal." We say "animals" when we should say "animals from species different from our own."

For this reason, in this book, terms such as "nonhuman animals" and other similar expressions are often used. Doing so allows us to use more accurate language and reminds us of the need to avoid this confusion.[1]

In fact, it's revealing that this remark is needed. It shows that many people feel uncomfortable with human beings being animals. We often want to think that we're special and apart from the rest,[2] which leads us to forget reality and to have a distorted view of the kind of beings humans are. However, this issue is not the main problem. The more serious issue is that we use this idea to try to justify our behavior toward other animals. Accordingly, we harm them in many different ways. We use them as we please and treat them in ways that we would never treat human beings. This difference in treatment has very serious consequences for them.

Introducing speciesism

This attitude toward nonhuman animals is very common. Therefore, it should be very easy to see, but it often goes unnoticed. This is because this attitude has traditionally been viewed as something normal, as everyday common sense, and it can be very hard for us to notice that our attitudes might be inappropriate or even harmful. In this regard, the lack of consideration for animals is not without precedent. Today and throughout history, human beings have been discriminated against for many reasons. These include sex or gender; skin color and physical features; social origin; sexual orientation; and intellectual and physical capabilities. Those who have benefited from this discrimination have usually considered these reasons legitimate. Today, however, many people believe they are totally unjustified, and with good reason. If someone suffers some harm, the fact that this individual has a certain skin color or is identified as a man or as a woman won't make them suffer any less, or make their suffering less important. What matters when it comes to respecting someone is not their circumstantial features such as their skin color; rather, it is the fact that they can suffer harm because of what we do. And our actions can cause very serious harm to the victims of discrimination. That's what matters.

In light of this, the question arises: Given the way we behave toward animals of species other than ours, couldn't we also be discriminating against them?

A growing number of people think so. In fact, there is a word for this belief. Among the names of the forms of discrimination suffered by human beings, the most well-known may be "racism" and "sexism." When it comes to our attitudes toward animals, there is a similar name, *speciesism*.

What is speciesism?

This word, "speciesism", has been in use for several decades and has been widely used in academia, research, and culture, as well as by the general public.[3] What does it mean? It's not difficult to guess, as it's analogous to other words we already know, such as those mentioned above: "racism" and "sexism." Let's change the words "sex" or "race," from which those terms derive, to "species," and we will understand its meaning. Speciesism is the discrimination against those who don't belong to a certain species. Discriminating against someone means treating them worse for unjustified reasons. If we discriminate against nonhuman animals, that is an instance of speciesism. So, in fact, we're dealing with a new word and using it to name something very old.

Increasingly, people believe that racism and sexism are unacceptable. What about speciesism? Is it acceptable? If so, how?

In the next section, we'll look at several answers to this question, and assess whether they are right.

"Humans matter most, just because"

Speciesism is often defended in a very simple way, which amounts to saying that humans matter "just because." This defense assumes that human beings are special *just* because we are human, that is, because of the species to which we belong, without any further reason.[4] This assumption doesn't provide reasons in favor of anything. It's just an affirmation without any justification.

This position is not always expressed clearly. For example, those who hold it sometimes state that ethics "by definition" only deals with human beings. However, in fact, this claim amounts to nothing more than stating that only human beings matter because we say so, without giving further explanation. This is what it means to defend something *just because*.

We usually think that this is not an appropriate way to defend any point of view. Suppose that someone said that racism is acceptable "just because." That would not be any justification at all. However, if it were valid to say "just because" in a certain case—for example, to defend speciesism—then it should be valid to do so to defend any other position. If we don't accept "just because" defenses of discrimination against certain human beings, then we shouldn't accept them in the case of speciesism either.

There are other reasons to deny that we should respect only those who belong to the species *Homo sapiens*. In fact, there is nothing magical that makes belonging to a certain species, by itself, something special. Consider the following.

Relatives in common

Imagine a row representing your ancestors on the maternal side. Your mother is in the first position. Just behind her is your grandmother and behind her your great-grandmother, followed by your great-great-grandmother, and so on. If we continue going backwards for only a few hundred generations, we will reach the Paleolithic. Now, if we keep traveling back through time, we will find the ancestor that humans have in common with animals of other species. We will reach a point where an ancestor of ours will also be the ancestor of other animals, such as chimpanzees and bonobos. In other words, suppose that next to the row with our ancestry, there is another row with the ancestry of chimpanzees. At some point we find an animal who is both our ancestor and the ancestor of chimpanzees, and the two rows will merge into one.

One might think that the line would have to be very long, perhaps long enough to circle the entire planet. In fact, the row would be a bit more than 90 miles long (close to 150 kilometers);[5] by train or car, we might pass it in less than one and a half hours. Furthermore, if we were to move further back in that line, beyond the point where we meet our common ancestor with chimpanzees, we would eventually reach other points where we would find our common ancestors with every other animal.

Now, think about all those ancestors of ours who we would pass in that hour and a half as we make our way along the row. They would be, so to speak, halfway between humans and other animals. Imagine that they still existed. Would we discriminate against them because they are not totally human? If so, at which point in the row would we do so? Would we draw a line somewhere dividing the row in two and say, "we will respect those before this point but not those who come after"?

The truth is that doing this would be quite arbitrary. In that row, there are no clear divisions at any particular point, only very small gradual differences from mothers to daughters. At present, different species are distinguished in a very marked way because the animals that once existed between each of them are no longer here. If they continued to exist, then there would be no clear point to make such a distinction.[6]

This argument suggests that belonging to a particular species is less important than it seems. However, in fact, we have even stronger reasons to affirm this. Consider the following case, which is, again, taken from a well-known story:

E.T. the extraterrestrial

An extraterrestrial being we call E.T. accidentally lands on Earth. Some human beings want to use him to do harmful research, and so they kidnap him. But there are others who care about him. A group of teenagers comes to the rescue. They finally manage to save him, and he's able to fly back home.

E.T. is not a human being. However, most people think that is not a reason for us not to care about him. Many people all around the world know the story of E.T., and most of them are happy that he is rescued, even though humans could benefit from experimenting on him. This happiness is clearly at odds with the idea that only human beings deserve full respect.[7]

In fact, there are many other examples of this in literature, cinema, and mythology. Let's take a look at some of them.

What happens if someone is not human?

Think about the following list of characters who appear in different stories (you may not know all these characters, but you probably know at least some of them): *The Lord of the Rings*'s hobbits, *Blade Runner's* replicants, the fairies featured in many tales, divinities such as Minerva or Venus, characters in films and shows such as Chewbacca or Spock, Pinocchio, Bambi, the androids in films and shows such as *Artificial Intelligence* or *Westworld*, or in Isaac Asimov's novels, Nemo the fish and so on.

These fictional characters have at least two things in common. The first is that they are not human beings. But this does not prevent us from caring about what happens to them when we see or read the stories in which they appear. This is due to the second thing they have in common: different as they are, all these characters can feel and suffer, and thus be affected by whatever may happen to them. This is true of many other celebrated characters from novels, movies, and popular traditions. We care about what happens to these characters, and we empathize with them. This shows that, for us to worry about what happens to someone, it is not necessary that they belong to the species *Homo sapiens*.

It may be argued that these are fictional characters. But that doesn't really make a difference here. If we see someone in a film torturing a child, we can tell whether that person is doing something morally objectionable without having to ask whether the film is entirely fictional or a true story. In fact, in some films and shows such as *Her*, *Tron*, or *Black Mirror*, there are even examples of pieces of software that feel and suffer, and we can see that in those films it's right to feel empathy for them and for other characters to defend them.

This being so, the conclusion is clear. There's nothing magical in human DNA that makes humans the only beings that are especially important. This means species alone can't be the reason to respect someone.

But maybe there's some other reason why we should give full respect only to humans. Maybe humans have some characteristics that other animals lack which makes them special. We will now see if this is so.

The idea that human beings matter more because of their intelligence, sympathy, or power

It's often claimed that we should respect only human beings because they are intelligent and other animals are not. According to this view, only human beings can have abstract thoughts, use a language, solve complex problems, etc., and due to this, other animals matter less or don't matter at all.

There is a different argument that is sometimes used to defend the same position. Some people say that we have a special feeling of sympathy or solidarity toward other human beings and that, in turn, we don't feel that sympathy toward other animals. According to this view, this sympathy justifies us in only respecting human beings.

In other cases, it is argued that humans are more powerful than other animals and it is legitimate for us to do what we please to animals[8] simply because we have the power to do so.

All these reasons (intelligence, sympathy, power, etc.) are very different, but they have been used to defend exactly the same position: that humans matter more than other animals. We will see next whether they are convincing or not.

False assumptions about the differences between humans and other animals

At first glance, the assumptions from which these arguments start may seem correct. On reflection though, we can see that they are not. To begin, consider intelligence. It's often said that only human beings are intelligent or rational, but this claim is inaccurate. It's incorrect to say that humans have intelligence or rationality and that other animals don't. Being intelligent or rational is not a matter of "all or nothing." Rather, there are differences in the degree and type of intelligence that we have. These differences are more marked among certain animals, and less so among others. But the fact that human beings possess a certain degree or type of intelligence doesn't mean that other animals don't have any. Each one has a different intelligence. This is something that was indicated already by a 3rd-century philosopher, Porphyry, who pointed out that while there are birds that fly higher than partridges, that doesn't mean that partridges don't fly.[9]

In addition, not all members of a species have the same level of intelligence. Not all dogs or all goats are equally intelligent. The same is true of humans. Some human beings have greater intellectual abilities than others. If we accept the claim that being smarter means deserving more respect, this will have serious consequences: there will be human beings who have moral priority over others. This doesn't sound good. Most of us think that the suffering of Marie Curie or Albert Einstein should not count more than that of other less intelligent human beings.

Those who don't want animals to be given full respect often say that in order for us to respect someone, they must have a certain *level* of intelligence. They also claim that level would be the one that human beings usually have. According to this argument, even though many nonhuman animals are very intelligent, none of them would reach that level.

By this reasoning, it may seem that we clearly separate human beings from other animals, and we justify having very different attitudes toward them. But this is not the case, because there are many human beings who don't reach that level of intelligence either. There are people with intellectual functional diversity who[10] because of some accident or disease, or perhaps for congenital reasons, have lower or much lower intellectual capacities than most adult human beings.

Traditionally, these people have suffered outrageous, humiliating, and discriminatory treatment, and they have been labeled with disrespectful slurs such as "feeble-minded" or "mentally retarded." Today, unfortunately, their situation is still far from optimal, and they continue to face a multitude of obstacles and inconsiderate and discriminatory attitudes. The struggle in their defense has been very long and continues today (for example, the United Nations Convention on the Rights of Persons with Disabilities did not become operative until 2008). Awareness of this form of discrimination has grown and attitudes are changing, though much remains to be done. However, this struggle is incompatible with the idea that those who are less intelligent deserve less respect. If we accept that idea, then we justify giving less respect to people with lower intellectual abilities.

Some might think that this issue is not very important because the number of human beings without complex intellectual capacities is very small. But that misses the point, for three important reasons:

First, even if it were the case, that wouldn't be of much comfort for all the human beings who suffer this discrimination. Even if they were few, they would still suffer. And the discrimination against them would be just as reprehensible.
Second, any human being (including you and me) might end up in such a situation in the future. It could happen to us at any time, for example, if we suffer an accident in which our brain is damaged.
Third, as a matter of fact, every human being has been in such a situation, at least at some point. At the beginning of their lives, babies and infants

have much lower intellectual abilities than adults, and their intelligence is lower than that of many nonhuman animals. This is not a simple opinion or an open question. It's a statement of fact. However, most of us understand that we must give infants full respect, no less than we give adult human beings.

There's a bad response to this argument and a good one. Some respond by saying that we must respect human children because they will become adults.[11] According to this claim, although babies and infants don't have intelligence equal to that of adults, they will when they grow up. This is the bad response, which doesn't work. To start with, the mere possibility of having a capacity in the future is not the same as having it. This is common sense. For example, I won't find a job as a pianist, because I can't play the piano. Nobody is going to hire me for that job just because I have the possibility of learning how to play, by taking lessons and practicing for a few years.

Furthermore, those who defend this argument seem to think that all human beings have the possibility of reaching adulthood and having complex intelligence, which, regrettably, is not so. Unfortunately, there are children who suffer from terminal diseases. They will never become adults. Moreover, if the only reason to give children respect is that in the future they will have certain capacities, then there would be no reason not to deprive these ill children of their lives.

For all the above reasons, this argument should be rejected. We can insist that children must be respected not because of the abilities that they will have in the future, but because, today, at the present moment, they can experience suffering and pleasure. This is the good response.

Similar considerations apply in the case of sympathy and power. There are many human beings with no relationships of solidarity, sympathy, or affection with anyone. Moreover, conflicts between human beings are widespread in the world. Human beings wage war and kill and enslave other humans. They inflict all kinds of harm on each other. You just need to watch the news to see that it's false that human beings in general feel sympathy for all the other members of their species. This may be the case for some, but not for everyone. If the only reason to respect someone was that others have actual sympathy for them, then many human beings would be in serious trouble. This would also be a very handy justification for racism, sexism, and other forms of discrimination. Those who defend such discrimination might simply claim that they feel more sympathy for those who have skin color or physical features similar to their own or more sympathy for men than for women. This doesn't seem acceptable at all. In fact, it seems very unfair that the respect someone deserves would depend on being liked by someone else or not.

We see something similar with power relations. There are many human beings in situations of weakness who suffer all kinds of exploitation, slavery, oppression, humiliation, etc. Does this justify our indifference to their fate? Does it justify their exploitation? Most of us would consider it to be totally unfair to harm someone by taking advantage of their weakness. But if we reject this idea, we can't use it as a reason not to respect animals. Here, the same thing happens as in the case of intelligence and sympathy.

This point can also be explained using the following analogy:

The fence

Think of a circle surrounded by a fence. Imagine that only those inside this circle should be respected. Imagine, further, that only those who fulfill a certain condition (intelligence, sympathy, power, etc.) will be able to enter the circle.

This is a way to visualize the arguments we've seen above. Those who use such arguments think that all human beings will meet those conditions and will enter the circle, and that the other animals are going to be left out. However, this is not what really happens. We have seen that many human beings do not meet these conditions. Thus, they will end up outside of the fence as well.

This exclusion has important consequences. If we think that all human beings should be respected, we will have to oppose the construction of this fence. But this requires rejecting the idea that intelligence, sympathy, or power is what matters when it comes to respecting someone.

Is there any other condition, different from those used to construct the fence, that guarantees that no human being will be discriminated against? Yes, there is. We can respect all the individuals who may be harmed or benefited by our actions. And these individuals are all those who can experience suffering or pleasure. This capacity is, therefore, what we should take into account. And this implies that we must also respect other animals that feel and suffer.

There are some who think that this explanation might be offensive to many human beings. They think that we are degrading them if we say that there are some humans who don't have certain intellectual capacities, that are in a position of weakness, or don't have positive relationships with anyone. But it's actually the other way around. We are *defending* them. By denouncing these arguments, we're vindicating the position that no one should be discriminated against because of their intelligence, sympathy, or power. Thus, not only are we siding with nonhuman animals, but we are also defending human beings who don't meet those conditions.

Those who argue in favor of speciesism can't defend other humans in this way. They claim that, in order to be respected, one must fulfill certain conditions that these human beings can't satisfy. They are promoting an idea that discriminates against these humans, even if they don't realize that they are doing so. We must show the flaws in this idea if we want all human beings to be respected. We must oppose the idea that, in order to be respected, one must have some degree of intelligence or power, or receive sympathy from others.[12]

In contrast, those who defend animals do have a reason to respect anyone who can feel suffering and enjoyment (whether human or not). The things we do have the potential to harm them.

What really matters?

In addition to what we have seen so far, there is another way to approach this issue. Consider the following cases, which are hypothetical but not impossible (they could, unfortunately, happen):

Twists that life can take

Imagine that we discovered that we have some condition that doesn't affect us now, but that will in the future. The disease has no cure. In addition, it will sooner or later substantially reduce our capacity to reason. However, we will continue to be able to experience suffering and pleasure.

Imagine now another situation. Suppose we know that in the future, for whatever reason, we will have to live in a place where nobody will have sympathy toward us. And we will find ourselves in a position of great weakness relative to other people.

Now, suppose that someone asks us whether we would consider it acceptable to be harmed and exploited from that moment onward if we were in those situations. Imagine that we can decide what is going to happen. In facing this decision, we find ourselves with two options:

Option 1. *No respect.* We can conclude that it's right to harm and exploit those who don't have a certain degree of intelligence, sympathy, or power. In this case, we will suffer that fate in the future. Meanwhile, we will be able to continue to harm nonhuman animals.

Option 2. *Respect everyone.* We can conclude that it's not fair to harm those who don't have that intelligence, sympathy, or power. Thus, we will be free from suffering that fate ourselves in the future. We will also be rejecting the claim that nonhuman animals can be harmed and discriminated against.

The truth is that in such a case, almost no one would find it acceptable to be exploited in the future. There may be some who think that it would be worth it for them to suffer this exploitation in order to be able to exploit animals first. However, the fact is that the cost of this exploitation would be much greater for these people than the benefit they would obtain from it. Maybe they don't see that now. But they would see it clearly if the time came for them to suffer all the things that animals suffer today.

Those who don't want to respect animals sometimes try to find an intermediate option. They want to find some way to grant themselves respect but without having to respect those who are in the same situation. As we have already seen, doing so is not possible. We have to choose either one option or the other. And, if we consider how our acts can harm other individuals, then we will choose the second: "Respect everyone." That is, respect everyone who needs it, regardless of their intelligence, whether we feel sympathy for them or not, or whether they belong to our own species or not.

In fact, this question is very simple. If we can harm someone, then why not try to avoid doing so? What is so special about intelligence, sympathy, or power that makes it the case that harming those who don't possess or receive them is OK?

Of course, no one denies that intelligence or the relationships we have with other people can cause us suffering or enjoyment in certain ways. Clearly, this is the case. For example, we can enjoy reading books or suffer thinking about political problems. But intelligence and relationships aren't necessary conditions for good or bad things to happen to us. It's possible to experience suffering and enjoyment even if we have very little intelligence, and even if no one has any sympathy toward us.[13]

The argument that speciesism is natural

Despite what we have just seen, there are some who say that we have to accept speciesism for a different reason, that is, that speciesism is inevitable because it's natural. They believe that it's natural or instinctive to have a special concern for those who belong to our own species.[14] They say that other animals also have it. According to this argument, there is nothing wrong with speciesism.

This argument doesn't work either, for two reasons.

First, our preferences do not justify discrimination against someone. It's sometimes said that we also tend to benefit members of our own family or our friends before others. But even those who accept this understand that it doesn't make it legitimate to kill or exploit other human beings, or to discriminate against them in other ways. For the same reason, it can't justify speciesism.

Second, the fact that a certain position is considered natural doesn't mean that it's good or that it has to be accepted or promoted. To start with, it's not exactly clear what it means to say that something is "natural," or that there are "natural" attitudes. People tend to think that it's something innate, which means that it's present in our genes. But this is very confusing, because our genetic constraints are always mediated by our education and socialization. In any case, the fact that something is natural doesn't necessarily mean that it is good or justifiable. There are many attitudes that are considered to arise from our natural tendencies that are undesirable or even reprehensible. Violent attitudes are a very clear example. Others could be selfishness, greed, or envy. When considering whether something is right or wrong, we should be indifferent to the fact that it is natural.

There are even more reasons that could be presented against this argument in favor of speciesism. This is because the same argument has been used to defend racism, homophobia, and sexism, among other forms of discrimination against groups of human beings. If we don't accept it in these cases, then we shouldn't do so in the case of animals either.

All this aside, there's no reason why we should accept that speciesism is something natural. There are people who oppose speciesism, which means that speciesism is not an inevitable attitude.[15] Moreover, it's also not true that all human beings have a tendency to respect all those who belong to their own species. Some may have that tendency, but it's not universal among humans. We have already seen that all over the world, human beings attack each other in a thousand different ways, which indicates that this tendency is not natural.

Finally, it's not right that speciesism is acceptable because animals of other species are speciesist. There are also reasons to reject this argument.

To start with, even if animals of other species were speciesist, that wouldn't justify you, I, or any other person who can take responsibility for their actions, being speciesist too. Many nonhuman animals act in ways that we would never consider acceptable, attacking each other violently, killing other animals in their own family, raping others, etc.

In addition, it is not true that nonhuman animals are speciesist. Contrary to what is sometimes believed, they don't act to favor members of their own species above the rest. Many animals simply care about themselves, not about others, whether or not they are members of their species. Others care only about themselves and their offspring. And others just care about their families or their own groups. But they don't care about other animals of their species, or privilege them (actually, they are often in conflict with these animals). They don't behave better toward them than toward animals of other species.

In short, it's not true that speciesism is natural. But even if it were, that wouldn't justify it in any way.

Tradition is no justification

Another way we may think that speciesism is justified is by considering that human societies have always been speciesist. But history provides many examples of things that were accepted by societies centuries ago which we now think are terrible, and this observation casts doubt on the idea that the fact that something is traditional or 'has always been like this' makes it ok.

A widely accepted injustice

Think of some society of the past in which human beings of certain minority groups were hunted down and exterminated. Suppose that this was accepted by the majority of the population. Does this acceptance mean that such discrimination is justified and that it would be legitimate for us to continue it?

In many societies of the past, people might have thought so. However, nowadays, opinions are usually different. To be sure, humans continue to discriminate against and harm each other terribly and there are many ways in which human beings are oppressed. But many people now see the horrors humans suffered in the past as unjustified. This shows that we can't trust something just because it's a tradition; the fact that some practice is traditional doesn't imply that it is justified.[16] Throughout history, human beings have routinely done and accepted things that now seem horrifying and unacceptable. Wars, massacres, mass rapes, and genocides have been carried out, and they were often considered perfectly acceptable by those who did them. But the fact that something has always been a certain way doesn't mean it's OK. What's more: the fact that in the past there have been so many societies that have seen nothing problematic in common practices that seem appalling to us today should lead us to question our own opinions of what is right and wrong. We are as likely to make mistakes as those who lived in the past were. Bear in mind, also, how many atrocities of the past have been relatively recent. It would be a remarkable coincidence if the moral views that are common today just happen to be the correct ones, especially if, as we see, there are also strong arguments against them.

Reasons that are impossible to demonstrate

Finally, there are some who want to justify speciesism by appealing to reasons different from those we have seen thus far. What these reasons have in common is that they can't be verified in any way. Along this line, there are some who claim that humans are "the chosen species" or that human beings have a "dignity" or "intrinsic value" that other beings lack.[17] These phrases may give us the impression that those who use them must be right since they speak so eloquently and use such high concepts. But this is not the case.

Extravagant wording can't be a substitute for arguments. Let's ask ourselves: what exactly gives all humans such "dignity"? We already saw that it can't be intelligence or any other such capacity. The only characteristic that all human beings (and only they) have is human DNA. But, as we have seen before, there's nothing magical in our DNA that gives us some special dignity.

Another common way of defending the view that humans are special for reasons that can't be corroborated is to appeal to religion.[18] Some people claim, for instance, that humans deserve special respect because only they have immortal souls. However, for several reasons, this claim is hardly convincing. First, we have no proof that souls exist. So, only people who believe in them could accept the argument. But religious people can also reject this argument. Suppose it were true that immortal souls exist. Why should only humans but no other beings who can suffer have them?[19] Having a soul can't be based on a capacity like intelligence or power because then some humans who lack those capacities wouldn't have souls.

What's more, consider what would really follow if that were the case:

If humans (alone) had immortal souls

Suppose that, for whatever supernatural reason, humans have souls that live forever. That would mean that for anything we do to a human being, she or he could be compensated in the afterlife. Suppose now that, on the contrary, nonhuman animals don't have souls. That means they can't be compensated for whatever we do to them. So think of those cases where very bad things are done to them. For instance, someone tortures them until they die. If they lack immortal souls, then there is no possible way they could be compensated for their suffering. This means that if only humans had immortal souls, it would be much worse to harm nonhuman animals than humans, because the harm inflicted on them would be beyond reparation.

This example shows that the argument doesn't work. In fact, it implies just the opposite of what it is intended to show.

In other cases, speciesism is defended by appealing to other religious arguments. Some people argue that the books and traditions they consider sacred make some claims that support speciesism. We must note, though, that sacred books also typically make other points that, if interpreted literally, entail things we find terrible. They often condone xenophobia, the domination of women, wars of conquest, genocide, and slavery, as well as killing people for their sexual practices, etc. For this reason, many people believe that these types of passages shouldn't be understood literally. But if this is the case, then there's no reason to have a different attitude when it comes to speciesism.

In addition, these religious traditions contain other ideas that are favorable toward sentient animals. Islam and Judaism hold that we should be compassionate toward other animals and not harm them unnecessarily. This is one reason there are growing numbers of Jewish and Muslim people who stop harming and using animals, as we don't need to do so. As for Christians, they believe that Jesus existed and acted in certain ways, which Christians take as their paradigm of moral behavior. They also believe Jesus often made sacrifices for the sake of those who were weaker than him, suffering torment in order to help human beings. So, what would it mean for us to behave like this? What would helping those who are in a position weaker than our own entail? For one thing, it would entail respecting and helping nonhuman animals who are in such a position.

In addition, many religious people think that the best possible state of affairs would be a paradise on earth like the one that existed at the beginning of time. In this earthly paradise, nonhuman animals neither killed each other nor were they killed by humans. Other religious traditions, though also compatible with speciesist views, hold more explicit views favoring concern for other animals. Certain Hindu, Buddhist, and especially Jain views are examples. Similar reasons could be presented in the case of other religious traditions as well. As a result, there are some who claim that religion gives them reasons to oppose animal exploitation.

In fact, among those who reject speciesism, there are both people who have religious views and those who don't. This shows that speciesism has to do with our attitudes, more than it does with religion. Those who support speciesism often want to use religion to justify it. For this reason, they see their religion through speciesist eyes, even though they could avoid doing so. This happens because those who have religious beliefs often project their values onto them.[20]

In the early 20th century an English priest, William Inge, assumed this idea in making a point aimed at denouncing our attitudes toward nonhuman animals. He wrote:

> We have enslaved the rest of the animal creation, and have treated our distant cousins in fur and feathers so badly that beyond doubt, if they were able to formulate a religion, they would depict the Devil in human form.[21]

This is indeed a thought we can all agree with, regardless of what our views about religion are.

Excuses are sometimes used, rather than arguments

So far, we have seen that quite a few arguments have been given to defend speciesism, and they differ significantly from each other. Among those who use them are people who intend to reflect honestly about the arguments in order to discover the truth. But in some cases, what they are actually looking for is an excuse not to respect animals. This happens when we are aiming to reach a conclusion that we like, and so we try to find the arguments that best fit our purposes.

It's no surprise that many people do this. We usually reject injustice when we are the victims of it. But it's harder to do so when others are the victims, especially when we are the ones benefitting from the harms they suffer.

It is for this reason that very strict requirements, such as having very complex intelligence, are sometimes claimed to be necessary for someone to deserve respect. These conditions are designed to be impossible to satisfy by nonhuman animals. But consider this. There are certain abilities that human beings don't have that animals do possess. For example, birds have the capacity to fly by flapping their wings. And animals such as bats and dolphins have the sense of echolocation ("sonar"), which enables them to use sound to determine where faraway objects are situated. Interestingly, no one ever says that in order to deserve respect, it's necessary to have any of those capacities. If that were so, then we would have to respect those animals who have them, and no others. We would have to respect bats more than dogs or humans. But no one ever defends this. Nonetheless, let's reflect on the following supposition:

If humans (alone) had wings

Imagine that only humans had wings to fly, or that only they had the sense of echolocation. We can bet that there would then be many people who would say that humans should be respected more than other animals because only humans have those capacities. People would say things like this: "After all, the capacity to fly is what has allowed humans to elevate ourselves over the rest of the animals and to see the world in a way no other animal can." Or: "Echolocation allows us to have a unique perspective of the world, without which we would be limited beings like all other animals."

Why would this happen? Because, among those who defend speciesism, there are many people who argue not with the aim of examining what is fair, but only with the intention of justifying the attitudes toward nonhuman animals they already have.[22]

This suggests that there's something very influential behind the fact that speciesism is still widely accepted. It's a bias we have, that is, an opinion we hold prior to having judged the matter in a neutral way. This is what the word "*prejudice*" means. We have a speciesist prejudice because it is sometimes hard for us to reflect deeply on whether what we do to animals of other species is fair, without simply taking our prior beliefs for granted.

Judging the issues without cheating

We may wonder whether there is a different way of examining this issue in an unbiased way. And there is. Consider the following example:

How to cut a cake

Suppose you have to cut a cake into four pieces that will be distributed among four people, including you. You want to eat as large a piece of the cake as possible. If you know that you can pick any piece you want and you are selfish, then you might cut the cake very unequally. You might cut a large piece for yourself and leave three very small pieces for the others.

But imagine you have to cut the cake into four pieces, and then the rest of the people will choose the pieces they want. You'll get the last remaining piece. If everyone, including you, wants to eat as large a piece as possible, then you will cut the cake into four very similarly sized pieces. You'll try to have four slices that are each as large as possible.

Now, suppose someone asked us which of the two forms of cutting the cake is more just. How would we respond? It seems pretty clear that the majority would agree that the second one is. But why is the second one more just? Because it makes you act impartially.[23] In the first case, you know your own future situation, and you favor yourself over the others. In the second one, you don't know, and you design a scenario in which everyone is considered fairly. So, in order to envision behavior toward nonhuman animals that would be just, consider the following case.

Which of these worlds would you prefer to live in?

Imagine now that we were able to decide between two worlds we could live in. In that extraordinary scenario, we could choose a world where people are speciesist or one where they are not. In the speciesist world, they give humans a high degree of respect, but they don't pay the same respect to other sentient beings. As a result, humans are benefited in many respects. But nonhuman animals are harmed in some particularly awful ways.

Many people would choose a speciesist world, which is clear, as many people today are speciesist. But let's add a further qualification to this scenario. Let's add a requirement of impartiality. The example of the cake shows that our decisions are more just when they are made impartially. Let's introduce a condition to enforce impartiality.

How could we do that? Suppose you didn't know if you were going to live as a human or as some other animal. There's a lottery and you could come into existence as any sentient being. It's not that you would have a 50% chance of being born as a human and a 50% chance of existing as a nonhuman animal. Rather, the lottery aims to represent reality more closely, so there's one ticket for each sentient being. There are currently approximately 7.9 billion humans. The number of domesticated animals is much higher, and the number of animals living in the wild is higher still. Consequently, the odds that you will come into existence as a human are very small.

Which world would you choose if you had to make your decision according to this impartial method?

If we are honest, we will hardly say that our decision would be to choose the world with speciesism. This decision is very revealing. It shows that if we think about speciesism in an impartial way, that is, in a just way, then we'll conclude that speciesism should not be accepted. In other words, this decision shows us that speciesism is unjust.

This conclusion may be surprising at first. But if we think about it, we can see it is quite intuitive. There are many people who protest when they are harmed for the benefit of others. They view it as an injustice. But we demonstrate truly just behavior when we have the opportunity to benefit ourselves by harming others, yet we refuse to do so.

The answer: leaving speciesism behind

Throughout this chapter, we have seen that speciesism is sometimes defended "just because," which means that no justification is given for it. In other cases, it is argued that only those who are very intelligent or strong, or only those for whom we feel sympathy deserve respect. But this entails failing to respect many human beings. In addition, what matters in order to be able to be harmed by what others do to us is being able to feel suffering and pleasure. How intelligent or powerful we are, or how much sympathy others feel for us, is not what causes us to feel pain if we are beaten, or to be harmed if we are killed. Accordingly, those reasons fail to justify speciesism, as does the appeal to what is natural or to religion. In contrast, if we imagine ourselves in the situation that the animals we discriminate against are in, then we can see that we wouldn't want to suffer what they suffer.

All this leads to the following conclusion: defending animals is not a matter of personal preference or a hobby. It is not a simple matter of beneficence and compassion either. Certainly, we usually understand that we should have a compassionate attitude toward others. This attitude should extend to animals of other species. But, in addition to this, most of us think that we shouldn't discriminate against anyone. If this is so with human beings, then it should be so in the case of other animals as well, because they can also feel suffering and pleasure. In the next chapter, we will see why this is so.

Notes

1 It would be more accurate to call those animals that do not belong to our species "non-*Homo sapiens* animals," although in this book, for simplicity, this point has not been argued for. In biology, species are classified into genera. Thus, for example, European bisons, *Bison bonasus*, and American bisons, *Bison Bison* (together with other species already extinct) are grouped within the genus *Bison*, that of bisons. The name of each species is made up of two terms. The first is that of the genus within which the species is found, and is therefore common to all species belonging to the same genus. The second, in turn, is the one that differentiates the species in particular, that is, it is the one that specifies it (thus, a *Bison bonasus* is a bison of the *bonasus* species, the European one). Similarly, the species *Homo sapiens* belongs to the genus *Homo*, to which other currently extinct species belong, including *Homo luzonensis*, *Homo floresiensis*, *Homo habilis*, or *Homo erectus*, among others. And, just as in Latin the term "*Bison*" means simply "bison," the Latin word "*Homo*" means "human." That is, it is those who belong to the human genus, *Homo*, that are humans. Today, the only humans left in the world are those who belong to the species *Homo sapiens*, because all the other species that belonged to this genus have become extinct. But the members of the other species, like those mentioned above, despite not being *Homo sapiens*, were also *Homo*, that is, human. Due to this, distinctions such as those that are sometimes made in the media between, for example, "humans and Neanderthals," or between humans and other members of the genus *Homo*, come from a confusion between a genus and a species, that is, between humanity and the species *Homo sapiens*.

2 See Dunayer, J. (2001) *Animal equality: Language and liberation*, Derwood: Ryce; Burgat, F. (2005) *Liberté et inquiétude de la vie animale*, Paris: Kimé; Yates, R. (2010) "Language, power and speciesism", *Critical Society*, 3, 11–19; Taylor, N. (2013) *Humans, animals, and society: An introduction to human-animal studies*, New York: Lantern and Leach, S.; Kitchin, A.; Sutton, R. & Dhont, K. (2021) "Speciesism in everyday language", *PsyArXiv*, http://doi.org/10.31234/osf.io/ktvgx.

3 The word "speciesism" was initially used in 1970 in a pamphlet that has been reprinted in Ryder, R. D. (2010 [1970]) "Speciesism again: The original leaflet", *Critical Society*, 2, 1–2. For a more detailed definition of this term, you can find some explanations of it in Horta, O. (2010a) "What is speciesism?", *Journal of Agricultural and Environmental Ethics*, 23, 243–266. See also Horta, O. & Albersmeier, F. (2020) "Defining speciesism", *Philosophy Compass*, 15, 1–9 and Albersmeier, F. (2021) "Speciesism and speciescentrism", *Ethical Theory and Moral Practice*, 24, 511–527.

Other useful works about speciesism include Gompertz, L. (1997 [1824]) *Moral inquiries on the situation of man and of brutes*, Lewiston: Edwin Mellen; Salt, H. S. (1980 [1892]) *Animals' rights: Considered in relation to social progress*, London: Centaur Press; Singer, P. (2009 [1975]) *Animal liberation: A new ethics for our treatment of animals*, New York: New York Review/Random House; Clark, S. R. L. (1984 [1977]) *The moral status of animals*, New York: Oxford University Press; Rollin, B. (2006 [1981]) *Animal rights and human morality*, Amherst: Prometheus; Regan, T. (2004 [1983]) *The case for animal rights*, Berkeley: University of California Press; Sapontzis, S. F. (1987) *Morals, reason, and animals*, Philadelphia: Temple University Press; Spiegel, M. (1988) *The dreaded comparison: Human and animal slavery*, London: Heretic Books; Regan, T. & Singer, P. (eds.) (1989) *Animal rights and human obligations*, Englewood Cliffs: Prentice Halls; Rachels, J. (1990) *Created from animals: The moral implications of Darwinism*, Oxford: Oxford University Press; Pluhar, E. B. (1995) *Beyond prejudice: The moral significance of human and nonhuman animals*, Durham: Duke University Press; DeGrazia, D. (1996) *Taking animals* seriously: Mental life and moral status, Cambridge: Cambridge University Press; Bernstein, M. H. (1998) On moral considerability: An essay on who morally matters, Oxford: Oxford University Press and (2015) The moral equality of humans and animals, Basingstoke: Palgrave Macmillan; Cavalieri, P. (2001) The animal question: Why nonhuman animals deserve human rights, Oxford: Oxford University Press; Steiner, G. (2005) Anthropocentrism and its discontents: The moral status of animals in the history of Western philosophy, Pittsburg: University of Pittsburg Press; Ryder, R. D. (2011) Speciesism, painism and happiness: A morality for the twenty-first century, Exeter: Imprint Academic; Lepeltier, T.; Bonnardel, Y. & Sigler, P. (2018) La révolution antispéciste, Paris: Presses Universitaires de France; Caviola, L. (2019) How we value animals: The psychology of speciesism, PhD thesis, Oxford: University of Oxford; Giroux, V. (2020) L'antispécisme, Paris: Presses Universitaires de France; Cunha, L. C. (2021) Uma breve introdução à ética animal: Desde as questões clássicas até o que vem sendo discutido atualmente, Curitiba: Appris and Jaquet, F. (2021) "A debunking argument against speciesism", Synthese, 198, 1011–1027.

4 This view has been held, for example, in Diamond, C. (1995) The realistic spirit: Wittgenstein, philosophy and the mind, Cambridge: MIT Press; Posner, R. A. (2004) "Animal rights: Legal, philosophical and pragmatic perspectives", in Sunstein, C. R. & Nussbaum, M. C. (eds.) Animal rights: Current debates and new directions, Oxford: Oxford University Press, 51–77 and in Williams, B. (2006) "The human prejudice", in his Philosophy as a humanistic discipline, Princeton: Princeton University Press, 135–152. This is a fairly common idea, even if it clashes with the idea that the way we treat others should have some kind of justification; see Caviola, L.; Everett, J. A. & Faber, N. S. (2019) "The moral standing of animals: Towards a psychology of speciesism", Journal of Personality and Social Psychology, 116, 1011–1029.

5 The calculation of the distance in the line is done by estimating that each mother occupies a bit more than one and a half feet (less than 50 centimeters) in length, that there is a new generation every 25 years, and that, according to what we know today, humans, chimpanzees, and bonobos may have separated approximately 7.5 million years ago (although they probably continued to mix until much later). Following the same criterion, before reaching that point, we would have found, for example, our common ancestry with Homo erectus less than 25 miles (around 40 kilometers) away and Neanderthals about 6 miles (almost 10 kilometers) away. On this see Dawkins, R. (1993) "Gaps in the mind", in Cavalieri, P. and Singer, P. (eds.) The Great Ape project: Equality beyond humanity, Nueva York: St. Martin's Griffin, pp. 80–87.

6 This may be seen, for example, in the scientific discussion that took place around whether to classify Neanderthals as a species different from ours or as just a subspecies within our own. The former position eventually became the pre-eminent one, even though the latter also has proponents—see Wolpoff, M. H. (2009) "How Neandertals inform human variation", American Journal of Physical Anthropology, 139, 91–102 or Hublin, J. J. (2009) "The origin of Neandertals", Proceedings of the National Academy of Sciences, 106, 16022–16027, p. 16023. Another subspecies of our species is Homo sapiens idaltu, the humans of Herto, whose remains of just over 150,000 years ago have been found in Ethiopia, see White, T. D.; Asfaw, B.; DeGusta, D.; Gilbert, H.; Richards, G. D.; Suwa, G. & Howell, F. C. (2003) "Pleistocene Homo sapiens from Middle Awash, Ethiopia", Nature, 423/6941, 742–747. Today the question remains about the species in which to classify other earlier but relatively recent members of the genus Homo.

7 This idea was also explored in Singer, P. (2017) "Do aliens have inalienable rights?: What ET teaches us about our moral obligations", Nautilus, April 6, http://nautil.us/do-aliens-have-inalienable-rights-6052.

8 The argument focusing on cognitive capacities has been defended, for instance, in Francis, L. P. & Norman, R. (1978) "Some animals are more equal than others", *Philosophy*, 53, 507–527; Frey, R. G. (1980) *Interests and rights: The case against animals*, Oxford: Oxford University Press; and in Carruthers, P. (1992) *The animal issue: Moral theory in practice*, Cambridge: Cambridge University Press. The argument focusing on sympathy has been defended in Gray, J. A. (1980) "In defense of speciesism", *Behavioral and Brain Sciences*, 13, 22–23; Becker, L. C. (1983) "The priority of human interests", in Miller, H. B. & Williams, W. H. (eds.) *Ethics and animals*, Clifton: Humana Press, 225–242 and in Callicott, J. B. (1989) *In defense of the land ethic: Essays in environmental philosophy*, Albany: SUNY Press. The argument appealing to power has been defended in Narveson, J. (1977) "Animal rights", *Canadian Journal of Philosophy*, 7, 161–178.

9 Porphyry; Clark, G. (ed.) (2014 [ca. 3rd century]) *On abstinence from killing animals*, London: Bloomsbury, 3, 8, 8.

10 Patston, P. (2008) "Constructive functional diversity: A new paradigm beyond disability and impairment", *Disability and Rehabilitation*, 29, 20–21, 1625–1633.

11 This idea has been defended in McCloskey, H. J. (1979) "Moral rights and animals", *Inquiry*, 22, 23–54, p. 42 and in Scanlon, T. M. (1998) *What we owe to each other*, Cambridge: Harvard University Press, pp. 184–185. Such arguments were answered already in Nelson, L. (1956) *System of ethics*, New Haven: Yale University Press, p. 143.

12 See on this for instance Singer, *Animal liberation*; Pluhar, *Beyond prejudice*; Sztybel, D. (2006) "A living will clause for supporters of animal experimentation", *Journal of Applied Philosophy*, 23, 173–189; Tanner, J. (2008) "Species as a relationship", *Acta Analytica*, 23, 337–347 or Horta, O. (2014) "The scope of the argument from species overlap", *Journal of Applied Philosophy*, 31, 142–154.

It is sometimes responded to this argument that all human beings must be respected; it doesn't matter if they can't reason much, if they are not in a situation of power, or if there is nobody who cares about them. However, we don't need to have the same attitude with other animals. This is claimed, for example, in Paske, G. H. (1991) "In defense of human 'chauvinism'", *Journal of Value Inquiry*, 25, 279–286; Scruton, R. (1996) *Animal rights and wrongs*, London: Metro and Lynch, T. & Wells, D. (1998) "Non-anthropocentrism? A killing objection", *Environmental Values*, 7, 151–163.

A close scrutiny shows that this allegation is deceptive. It contradicts all the claims made before to defend giving humans more consideration than animals (that is, those that assume that what matters is intelligence, sympathy, or power), and insists instead again that humans deserve special respect only for being human, that is, "just because." However, as we have seen above, by saying "just because," we are not providing any kind of justification for the view that we hold. On the contrary, by doing so, we're just restating the view we want to defend without giving any reason in favor of it.

It has also been argued in some cases that we must fully respect only human beings because they belong to the same species as those who have a certain intelligence, power, etc. Different versions of this kind of argument have been presented during the last decades, sometimes more openly and sometimes in more obscure ways, for instance, in Fox, M. A. (1978) "Animal liberation: A critique", *Ethics*, 88, 106–118; Schmidtz, D. (1998) "Are all species equal?", *Journal of Applied Philosophy*, 15, 57–67 and Cohen, C. (2001) "In defense of the use of animals", in Cohen, C. & Regan, T. *The animal rights debate*, Lanham: Rowman & Littlefield, 3–123. Two recent versions of this old argument can be found in Hsiao, T. (2017) "Industrial farming is not cruel to animals", *Journal of Agricultural and Environmental Ethics*, 30, 37–54 and Kagan, S. (2019) *How to count animals, more or less*, Oxford: Oxford University Press. This argument is also deceptive because what those who use it really mean at the end of the day is simply that we should respect all humans. But belonging to a group in which other people have a certain capacity is not the same as having that capacity, neither does it mean "half-having" it or having it in some strange latent form. The fact that someone of my species has a certain capacity doesn't make me have it. For this reason, the only way to guarantee someone respect implies rejecting the idea that having that capacity is necessary for being respected. For rebuttals of the argument see Nobis, N. (2004) "Carl Cohen's 'kind' arguments *for* animal rights and *against* human rights", *Journal of Applied Philosophy*, 21, 43–59; McMahan, J. (2005) "Our fellow creatures", *The Journal of Ethics*, 9, 353–380 and Tanner, J. (2007) *Animals, moral risk and moral considerability*, PhD thesis, Durham: Durham University.

It's interesting to note the case of one of the authors cited above who defended this position, Michael Allen Fox. After debating for some time with those who argued in favor of nonhuman animals, he concluded that the arguments for speciesism didn't really have a sound basis. He revised his own position in depth and came to the conclusion that, indeed, speciesism has no justification. For this reason, he changed his view, and ever since, he has been defending animals. See Fox, M. A. (1999) *Deep vegetarianism*, Philadelphia: Temple University Press.

13 Most people writing about speciesism have made this point in one way or another. One way to defend it is by arguing that what is relevant to respecting someone is just how that individual may be harmed or benefited by what we do, or fail to do. We may call this, therefore, the "argument from relevance." This point has been in Horta, O. (2018) "Moral considerability and the argument from relevance", *Journal of Agricultural and Environmental Ethics*, 31, 369–388, see also Bernstein, *On moral considerability*.

14 Petrinovich, L. (1999) *Darwinian dominion: Animal welfare and human interests*, Cambridge: MIT Press, 55.

15 It is interesting to point out here that children typically appear to be less speciesists than adults. If this is actually the case, it would suggest that socialization may play an important role in the degree of speciesism present in a certain society. See Wilks, M.; Caviola, L.; Kahane, G. & Bloom, P. (2021) "Children prioritize humans over animals less than adults do", *Psychological Science*, 32, 27–38.

16 Chinese philosopher Mozi argued for this in the 5th century BC, indicating that everything that is now traditional was an innovation at some point, so if we should accept only that which is traditional current traditions would never have been considered acceptable. See Mozi; Johnston, I. (ed.) (2010 [ca. 5th century BC]) *The Mozi: A Complete Translation*, New York: Columbia University Press, ch. 39.

17 Machan, T. (2004) *Putting humans first: Why we are nature's favorite*, Oxford: Rowman and Littlefield.

18 See Reichmann, J. (2000) *Evolution, animal 'rights' and the environment*, Washington, DC: The Catholic University of America Press. The relation between religious views and the moral consideration of nonhuman animals has been examined in Waldau, P. (2001) *The specter of speciesism: Buddhist and Christian views of animals*, Oxford: Oxford University Press; Waldau, P. & Patton, K. C. (eds.) (2006) *A communion of subjects: Animals in religion, science, and ethics*, New York: Columbia University Press and Oliveira, F. C. S. (2011) "Especismo religioso", *Revista Brasileira de Direito Animal*, 8, 161–220. See also Regan, T. (ed.) (1986) *Animal sacrifices: Religious perspectives on the use of animals in science*, Philadelphia: Temple University Press and Linzey, A. (2013) *Why animal suffering matters: Philosophy, theology, and practical ethics*, Oxford: Oxford University Press.

19 As has been pointed out above already, there's nothing in our DNA that indicates the capacity of having a soul. Moreover, if this were so, then alterations in our

DNA could make it possible that there existed humans without souls, something with which those who believe in souls commonly disagree. If, instead, the relevant factor to have a soul were having a subjectivity, that is, that which allows us to have experiences, then not only human beings would possess souls.

20 See Perlo, K. W. (2009) *Kinship and killing: The animal in world religions*, New York: Columbia University Press.

21 Inge, W. (1920) *The idea of progress*, The Romanes Lectures, Oxford: Oxford University Press, pp. 13–14.

22 See in relation to this Bruers, S. (2021) "Speciesism, arbitrariness and moral illusions", *Philosophia*, 49, 957–975; Jaquet, F. (forthcoming) "Speciesism and tribalism: Embarrassing origins", *Philosophical Studies*, see also Bastian, B.; Loughnan, S.; Haslam, N. & Radke, H. R. (2012) "Don't mind meat? The denial of mind to animals used for human consumption", *Personality and Social Psychology Bulletin*, 38, 247–256. There are reasons to think that we look for a solid and clear justification of the view that we may disregard sentient animals because we want such a justification to exist. But the fact that such a solid justification has not been found yet, despite many years of trying so many different arguments, suggests it may never be found because it appears that it doesn't exist. On this, see Singer, P. (1999) "A response", in Jamieson, D. (ed.), *Singer and his critics*, Oxford: Blackwell, 269–335, pp. 295–296.

23 Regarding this point, see VanDeVeer, D. (1979) "On beasts, persons and the original position", *The Monist*, 62, 368–377 and Rowlands, M. (2009 [1998]) *Animal rights: Moral theory and practice*, Basingstoke: Palgrave Macmillan.

Chapter 2

Feeling and suffering

We can't deny the obvious any longer

In July 2012, a conference was held in Cambridge, UK, in which some of the most accomplished scientists in different fields of science gathered. At that conference, a declaration about animal consciousness was made that has been much cited since then. It has become known as *The Cambridge Declaration on Consciousness*, and it states the following:

> Humans are not unique in possessing the neurological substrates that generate consciousness. Nonhuman animals, including all mammals and birds, and many other creatures, including octopuses, also possess these neurological substrates.[1]

This declaration granted scientific recognition to an idea that wasn't really new.[2] The idea is simple: not only human beings, but also a huge number of animals of other species, can experience suffering and pleasure. They are not unconscious objects, like teddy bears. This is what it means to say they are conscious beings.

For a very long time, most people, including, of course, scientists, had already been convinced of this. So perhaps to many people, this declaration did not provide any new information. However, it accomplished something important: we can now point out that the scientific community has found good evidence that animals of other species feel and suffer, just like human beings. This is good news for those who defend conscious nonhuman animals, and even more so for the animals themselves.

Why is this important? What is special about the capacity to suffer and enjoy? What evidence led to the Cambridge Declaration? How can we know who can suffer? The following sections will try to clarify these questions.

Why the capacity to feel and suffer is what matters

We have seen that when it comes to respecting others, we shouldn't take into account their intelligence or likeability. But why does it matter that they can

DOI: 10.4324/9781003285922-3

suffer? Why is this the reason we should respect them, rather than the fact that they are living beings, for instance? To think about this problem, consider the following example.

Irreversible coma
Suppose that you and I suffer brain damage so severe that we lose consciousness irreversibly. We enter a coma from which we will never wake up. It's impossible for us to have any experiences again, not even dreams. But our body remains alive for several weeks afterwards.

What value would our lives have for us in that state while our bodies are still alive? Would they be as valuable as our current lives?

Most of us would not think so. In fact, most of us understand that living such a life would have no value at all for us. It seems that in a case like this, what would continue to be alive would be our organism, our body. But you and I, as such, would have disappeared.

Why do we think this? Life has value because of what happens to us. A life without any kind of experience, in a state of total unconsciousness, holds nothing positive for those who live it. Another example suggests this.

The permanent sleeping drug
Suppose we lived our entire lives under the effect of a powerful sleeping drug that prevented us from waking up, and even prevented us from dreaming. Our whole lives would be spent like that, from womb to death.

When we reflect on this, we see that living such a life would really be like living no life at all. Nothing really good or bad could ever happen to us. This shows that merely being alive isn't something that has value in itself. What has value are the things that happen to us throughout our lives. That is, the experiences we have are what make us value our lives.

If we lost consciousness forever, as in the example of the irreversible coma, our bodies would be like empty shells with no one living inside. That's why the lives of organisms that can't have experiences are like those in the two examples above. Although these organisms are alive, there's no one in them experiencing good or bad things. That is what the lives of plants, fungi, and bacteria are like.

What does it mean to be sentient?

In order for good or bad things to happen to us, it's necessary that we are able to suffer and enjoy experiences. There's another name for this. It's a word that may sound strange at first, but is widely used in debates on this issue. That word is *sentience*.

What is sentience?

Sentience is the capacity to experience things, that is, to be able to feel what happens to us. Sentience doesn't consist in simply being able to detect or respond to changes in one's environment. A thermostat or a plant can do that, but they don't have any conscious experiences when they do so—it all happens "in the dark" without any feelings. On the other hand, beings with sentience (that is, sentient beings) experience what happens to them.[3] An animal who sees something experiences it. Someone who has a thought or memory experiences something—there is something that it feels like to think about or remember something. Sentient beings are all beings who have experiences, regardless of the types of beings they are or the kinds of experiences they might have. Sometimes those experiences are good, pleasant ones. In other cases, they are negative and unpleasant.

There is another way of expressing the idea that we can experience positive and negative things: by simply saying that we can feel suffering and pleasure. We understand the meaning of these words very broadly. We call suffering not only the physical pain we feel when we are hurt, but any experience that feels bad to us. Negative emotions such as fear, grief or anguish, dissatisfaction, frustration, discontent, boredom, and uncomfortable feelings such as cold and discomfort are also examples of suffering. Likewise, we call pleasure any nice experience, such as those of satisfaction, fun, and tranquility.[4] Sentient beings are those who can feel suffering and pleasure of any kind.

We might think that suffering isn't always bad. Sometimes suffering saves us from enduring a greater harm. For example, feeling the pain of a burn makes us avoid getting burned again. But why does that happen? Well, pain is a very unpleasant experience, so we don't want to experience it. If suffering were pleasant, we would not move our hand away from the fire. It may, in certain cases, have positive indirect effects, as in this one. But suffering has these effects precisely because we feel it as negative, as disagreeable in itself, and thus it motivates us to avoid it.

The suffering and death of sentient beings

Just as many human beings suffer, so do a large number of other animals. This gives us reasons to reduce the suffering that exists in the world. It's sometimes pointed out that it's good that there are also those who can experience enjoyment. But we must take something else into account. In a world such as ours where there's so much suffering, ending it is a very important task. Even if it's good to have more enjoyment, it seems much more pressing that there's less suffering. Suppose we had to choose between two options: someone stops suffering a terrible pain or someone else begins to experience an equally intense pleasure. In general, it seems that the former would be a greater priority.[5]

Despite this, human beings inflict a great deal of suffering on many animals every day. In addition, they often kill them in large numbers. There are those who say that by killing animals we are not doing anything wrong, or that we only cause them a very small harm. One way to try to justify this is by saying that nonhuman animals don't realize they are alive or that they can't make long-term plans or imagine themselves living in the future, and so we don't seriously harm them when we kill them painlessly. If this reasoning were correct, the slaughter of animals would be acceptable as long as it was done without causing them pain. However, this doesn't seem to be the case, for two reasons.

First, it's important to note that the slaughter of animals isn't painless. In the next chapter, we will see how the vast majority of animals are actually killed, and we will find out that doing so causes them unimaginable suffering.

Second, it isn't credible that death is not a harm for nonhuman animals. Most people, in fact, think otherwise, especially those who have ever lived with an animal, such as a dog. And they have compelling reasons to think so. As we have seen, if death harms us, it's because it takes away the good things in life. If this is correct, then dying is generally bad for all beings who can enjoy positive things. An animal with a very simple mind won't be able to make long-term plans or imagine themselves in the future, but will indeed be able to enjoy the things that happen to her.[6]

Death harms humans, not because of the mere fact that our bodies are alive but because we are sentient. Sentience is what makes it possible for our lives to be better or worse. It's the same for other sentient animals.

The question about who can experience suffering and pleasure

In light of this, a question sometimes arises: how do we know that animals can experience suffering and pleasure? Is this certain? What if only humans have that capacity? Another question sometimes arises when discussing respect for animals: what about plants? Don't they also have the capacity to experience suffering and pleasure?

Although these two questions are different, they can be answered at the same time. Both can be reduced to a single question: who can experience suffering and pleasure?

Most of us understand that animals, or at least many, many animals, experience suffering and pleasure. They are sentient. We also understand that other living beings, such as plants, do not. They can no doubt interact with their environment. However, unlike animals, they can't feel what happens to them. They can't have any experiences, such as suffering and enjoyment, at all.

A plant that grows toward the light is responding to an external stimulus. It reacts to light, but it doesn't see it. A thermostat is sensitive to temperature, but it doesn't feel cold or hot. On the other hand, when an animal is heading toward a meal that smells enticing, something else happens. The animal has the experience of smell. That is why he consciously decides to go toward the meal.

Many people find this obvious. However, there is also a minority who deny this, despite the scientific agreement. This case is similar to that of people who refuse to believe in other matters about which there is a wide scientific consensus such as biological evolution. Due to this, to clear up some doubts that may arise here, the following sections will explain this issue in more detail. To do so, they will review the evidence indicating that someone is sentient.

What the ways animals behave shows

What are the grounds for thinking that someone can experience suffering and pleasure? Why do we believe many animals have these capacities? The first thing to look at is their behavior. This seems to show us clearly that they experience suffering and pleasure. We observe an animal moaning pitifully and think she is suffering. If we see her running and jumping in an animated way, we realize that she is enjoying the moment. This is easy to understand.

In addition, animals behave very differently in different situations. The ways they react are not automatic, but vary according to what happens to them. Think about two piglets playing chase or a bird selecting branches and making a nest with them. Their behaviors in doing so are so complex and adjusted to the context in which they are that it would be very odd if these animals just acted automatically, without feeling or thinking. It seems they do it because they are thinking about what is going on and deciding to act in a particular way.

In addition, sometimes the behavior of many nonhuman animals shows that they solve problems and perform calculations.[7] This is seen in some animals who have the misfortune of being used in laboratory experiments. For example, rats and octopuses are put in mazes and observed. These animals seek out the exit, think about how to find it, and are often successful in doing so. Many other animals also show remarkable cognitive abilities. For example, squirrels who store food for the future depend on memory to survive. If they couldn't remember and recognize the places where the food was hidden, they would starve to death.

Some believe that these behaviors don't imply that animals are sentient, unlike the case of humans. They say that we can talk with other humans, and they can tell us if they are suffering or if they are well.[8] In contrast, no other animal can do that.

In response to this claim, it can be said that animals of other species often do express their suffering. They simply do it in other ways.[9] Think, for example, of a dog who goes first to the door, then comes over to us and nudges us, and finally returns to the door to look at us insistently. Or, consider another dog who whines looking at us insistently with a pitiful expression on his face. Anyone will understand that these animals want to communicate something to us. The first one is trying to say something like, "I want you to open the door so we can go outside." The second would be indicating to us that he isn't well, is restless, or wants us to do something for him.[10] There are primates who have been taught to use sign language used by deaf humans. This has not been done to benefit these animals who have been kept as the property of certain institutions. It has been done, rather, for human benefit, to discover what these primates can think and communicate. Through the use of sign language, they have been able to express themselves, manifesting their emotions, discomfort, and wellbeing many times. This was the case, for example, of Koko.

Koko was a gorilla who was born in a San Francisco Zoo in 1971 and lived most of her life in the facilities of the Gorilla Foundation, near the place where she was born. Over many years, different people had sign language conversations with Koko and the conversations were transcribed. One of these transcriptions reads as follows:

> In December of 1984 a tragic accident indicated the extent to which gorillas may grieve over the death of their loved ones. Koko's favorite kitten, All Ball, slipped out of the door and was killed by a speeding car. Koko cried shortly after she was told of his death. Three days later, when asked, 'Do you want to talk about your kitty?' Koko signed, 'CRY.' 'What happened to your kitty?' Koko answered, 'SLEEP CAT.' When she saw a picture of a cat who looked very much like All Ball, Koko pointed to the picture and signed, 'CRY, SAD, FROWN.' Her grief was not soon forgotten.
> *17 March 1985, with Francine Patterson*
>
> F: How did you feel when you lost Ball?
> K: WANT.
> F: How did you feel when you lost him?
> K: OPEN TROUBLE VISIT SORRY.
> F: When he died, remember when Ball died, how did you feel?
> K: RED RED RED BAD SORRY KOKO-LOVE GOOD.[11]

This shows us that animals can tell us what they feel (and that they may feel much more than many people would expect). We can thus see how awful the way humans behave toward these animals is, as it typically consists in locking them up and harming them in other ways. It's not bad just because these animals can communicate with us. It's bad because they suffer, and the fact that they communicate what they feel gives us an idea of what they can suffer. This challenges the idea that only human beings can suffer, leaving the possibility open that many other animals can suffer too.

This also shows that the assumption that only humans can communicate what they feel is false. Moreover, the ability to communicate isn't a necessary condition for being sentient. The crucial thing is that, even if an animal doesn't use a language, we can still conclude that she or he experiences suffering or pleasure. In fact, in order to know if someone suffers, language isn't as important as it might seem. Consider, for example, the following:

Language isn't the key

Imagine that we see someone crying and whining. We approach her and she tells us, without ceasing to cry, that she is having a great time. Or imagine that we hear someone laughing out loud. We ask her how she is and she tells us, with a cheerful smile, that she is suffering terribly. These statements would not be credible. Why? Because the behavior of these people contradicts what they are telling us.

This shows that someone's behavior may indicate a person's mood more reliably than his or her words. Language isn't indispensable for us to know that someone feels suffering or pleasure.

Therefore, an animal's inability to use a language is not a reason to conclude that the animal doesn't feel. The reasons to think that someone suffers or experiences enjoyment are just as credible for other animals as they are for human beings.

In addition, there's something more that the behavior of nonhuman animals can show us. Consider the next case.

Rats know that other rats are sentient—and science agrees

An experiment carried out in the late 1950s at Brown University showed the contrast between the attitude of many human beings and other animals. In this experiment, some caged rats needed to push a lever to get food. The rats learned to do this, and did so regularly in order to eat. Then, other rats were set beside them in a different cage. From that moment on, every time the first rats pressed the lever, the second ones received painful electric shocks. When the first group of rats saw this, they stopped pressing the lever, even though this meant they couldn't get any more food.

Other experiments showed similar results. In these experiments, rats helped other rats who were in distress. For instance, in another experiment carried out several decades later, when forced to choose between getting food or freeing other rats from a tank filled with water, rats chose the latter in most cases.[12]

These experiments show several things. We saw in the previous chapter that speciesism is often defended by appealing to the capacities human beings have. It's sometimes claimed, for instance, that only human beings can be altruistic and care about what happens to other beings. What we have just seen indicates that this is not so.

In addition, these experiments show the indifference that is often displayed by humans toward other animals. They are treated as if they were things; they are disregarded and made to suffer physically and psychologically, in ways that would be considered criminal if they were human beings. In the next chapter, we will see what the most important consequences of this indifference are, in the fields where animals are exploited on a larger scale.

Finally, these experiments show something else. As mentioned above, there are still some human beings who doubt whether animals of other species can feel and suffer. In contrast, what we have just seen shows that other animals have no such doubts. The rats used in these experiments don't seem to have any doubts whether other rats can suffer. Their behavior shows this very clearly. And, as we have seen, science backs them on this point. Scientific consensus indicates that these rats are the ones who get this right, not people who still have doubts about animal suffering.

Evolutionary explanations of sentience

What we have just seen makes perfect sense if we think about the following: What is the ultimate reason why human beings can experience suffering and pleasure? The answer is that we have evolved to do so because this makes it easier for us to survive, and for our genes to be passed on to following generations. This also explains why other animals also experience suffering and pleasure.

Experiences, good and bad, motivate us to act. Suffering when negative things happen to us motivates us to avoid them. Enjoying the things that are good for us moves us to seek them out. Likewise, having desires motivates us to try to fulfill them. For example, if a mother desires that her pups survive, she will take care of them.

In addition, having experiences allows us to act in a variety of ways, depending on what turns out to be most advantageous in each case. This makes it easier for sentient animals to survive and reproduce. It also makes social animals help other members of their group (not their species, as we saw in the previous chapter) to survive.[13]

This entails two important things:

First, it would make no sense if beings unable to move felt suffering and pleasure. It's perfectly understandable that a burn hurts an animal, since this animal can act to avoid being burned. But if a tree suffered when it was burned, what good would that do for it? Since the tree wouldn't be able to escape, it would burn all the same. Therefore, it would not make sense that beings incapable of making relatively rapid movements, such as plants or fungi, could be sentient. Since sentience requires complex neural structures which consume a lot of energy, a creature that was sentient but unable to move would be less able to survive than an insentient one which required less energy.

Second, it isn't credible that only human beings are sentient. Humans are not the only animals who can move or exhibit complex and flexible behavior. Many other animals can. In addition, the idea that sentience would have arisen suddenly, with the appearance of human beings, isn't very plausible. Sentience isn't only evolutionarily useful for the survival of human beings; it's useful for the survival of other animals too, many of whom existed before the emergence of humans.

This indicates that not only human beings but also other animals can experience suffering and pleasure. Even so, this isn't entirely conclusive. There are plants, such as carnivorous ones, that are capable of fast movements. Their ability to move is similar to that of some animals, such as bivalves. There are also microorganisms that move, such as some bacteria. However, there are other reasons to deny that they can suffer.

What makes the experience of suffering and pleasure possible?

The crucial question is the following: What is it that allows a creature to be sentient? To date, there's still a lot we don't know about this. But there are some things we do know. We know that our capacity to suffer isn't based on some non-natural thing, like the possession of an immaterial soul. Rather, it is our nervous systems performing certain functions that make it possible for us to have experiences.

How do we know this? There are many sources of evidence. We know that if someone suffers certain kinds of damage to the brain (the central organ of the nervous system), her experiences are altered. For instance, damage in a particular area of the brain can cause someone to lose her sight, even if her eyes work perfectly. We also know that if we suffer some very serious brain injury, we cease to be conscious, even if our bodies remain alive. We know that certain drugs cause chemical processes that change the way our brains function, which, in turn, alters our experiences. This doesn't happen by chance. It happens because the functioning of our brains generates our experiences.

Complex information processing in our nervous systems enables us to have experiences. At present, we do not know exactly how this takes place. But we do know that without complex information processing, we cannot have experiences. All this leads to the conclusion that the structures in the biological world that can generate experiences are nervous systems.

Which animals are sentient?

Some nervous systems are very simple and lack any form of general coordination or centralization. For this reason, they can't process complex information. They simply transmit nervous information from sensitive cells to motor cells, which move some part of the body automatically. Animals that have this type of nervous system can react reflexively, for example, moving when something touches them. But they don't experience what happens to them, because, in the absence of complex information processing, it appears that there can be no experience. That is why we may infer that animals with these very simple nervous systems can't suffer.

What kind of nervous system is necessary for an animal to be sentient? Currently, we don't know exactly. Therefore, we can't know for sure where exactly the boundary is between animals who can suffer and those who can't (and it will likely be a long time before we know this). However, we can make some reasonable guesses given what we do know, in cases such as the following.

Animals with complex brains. Vertebrates and a wide range of invertebrates have nervous systems with a highly developed central organ (the brain). Therefore, it doesn't seem plausible that they don't experience what happens to them. These animals are often very different from one another. Sardines, bats, jaybirds, octopuses, and humans are very different, but they all have complex nervous structures (including many aquatic animals, such as all kinds of fishes and cephalopods, even if this is something some people still aren't aware of).[14] All of them display complex behaviors. It doesn't seem reasonable to deny that they can have experiences.

Animals with simpler brains. There are other animals with less complex centralized nervous systems. Many invertebrates have simple brains. Arthropods are an example. This is a very numerous group (a "phylum" in biology) of invertebrates. It includes, among others, insects and crustaceans, such as lobsters or crabs. These animals sometimes exhibit complex behavior as the example below indicates.[15]

The dance of the bees

When a bee discovers a place where there are flowers from which it's possible to obtain food for the hive, she returns to the hive and, gaining the attention of the other bees, begins making a series of movements resembling a dance. The bee heads in a certain direction and makes movements with her abdomen, waggling her body. The orientation of her body identifies the direction of the flowers, and the duration of the "dance," their distance. Likewise, the degree of agitation with which she moves indicates how profitable she thinks a trip to the flowers would be. The bees can also use this dance to communicate other kinds of information. For example, if the colony is going to move to a new location, a bee can indicate where she thinks this should be. Bees can also use these dances to debate if they have a disagreement about the direction in which they think they should go. In these cases, each bee does the dance in the direction that seems most promising to her, and the option that ends up prevailing is the one that gets the most support from the bees involved.

When the other bees see these movements, they know how to recognize that information. They interpret the meaning of the movements. In fact, successfully interpreting the dance can be crucial. Life in nature, as we'll see in chapter 6, isn't idyllic at all, but is very hard for animals. Most of them don't manage to survive. Bees need to clearly understand what their hive mates want to tell them; otherwise, they could die.

This shows how bees communicate with each other. They transmit information to each other visually, using signs that correspond to different movements. In fact, different varieties of bees have different kinds of dances, as if they have different dialects. What is more, they don't just accept the information they receive; they can actually question it. In a well-known experiment, food was placed in a boat located at the shore of a lake and the boat was afterward moved to the middle of the lake. When some of the bees went back to the hive and reported to the other bees that there was food in the middle of the lake, the other bees dismissed that information.[16] This suggests that they didn't regard the information as reliable in light of their previous knowledge.

It seems very difficult to explain this form of communication on the assumption that bees are unconscious automata. Communication of this kind seems to imply that these animals are indeed performing their dance intentionally. It appears they also experience the sight of another bee dancing and are interpreting what that bee says. Like bees, there are many other invertebrates with simple brains but more or less complex behaviors. Are they strong candidates for sentience? Yes, they are.[17]

Animals without brains, but with centralized nervous systems. Other animals, such as bivalve mollusks (for example, mussels, oysters, and clams), don't process information through brains. Instead, they have only a few nerve ganglia. Is this enough for them to be sentient? At this time, we don't know.

There are other indicators that we could consider. Some bivalves have eyes, which suggests they have some visual experience. Moreover, it has been proven that the heart rate of some of these animals increases in the presence of predators. Also, many animals with these simple nervous systems seem to react to opioids known to reduce pain in other animals. This seems to suggest that they could also experience pain, even though it doesn't prove it conclusively. Perhaps the nervous activity that takes place in the nerve ganglia of these animals is enough for the processing of information required for consciousness to arise.[18] Due to these factors, their case is very different from that of organisms without any nervous system, and the question of their sentience remains unresolved.

This leaves open a couple of questions. We still don't know exactly which beings can experience suffering and pleasure. We don't know precisely what their experiences are like. (We also don't know this for sure in the case of other human beings.) We don't know how intensely they experience their suffering. However, while it's desirable to know as much as possible about these questions, we don't have to wait for all the answers to respect animals. If we know or suspect that they suffer, that is enough. In addition, we can make more or less reasonable estimates of what their suffering feels like in a whole range of circumstances. Although we don't know precisely what a pig, an octopus, or a fish feels, we know that by stabbing them, beating them to death, or boiling them alive, we are surely causing them great pain.

Likewise, in cases in which we don't know with certainty whether an animal can suffer, we know that if we treat these animals as if they did not suffer and they do, we could be causing them tremendous harm. On the other hand, if we consider the possibility that they do, we can avoid causing such harm to them.[19]

There are overwhelming reasons to conclude that many animals can feel and suffer, and we should take this into account when we ask ourselves how to act toward them.

Are there other living things that could be sentient?

What about other living things? Many plants have complex physiologies. Sometimes they also respond in surprising ways to their environment. How can we say that they don't experience suffering or pleasure? Because they don't have nervous systems or any other structure that processes complex information. Without these, we lack a sound basis for thinking a being can have experiences.[20] Some animals, such as sponges, also lack nervous systems. Animals don't suffer simply because they are animals. They suffer because of complex physical processes in their nervous systems. In fact, if we were to construct machines with a system that performed the same functions that centralized nervous systems perform, those machines would also have experiences, and we could also cause them harm.[21] Some people may consider this counterintuitive, but it's important to keep in mind that sentience doesn't arise simply because our body is alive. Recall the example in which we could lose consciousness forever but continue to live. The same is true of plants and other living organisms without nervous systems (fungi, protists, archaea, and bacteria). They perform different physiological functions, but they do so without conscious awareness. This is why it's appropriate to call certain states in which we lose consciousness "vegetative," because vegetables are not conscious either.

Should we care more about some animals than others?

We have seen that no being who suffers should be discriminated against. But at this point, a question may arise. Perhaps there are some animals who can suffer and enjoy their lives more than others. If so, we might think that they matter more, since they can suffer more significant harms.

However, this isn't necessarily so. Let's see what happens in the following example.

The cow and the crab

Think of two very different animals: a cow and a crab. Both animals are suffering, and we can only help one of them. Someone suggests that we should help the cow because she has a greater capacity to suffer than the crab. But we find out that the cow is undergoing a very slight pain, which will pass quickly. It's a minor nuisance. Meanwhile, the crab is suffering a very intense pain, the greatest of which she is capable. It's a much greater pain than the one the cow is suffering.

In a case like this, there would be no reason to pay more attention to the cow than to the crab. There will be many situations in which the cow could suffer more, but not in this case. Therefore, it would be a mistake to think that the cow has priority on this occasion. Whether helping one animal or the other has priority will depend on how much they are suffering in each case, not on their general capacity for suffering.

Thus, even though some beings have a greater capacity to experience suffering and pleasure than others, this doesn't mean they count more. Their needs will be more important when they are in a worse situation, but the opposite may be the case, as in the above example.

Why the suffering of nonhuman animals isn't less important than ours

The example of the cow and the crab isn't valid only for cases in which we compare the suffering of two nonhuman animals. It's also valid when we compare the suffering of a human being and another animal. It's sometimes said that although nonhuman animals experience suffering and pleasure, they don't really suffer a great deal. Those who claim this may accept that animals of other species should be respected, but they think that human beings, because of their greater intelligence, can experience suffering and pleasure much more intensely.[22] Take the following as an example. Suppose we know that we have to go through a very painful treatment. We will suffer not only while this pain lasts but also beforehand, from anticipating it. Or, suppose we remember something bad that happened to us. We will feel sad about it.

What does this mean? Will humans always count more as a result? If so, that would not mean we shouldn't respect other animals. However, it could imply that we should have a special respect for humans, greater than we give to other animals.

It could be argued that many animals remember their past sufferings and enjoyments. Some may also anticipate future suffering and enjoyments. But this is by no means the crucial point here. What's important is that the suffering of other animals shouldn't matter less. There are several reasons to claim this.

First, remember what we saw in the example of the cow and the crab. Imagine the same case, but with a human instead of a cow. Suppose we can prevent a human being from suffering a minimal discomfort that hardly bothers her at all or a crab from suffering the most intense pain this crab is capable of feeling. Even though the human being may suffer more in other cases, that would not change the situation in this one. In such a situation, the crab would suffer more.

Second, in many cases, having greater intelligence doesn't make us suffer more but rather less. If, for example, we cage a deer and a human being, we can explain to the human being that it's temporary and that it will all be over soon. But we can't explain this to the deer. In that circumstance, the deer could be terrified. In fact, many captured and imprisoned animals die from stress in such situations. In contrast, a human being could be freed from such anguish with a few words.

Third, we should remember something else that we have seen before. Many human beings lack complex intellectual capacities. Thus, if this argument were correct, it would mean that their ability to suffer would be less than that of others. However, this doesn't appear to be the case. It doesn't seem that a little girl can suffer much less than an adult woman.

Fourth, we may doubt the idea that human beings have an incomparably greater capacity to suffer than that of less intelligent beings. Consider the following question: are the purely physical pain and pleasure that human beings can feel greater than those of other animals? There's no clear physiological evidence to conclude this, at least in the case of animals with a sufficiently developed nervous system.

We may respond that human beings also experience psychological suffering and enjoyment. However, human beings don't just care about intellectual suffering or enjoyment; pain and physical pleasure are also important. It's clear that we can suffer in special ways because of our intelligence. But we can also suffer terrible physical pains. Those who have suffered a very painful illness know this well, not to mention those who have suffered torture. It's true that some intellectual or psychological sufferings are greater than many physical sufferings. However, the opposite is also the case. For example, many people are afraid to go to the dentist, but that psychological distress is much less significant than the suffering caused by an acute toothache.

Something similar happens, in reverse, with the things we enjoy. Some may give us intellectual enjoyment, such as reading books or watching movies. But other things give us physical pleasure. We can, for example, eat and drink, do some activity like running or swimming, have sex, etc. We may experience many purely intellectual pleasures, but this doesn't mean that the physical ones don't count for anything compared to them. Suppose that, in exchange for reading a very good novel, we had to stop enjoying the taste of food forever. Would we accept something like that? Maybe some would, but the vast majority would not.

In light of all this, the logic of the argument is very clear. First, it isn't true that our intellectual or psychological suffering and enjoyment must necessarily be greater than our physical suffering and enjoyment. Sometimes this is indeed so, but in other cases it isn't. Second, it isn't true either that our physical suffering and enjoyment are greater than those of all other animals. When we add this up, we can infer that there's no reason to believe that our intellectual suffering and pleasure must, in all cases, be greater than the physical suffering and pleasure of other animals. There are some cases in which this is so, but others where it isn't. Therefore, we can't say that human beings count more for this reason.

Animals matter because sentience matters

In this chapter, we have seen that the capacity to experience suffering and pleasure, also called sentience, is what counts when it comes to not harming someone. All animals with this capacity, not only humans, have an interest in not suffering. Likewise, if death harms human beings, it also harms other animals who can enjoy their lives. We have also seen that a very large number of animals are sentient, even if we don't know exactly which animals are not. And we have seen that although many human beings have very complex intellectual capacities, this doesn't make what happens to other animals less important.

All this reinforces the conclusion we reached already in the previous chapter, which is that speciesism should be rejected. However, at present, speciesism continues to exist and to have very serious consequences for animals. In the next chapter, we will look at some of these.

Notes

1 Low, P. et al. (2012) *The Cambridge Declaration on Consciousness*, http://fcmconference.org/img/CambridgeDeclarationOnConsciousness.pdf. You can find an extensive bibliography about this at PhilPapers (2016 [2013]) "Animal consciousness", *Bibliographies, PhilPapers*, http://philpapers.org/browse/animal-consciousness. For a general analysis of the different indicators and arguments implied in this question see Allen, C. & Trestman, M. (2014 [1995]) "Animal consciousness", in Zalta, E. N. (ed.) *The Stanford Encyclopedia of Philosophy*, Stanford: Stanford University, http://plato.stanford.edu/archives/sum2014/

entries/consciousness-animal or Tye, M. (2017) *Tense bees and shell-shocked crabs: Are animals conscious?* New York: Oxford University Press, see also Animal Ethics (2014) *Sentience, Animal Ethics*, http://animal-ethics.org/sentience.

2 Bekoff, M. (2013) "After 2,500 studies, it's time to declare animal sentience proven", *Live Science*, September 6, http://livescience.com/39481-time-to-declare-animal-sentience.html.

3 On this, see Allen and Trestman "Animal consciousness." The terms "sentience" and "consciousness" are commonly used as synonyms. Sometimes they are defined in ways in which they differ in some details (such as when sentience is identified with the capacity to have positive and negative experiences and consciousness simply with the capacity to have experiences). In the debates about animal suffering and the reasons to respect them, the word "sentience" tends to be used more frequently.

4 There may be sensations that are unpleasant to some people and not to others. That doesn't mean that suffering is bad for some people but not for others, but that there are things that cause some people to suffer but not others. If suffering were not unpleasant, if it were not a bad thing, we would not call it suffering. It would be something different. The same thing happens with pleasure; if we did not feel it as pleasing in some way, we would not call it so.

5 On this, see Ryder, *Speciesism, painism and happiness*; Shriver, A. J. (2014) "The asymmetrical contributions of pleasure and pain to animal welfare", *Cambridge Quarterly of Healthcare Ethics*, 23, 152–162; Gloor, L. (2019 [2016]) "The case for suffering-focused ethics", *Center on Long-Term Risk*, http://longtermrisk.org/the-case-for-suffering-focused-ethics; Mayerfeld, J. (2002) *Suffering and moral responsibility*, Oxford: Oxford University Press or Vinding, M. (2020) *Suffering-focused ethics: Defense and implications*, Copenhagen: Ratio Ethica. For more information see *Suffering-Focused Ethics (SFE) Resources*, http://suffering-focused-ethics.surge.sh.

6 The view that death is not harmful to animals for reasons like the ones mentioned above has been defended in Cigman, R. (1981) "Death, misfortune and species inequality", *Philosophy and Public Affairs*, 10, 47–54 and Ferré, F. (1986) "Moderation, morals and meat", *Inquiry*, 29, 391–406. For a rebuttal of the idea that nonhuman animals can't understand death see Monsó, S. (2021) *La zarigüeya de Schrödinger: cómo viven y entienden la muerte los animales*, Madrid: Plaza y Valdés. For defenses of the view that death harms us because it means we will not be able to enjoy future goods see for instance Nagel, T. (1970) "Death", *Noûs*, 4, 73–80 and Scarre, G. (2007) *Death*, Stocksfield: Acumen. For defenses of the view that animals are harmed by death because they are sentient, see Rodd, R. (1990) *Biology, ethics, and animals*, Oxford: Oxford University Press; McMahan, J. (2008) "Eating animals the nice way", *Daedalus*, 137, 66–76; Kaldewaij, F. (2006) "Animals and the harm of death", in Kaiser, M. & Lien, M. (eds.) *Ethics and the politics of food*, Wageningen: Wageningen Academic Publishers, 528–532; Cavalieri, P. (2009) *The death of the animal: A dialogue*, New York: Columbia University Press; Bradley, B. (2016) "Is death bad for a cow?", in Višak, T. & Garner, R. (eds.) *The ethics of killing animals*, New York: Oxford University Press, 51–64.

7 On this, see Griffin, D. R. (1992) *Animal minds: Beyond cognition to consciousness*, Chicago: Chicago University Press; Allen, C. & Bekoff, M. (1997) *Species of mind: The philosophy and biology of cognitive ethology*, Cambridge: MIT Press and Bekoff, M. (2007) *The emotional lives of animals: A leading scientist explores animal joy, sorrow, and empathy—and why they matter*, Novato: New World Library; see also Andrews, K. & Monsó, S. (2021) "Animal cognition", in Zalta, E. N. (ed.)

The Stanford Encyclopedia of Philosophy, Stanford: Stanford University, http://plato. stanford.edu/entries/cognition-animal.

8   Leahy, M. P. T. (1991) *Against liberation: Putting animals in perspective*, London: Routledge. For an opposing approach, see Rollin, B. (1989) *The unheeded cry: Animal consciousness, animal pain and science*, Oxford: Oxford University Press, see also Aaltola, E. (2012) *Animal suffering: Philosophy and culture*, Basingstoke: Palgrave Macmillan.

9   See in particular Meijer, E. (2019) *When animals speak*, New York: New York University Press and (2020) *Animal languages*, Cambridge: MIT Press. See also Freeman, C. P.; Bekoff, M. & Bexell, S. M. (2011) "Giving voice to the 'voiceless': Incorporating nonhuman animal perspectives as journalistic sources", *Journalism Studies*, 12, 590–607 or Fenton, A. & Shriver, A. (2018) "Animal minds: The neuroethics of nonhuman dissent", in Johnson, L. S. M. & Rommelfanger, K. S. (eds.) *The Routledge handbook of neuroethics*, London: Routledge, 484–498.

10 This, in fact, suggests that many nonhuman animals realize that other individuals (such as us) also have thoughts. See Lurz, R. W. (2011) *Mindreading animals: The debate over what animals know about other minds*, Cambridge: MIT Press.

11 Gordon, F. & Gordon, W. (1993) "The case for the personhood of gorillas", in Cavalieri, P. & Singer, P. (eds.), *The Great Ape project: Equality beyond humanity*, New York: St. Martin's Griffin, 58–77, p. 67. There are many other dialogues in which Koko, who defined herself as FINE ANIMAL GORILLA (ibid., p. 76), shows she has a clear mastery of the sign language she uses. She even makes jokes and plays tricks in this way. In another case, another person, Barbara Hiller, showed her a photograph of a bird, and Koko replied:

> K: THAT ME [to the adult bird].
> B: Is that really you?
> K: KOKO GOOD BIRD.
> B: I thought you were a gorilla.
> K: KOKO BIRD…
> B: You're teasing me. [Koko laughs.]
> B: What are you really? Koko laughs again, and after a minute signs
> K: GORILLA KOKO.
>   Ibid., p. 67.

Other animals, including chimpanzees, bonobos, and orangutans, have been shown to be capable of learning sign language as well. In any case, as noted above, this should only lead us to reject the idea that humans are unique regarding this and should not lead us to think these animals are more sentient or deserve more consideration than other sentient animals.

12 Church, R. M. (1959) "Emotional reactions of rats to the pain of others", *Journal of Comparative and Physiological Psychology*, 52,132–134; Sato, N.; Tan, L.; Tate, K. & Okada, M. (2015) "Rats demonstrate helping behavior toward a soaked conspecific", *Animal Cognition*, 18, 1039–1047; See also Bartal, I. B. A.; Decety, J. & Mason, P. (2011) "Empathy and pro-social behavior in rats", *Science*, 334, 1427–1430.

13 This is explained in Ng, Y.-K. (1995) "Towards welfare biology: Evolutionary economics of animal consciousness and suffering", *Biology and Philosophy*, 10, 255–285; Damásio, A. R. (1999) *The feeling of what happens: Body and emotion in the making of consciousness*, San Diego: Harcourt and Denton, D. A.; McKinley, M. J.; Farrell, M. & Egan, G. F. (2009) "The role of primordial emotions in the evolutionary origin of consciousness", *Consciousness and Cognition*, 18, 500–514.

14 For a general overview of this, see, for example, Gregory, N. G. (2004) *Physiology and behaviour of animal suffering*, Ames: Blackwell; Panksepp, J. (2004)

Affective neuroscience: The foundations of human and animal emotions, New York: Oxford University Press; Broom, D. M. (2014) *Sentience and animal welfare*, Wallingford: CABI. For more specific studies concerning different classes of vertebrates, see Willis, W. D. (1985) *The pain system: The neural basis of nociceptive transmission in the mammalian nervous system*, Basel: Karger; Gentle, M. J. (1992) "Pain in birds", *Animal Welfare*, 1, 235–247; Machin, K. L. (1999) "Amphibian pain and analgesia", *Journal of Zoo and Wildlife*, 30, 2–10 or Mosley, C. (2011) "Pain and nociception in reptiles", *Veterinary Clinics of North America: Exotic Animal Practice*, 14, 45–60, in addition to the already extensive literature about fish sentience, such as Chandroo, I. J. H. & Moccia, R. D. (2004) "Can fish suffer? Perspectives on sentience, pain, fear and stress", *Applied Animal Behaviour Science*, 86, 225–250 or Braithwaite, V. (2004) *Do fish feel pain?*, Oxford: Oxford University Press. Regarding invertebrates with complex nervous systems, see Budelmann, B. U. (1995) "Cephalopod sense organs, nerves and the brain: Adaptations for high performance and life style", *Marine and Freshwater Behaviour and Physiology*, 25, 13–33 or Mather, J. A. (2001) "Animal suffering: An invertebrate perspective", *Journal of Applied Animal Welfare Science*, 4, 151–156; Mikhalevich, I. & Powell, R. (2020) "Minds without spines: Evolutionarily inclusive animal ethics", *Animal Sentience*, 29/1, a. 329; Villamor Iglesias, A. (2021) "The suffering of invertebrates: An approach from animal ethics", *Tópicos*, 61, 403–420.

In addition, a large number of animals, both vertebrates and invertebrates, secrete substances to reduce their suffering in situations of extreme pain. The fact that an animal has receptors for these substances suggests that the animal may suffer. See, for instance, Dreborg, S.; Sundström, G.; Larsson, T. A. & Larhammar, D. (2008) "Evolution of vertebrate opioid receptors", *Proceedings of the National Academy of Sciences*, 105, 15487–15492 or Elwood, R. W. (2011) "Pain and suffering in invertebrates?", *Institute for Laboratory Animal Research Journal*, 52, 175–184.

15 Von Frisch, K. (1967) *The dance language and orientation of bees*, Cambridge: Harvard University Press.

16 See Gould, J. L. & Gould, C. G. (1988) *The honey bee*, New York: W. H. Freeman.

17 For a general view on invertebrate animals' sentience, see Lockwood, J. (1988) "Not to harm a fly: Our ethical obligations to insects", *Between the Species*, 2, 204–211, http://digitalcommons.calpoly.edu/cgi/viewcontent.cgi?article=1712&context=bts; Smith, J. A. (1991) "A question of pain in invertebrates", *Institute for Laboratory Animal Research Journal*, 33, 25–32, http://ilarjournal.oxfordjournals.org/content/33/1–2/25.full or Mather, J. A. (2001) "Animal suffering: An invertebrate perspective", *Journal of Applied Animal Welfare Science*, 4, 151–56; Barron, A. B. & Klein, C. (2016) "What insects can tell us about the origins of consciousness", *Proceedings of the National Academy of Sciences*, 113, 4900–4908; Tomasik, B. (2015) "The importance of insect suffering", *Essays on Reducing Suffering*, http://reducing-suffering.org/the-importance-of-insect-suffering or Crustacean Compassion (2021) *The case for the legal protection of decapod crustaceans*, Crustacean Compassion, http://crustaceancompassion.org.uk/our-report. For a comprehensive report on this see Knutsson, S. (2016) *Reducing suffering among invertebrates such as insects. Policy paper by Sentience Politics*, Berlin: Sentience Politics, http://sentience-politics.org/files/reducing-suffering-invertebrates-6.pdf. There is a series of papers about this question in Rethink Priorities (2019) "Invertebrate welfare", *Publications, Rethink Priorities*, http://rethinkpriorities.org/publications/category/Invertebrate+Welfare.

According to a common idea, we don't need to care about what happens to invertebrates because, since they are so different from us, it is difficult for us to feel empathy for them, and to therefore give them moral consideration. One way to respond to this is by arguing that we should give moral consideration to all sentient beings regardless of whether we can feel empathy for them or not. Another way to respond is by arguing that we can, and should, develop an empathetic response for all sentient beings; see Gruen, L. (2015) *Entangled empathy: An alternative ethic for our relationships with animals*, New York: Lantern Books and Aaltola, E. (2018) *Varieties of empathy: Moral psychology and animal ethics*, London: Rowman & Littlefield.

18 These two points are explained respectively in Kamenos, N. A.; Calosi, P. & Moore, P. G. (2006) "Substratum-mediated heart rate responses of an invertebrate to predation threat", *Animal Behaviour*, 71, 809–813 and Stefano, G. B.; Fricchione, G.; Goumon, Y. & Esch, T. (2005) "Pain, immunity, opiate and opioid compounds and health", *Medical Science Monitor*, 11, MS47–MS53.

Bivalves belong to the group (the phylum) of mollusks, in which there are animals with very diverse nervous systems. These also include gastropods, such as snails, whose nervous systems are very similar to, even if not exactly like, those of bivalves. There is evidence that they may suffer (which could be a reason to think that bivalves do too), as pointed out in Kavaliers, M.; Hirst, M. & Teskey, G. C. (1983) "A functional role for an opiate system in snail thermal behavior", *Science*, 220, 99–101 and Crossley, M.; Staras, K. & Kemenes, G. (2016) "A two-neuron system for adaptive goal-directed decision-making in *Lymnaea*", *Nature Communications*, 7, 11793, 1–13. In addition, among mollusks, we can also find cephalopods, such as octopuses and squids. As mentioned, these are animals with highly developed nervous systems and with highly complex behavior who can think about how to act. Thus, as we have seen, they are explicitly listed in the Cambridge Declaration on Consciousness as an example of animals who feel and suffer. In any case, although bivalves have much simpler nervous systems, we have already seen that this doesn't necessarily imply that they lack sentience.

19 See Birch, J. (2017) "Animal sentience and the precautionary principle", *Animal Sentience*, 16/1, a. 017; Knutsson, S. & Munthe, C. (2017) "A virtue of precaution regarding the moral status of animals with uncertain sentience", *Journal of Agricultural and Environmental Ethics*, 30, 213–224 or Sebo, J. (2018) "The moral problem of other minds", *Harvard Review of Philosophy*, 25, 51–70.

20 It is important to keep in mind that it is not that there is something magical about nervous systems which makes them necessary for experience. What matters is that they perform certain functions. The crucial point in the case of plants and other living organisms is not that they lack nervous systems but that they also have no other structure that performs these functions.

21 See Winsby, M. (2013) "Suffering subroutines: On the humanity of making a computer that feels pain", *Proceedings of the 2013 Meeting of the International Association for Computing and Philosophy*, 48, http://iacap.org/proceedings_IACAP13/paper_48.pdf; Mannino, A.; Althaus, D.; Erhardt, J.; Gloor, L.; Hutter, A. & Metzinger, T. (2015) *Artificial intelligence: Opportunities and risks. Policy paper of the Effective Altruism Foundation*, Berlin: Effective Altruism Foundation, http://ea-stiftung.org/files/ai-opportunities-and-risks.pdf, p. 9; Jaquet, F. & Cova, F. (2018) "Of hosts and men: Westworld and speciesism", in South, J. B. & Engels, K. S. (eds.) *Westworld and philosophy: If you go looking for the truth, get the whole thing*, New York: John Wiley and Sons, 217–228; Gibert, M. & Martin, D. (2021) "In search of the moral status of AI: Why sentience is a strong argument", *AI and Society*, 1, 1–12 and Owe, A. & Baum, S. D. (2021) "Moral consideration of

nonhumans in the ethics of artificial intelligence", *AI and Ethics*, 1, 517–28. For an overview see Harris, J. & Reese Anthis, J. (2021) "The moral consideration of artificial entities: A literature review", *Science and Engineering Ethics*, 27, a. 53.

22 These arguments are challenged in Rollin *The unheeded cry* and Cavalieri, *The animal question*.

Chapter 3

Harming animals

Into the farm

The first thing that strikes you as you approach it is the smell, which is hard to bear even at a distance. As you get closer, it becomes unbearable even if your nose and mouth are covered. The next thing that hits you is the noise made by all the animals crowded together. When you finally enter the farm, it's your eyes' turn to shock you. In every direction you look you see masses of animals packed together in tiny spaces, many of them with open wounds and clear signs of disease. There's dirt all around, and here and there you see dead animals lying on the ground. The air is heavy and smothering, and the noise and the stench continue to assault your ears and your nose.

It's hard to believe at first that something like this can really be happening, that such a place could be real. It feels like you're visiting hell. But you can see it is indeed real. And then the thought hits you that until this moment there was a very important part of reality you were totally unaware of. But not anymore. Now you can see it. You can see its victims too. And you won't forget them.

Direct acquaintance with the lives of the animals we use is something that makes a lasting impression on you. The first time you walk into a modern farm with hundreds or thousands of animals is a shocking experience which is not easy to forget. Many animal activists can attest to this.

There's something quite disconcerting about this, which is related to the fact that people use animal products every day. That being so, shouldn't we know more about something that is so central to our lives? However, most people have no idea of what this means for the animals. Of course, most people have no interest in the issue. Many have never thought about it, others may prefer not to know. But the fact is that people typically know about other issues even when they don't find them particularly interesting. There are a number of things we learn about at some point in our lives, whether we like it or not, maybe at school or through the media, because they are considered important in our society. Nothing like this happens in the case of animal exploitation, though.

DOI: 10.4324/9781003285922-4

Why is that? After all, it is widely believed that it's perfectly ethical to use animals as we do, especially by the people directly involved in animal exploitation industries. But, if this is so, there shouldn't be anything to be ashamed of in doing so. There should be nothing to hide. However, farms and slaughterhouses, as well as many other facilities where nonhuman animals are used, are not in the public eye. In fact, it can be difficult to find out exactly what happens in them. Modern farm owners aren't very keen on opening up their farms to public scrutiny. The footage one can see on the internet about how modern animal farms and slaughterhouses operate has been mostly taken by animal advocates who wanted people to know about them.[1] Otherwise, they would remain mostly invisible. This is totally at odds with the view that there's nothing unethical about animal exploitation. Why all the secrecy? Perhaps the reason is that there actually *is* something wrong with animal exploitation. In fact, we may ask ourselves, if we don't know what actually happens to the animals we use, how can we assume that such use is perfectly acceptable?

This chapter will try to address this by describing briefly what animal exploitation actually consists in. Describing this in detail would require a large amount of space, and for this reason, it is necessary to summarize. This means there will be many forms of animal exploitation that won't be discussed here. Only those ways of exploiting nonhuman animals which most people take part in will be addressed. With some exceptions, these are also the practices that affect the most animals. We will first look at what happens to those who suffer for our entertainment. We will then look at the situation of those animals exploited in the most common way: those that are killed for the production of food and cooking products, as well as for clothing.

The chapter won't cover what happens in other areas in which animals are exploited, such as for ornaments, as companions that can be bought and sold, as working tools, for experimentation, or in wars.[2] Neither will it explain all the ways nonhuman animals are exploited for entertainment, food, or clothing, nor all the aspects of those forms of exploitation that we will examine. Otherwise, this chapter would become an encyclopedia. Nevertheless, as mentioned already above, we will look at the most basic aspects of the most representative forms of animal exploitation. This will give us an idea of what animal exploitation as a whole is like.

Harming animals for entertainment

Let's start with the ways people entertain themselves that harm animals. Many people today are appalled when they consider the harms that animals suffer in activities such as bullfights and dog fights. Such activities are now banned in many countries, though they remain legal in others. But there are other forms of entertainment that affect many more animals. In the vast majority of cases, people don't carry out these activities because they want animals to suffer and die. Rather, they just want to have fun in particular ways that entail that animals are harmed terribly. We will now examine how this happens.

Hunting

One form of entertainment that kills a huge number of animals is hunting. In many countries, there are no registered figures of the animals that are victims of this practice, but it has been estimated that hundreds or even thousands, of millions of animals are hunted annually.[3] Note also that when these animals are raising young, the latter also typically die (they often starve, or are eaten by other animals).[4]

In addition to being killed, animals also suffer a great deal when they are hunted, even when they manage to escape. When chased, animals will run as hard as they can, to their very limits, as they are terribly distressed and terrified during the hunt, just as we would be if we were chased by someone who wanted to kill us.[5] They also suffer physically. This will happen, for instance, to a hare or a deer when chased for a long time. These animals have not evolved to be long distance runners, but to escape through quick bursts over short distances. This, however, is often insufficient to escape from humans, so they have to run for much longer than they can stand without becoming terribly exhausted. In addition to this, the animals have to endure the pain of the wounds inflicted on them during the hunt, which may be numerous.

Sometimes animals aren't caught by their hunters and yet die days or even weeks afterwards because of their wounds. They may die because those wounds left them incapable of finding food, or left them defenseless against attacks by other animals. In other cases, they survive, but the injuries they suffer leave them maimed, or cause them to undergo chronic pain for the rest of their lives.

Another effect of hunting that people often fail to notice is that animals, out of fear, refrain from entering areas in which there are predators. This also happens when their predators are humans. We may think this is safer for them, but it also means they are sometimes half-starved or at least malnourished even when there's food available, as[6] they don't dare to enter places where they could feed for fear that they may be attacked. Hunting thus causes distress and anguish to animals, and worsens their capacity to find food and to nourish themselves adequately.

Finally, dogs used for hunting are also victims. They are bred for this purpose and often killed when they are no longer young. They suffer from the cold while transported to the hunting grounds, and are sometimes shot by mistake. As a result of all this, their lives are often short and full of hardships.

Sport fishing

Another form of entertainment that harms many animals is sport fishing. In fact, this is the one that kills the most animals. The total number may be up to tens of billions a year.[7]

Angling is the most popular form of sport fishing. Animals that just happen to be swimming around bite what they believe to be food, but is in fact bait attached to a hook. And then their nightmare begins. The hooks pierce their mouths or other parts of their body, which causes them significant pain. We can imagine how painful this must be, as when they are dragged out of the water the hooks hold their entire weight. In this way, the hooks usually get deeper and deeper, and tear apart the body parts they are attached to. Then, they start to suffocate. They struggle frantically to get back to the water as long as they have enough strength, which shows how distressed they are. Scientific studies indicate they suffer very significantly during this whole process, until they die.[8]

In recent decades, the practice of "catch and release" has spread. However, many animals that are captured do not survive when returned to the water. This is often a consequence of the severity of the injuries inflicted on them by the hook. They can suffer infections or severe hemorrhages. Sometimes their mouths are hurt so much by the hooks that they can no longer feed properly and they starve. They can also die because they lose too many scales due to handling by fishers, or simply because they are exhausted after the stress of their capture. In other cases, they are left too weak after their frantic struggle to flee, and are rendered easy prey for other animals, or without enough energy left to find food.[9]

In addition to this, anglers often use other small animals as bait. They are impaled on the hooks. An animal that doesn't die from this may be eaten alive by the captured fish. Furthermore, loose angles and fishing lines continue to harm and kill many animals, years after the fishers leave them behind or lose them.

Other fishers do not use hooks, but nets. The animals that are captured in them also have miserable deaths. Once captured, the nets tighten on their bodies, so the animals are squeezed together, chafing each other intensely. This not only causes injuries to their scales: it also drives them to feel much pain and distress as they suffocate. Others are killed by divers with spears and other weapons, which make them suffer just as we would if we were impaled.[10]

Other sentient animals that are also captured in large numbers by fishers are crustaceans, such as lobsters or crabs. Like a trapped fish, they'll desperately try to flee when captured. Afterwards, to keep them "fresh," they are sometimes kept in ice, thus suffering considerably from the cold. Finally, they typically endure horrible deaths as they are often cooked alive.

Defenses of hunting and fishing

Hunting and fishing are often defended as traditions and as healthy ways to engage in sport. But this is clearly irrelevant for the animals involved. While for the hunter the hunt may just be a few hours of entertainment, or a way of exercising outdoors, for the animal who is hunted and killed it is an experience of intense pain, fear, distress, and death.

Sometimes these practices are defended by claiming that they are necessary to manage animal populations. This view rests on a conservationist idea according to which we should not care about individual sentient animals, but about ecosystems and species conservation.[11] According to this position, if killing some animals allows us to keep a certain ecosystem in a given way, it's perfectly justified to do so.

Would we ever accept killing human beings in order to conserve a particular ecosystem? Of course not. Accordingly, if we reject speciesism, it seems we can't accept that it is perfectly acceptable to kill other sentient animals for that purpose. In fact, those holding this view almost never claim that humans should be significantly harmed or killed to keep an ecosystem in a certain way. They would find such a view repulsive. They only accept these conservationist killings when nonhuman animals are the ones to be killed, even though humans impact the environment much more. The reason for this is, simply, a speciesist bias.

We must bear in mind that it is individual sentient animals that can suffer, not ecosystems or species. This is why it should not be acceptable to kill and inflict terrible suffering on sentient beings in order to maintain a certain ecosystem in its current state. If we think it is not acceptable to do so in the case of human beings, we can't accept it in the case of other animals either.

Hunters sometimes argue that they just behave as natural predators do and that in nature it's normal that animals die continually. However, this provides no justification for hunting or fishing. Life in the wild is not idyllic for animals at all: there are many ways in which animals suffer and die in nature. But this doesn't give us a reason to add even more suffering and death to what already exists. We will come back to this again in Chapter 6.

Circuses and shows with nonhuman animals

Let's take a look now at what happens in the case of shows that use animals. We can start by examining what happens in circuses. When people attend circuses, they often fail to imagine what happens when the show is over. Moreover, they also fail to see what's really going on during the show. Let's think about it for a moment. Can we really believe that animals perform because they enjoy it? This is a good question we should consider. And there's another one which is also important when we think about animals in circuses: what happens to them when they are not performing?

Answering these two questions can give us a glimpse of what the lives of these animals are like. Consider the latter question first. When animals are not performing, they aren't hanging around enjoying themselves. They spend most of their lives in trucks, in which they have very little space to move, being transported from town to town. Sometimes big animals such as elephants or horses don't even have enough room to turn around. This is terribly boring and frustrating for them. On top of that, it's also bad for their health.

Social animals also suffer from loneliness, just as we would if we were in their situation.[12] In addition, they have to deal with stress, the never-ending discomfort and tiredness of having to travel thousands of miles. This is even tougher when they have to suffer from the cold or the heat, especially in the case of animals that are better suited for a different climate.[13]

Even worse than this is what they have to undergo in order to perform. The tricks they have to do in shows are very difficult and stressful for them. In some shows, for instance, animals such as lions stand on the back of horses. In other shows, elephants are made to do things such as standing on a single leg. This is very difficult and painful for them, as they are so heavy, and can cause them serious injuries. So let's consider the first question asked above. How is it possible that the lions do this and that the horses don't panic and flee? How can elephants agree to do something so painful for them? The answer is simple: because they've been systematically tortured and punished until their will is totally broken.

From the first moment a lion cub or a baby elephant arrives in the circus, she is taught to obey by being beaten up regularly with instruments such as whips, sticks, metal hooks, and even electric prods. They suffer this torture daily not as a punishment for not doing something, but only so they get accustomed to fear, and so their wills are totally broken down. This is also the reason why this is done to them from infancy. In this way, they end up so scared of their trainers that they accept being made to do a wide range of painful and scary tricks, both for fear of the pain of the punishments they get and because their will to disobey has been broken.[14] In addition to this, the teeth and claws of many of these animals are often taken out (something which is usually done without any anesthetics or painkillers), though even this is but a small part of the huge suffering inflicted on them every day of their lives.

As a result of all this, these animals often suffer from serious psychological disorders, which are made worse by the stress of having to perform in front of noisy crowds.[15] For this reason, sometimes an animal can't stand it any longer and rebels, attacking the trainers or fleeing. This usually results in the animal being killed. Animals who can't perform any longer are also killed, or sold.

Circuses are not the only establishments where animals are kept for entertainment. Other businesses of this type include aquariums and zoos. These are sometimes defended by claiming that the animals living in them are well cared for, and thus free from the harms they suffer in nature.[16] But this argument isn't convincing. It is completely true (despite what some people believe) that animals in nature usually suffer a lot and have very short lives. It is common for them to face many difficulties and injuries. However, this does not mean that animals in aquariums and zoos live well. They are often locked up in small cages or other tiny spaces in which they can hardly move, and they suffer from adverse environmental conditions. Their continuous exposure to visitors can be very stressful for many of these animals. In turn, those who are social and live alone can suffer greatly from loneliness.[17] Aquatic animals, on the other hand, are especially stressed because the pools they are in are very small, which is a major source of suffering for animals with a sense of echolocation, such as dolphins. They also suffer from various health problems, especially in their eyes and skin, due to the quality of the water in the pools and the chemicals in it.

Another argument that is used to defend these establishments is that they help to preserve the species whose members die in the wild without reproducing.[18] According to this position, it is justified to harm sentient animals if this furthers conservation efforts. This is the same argument used to defend hunting. Those who use it are displaying a speciesist attitude, since they would never feel justified in harming innocent human beings for the same purpose. Sentient beings matter, and so they should not be harmed and killed to promote the existence of entities that cannot feel suffering or wellbeing, such as ecosystems or species.

Finally, we must not forget that, in addition to all we have seen, keeping animals entails feeding them, and they are often fed other animals, or animal products. As a result, these other animals are also exploited and killed. This means that for each animal kept in a circus, zoo, or aquarium, there are many others who suffer and die.[19]

Something similar can be said in the case of other uses of animals for fun which, at first sight, may also seem harmless for animals. This is what happens in the case of horse and dog races. Many people believe that the animals competing in them are happy ones who enjoy racing. However, the fact is that they are forced to compete and heavily trained from a very young age. At those ages, their bodies aren't properly developed, so they are more vulnerable to injuries. And when they suffer serious injuries that prevent them from racing, they aren't saved, but killed.

So, to conclude: there are many different ways human beings can have fun, and some of them cause nonhuman animals to suffer terribly. However, we can choose those forms of entertainment that are harmless to others, including other animals.

Exploiting animals for their consumption as food

The use of animals for entertainment often provokes disapproval. But the main way in which animals are exploited and harmed by humans is different: it is their use for food. Almost every animal raised to be eaten is bred on a factory farm. This is by far the most common way of raising animals in Western countries, and it's starting to become so in the rest of the world as well. This shouldn't surprise us. Many people all around the world eat animals, often several times a day. This requires that enormous numbers of animals are bred to be killed. These animals vastly outnumber humans (which is easy to understand, if we bear in mind that human beings typically eat many animals each year). Consider that today more than 70 billion animals are killed every year in slaughterhouses.[20] However, we never see these animals. If we are in the countryside or on the road, we may see some of them, but we don't usually see large numbers of them. Why is this? For a simple reason: because they are confined in farms.

Today, farms are organized so they can breed the highest possible number of animals in the smallest possible space and at the lowest possible cost. The number of animals eaten every day is so huge that it wouldn't be possible to raise them differently. This means that the space animals have is incredibly small. Most animals lack any room to move. In some cases, they can't even turn around. Many of them never see the sun light (until they are carried out to the slaughterhouse). All this is terribly frustrating for them, of course. Moreover, in modern farms, there's nothing for animals to do, they have nothing different to explore. This means they are extremely bored and depressed all the time.

For the same reasons, the places in which they are confined are rarely made with materials that are comfortable for them, such as grass or earth. Rather, they live on uncomfortable concrete slatted floors. This makes it easier for farmers to clean their excrement. But it means that animals have to live continually over their excrement. Not only must they endure the terrible smell, but since farms are poorly ventilated, this negatively affects their respiration too. In addition, sometimes the excrement isn't cleared away, so it accumulates and emerges up through the railings of the animals' cages or crates. Other animals, such as broiler chickens, live in industrial units, in non-compartmentalized spaces, and have to step on excrement piled on the ground all the time.

The awful conditions on large farms mean that animals are often in very poor health, and they suffer from many different illnesses. They are very vulnerable to infections, and they would suffer many more if they weren't routinely given large doses of antibiotics.[21] Even this doesn't stop them from getting sick anyway. Moreover, those big doses of antibiotics can also have negative effects on their health. And if they are sick, they often just die, as they do not get proper veterinary care. In some cases, it is the disease itself that kills them, in others, they die because the disease makes it impossible for them to feed. For instance, on pig farms, sick piglets may not have the strength needed to get their food, and they end up being too weak to stand up from the floor. When this happens, they suffer terribly. They can do nothing but lie on the ground as the other piglets continually step on them as they move around the pen. This causes them terrible pain as they suffer from both disease and starvation. The same happens to sick chickens. As for sick hens, they can be pecked continually by other hens as they are not strong enough to defend themselves. In certain cases, farmers kill sick animals who are not going to make it. They can do this by thrashing their small heads against a wall. In other cases they just remove them from the living spaces and leave them in the corridors in between. They no longer have access to food there, so they slowly starve or succumb to their disease or injury.

Disease can spread rapidly on factory farms, sometimes giving rise to epidemics. When this happens massive slaughters of animals commonly take place, including the killing of healthy animals too, to stop the disease from spreading more. This is done even when those conditions can be treated, since it's more expensive to treat the animals than to kill them and replace them with new animals. This is often done by burying the animals alive, throwing them into pits and covering them with quicklime.[22]

The terrible stress and boredom endured by animals on factory farms frequently makes them engage in aggressive behavior, which threatens their health. Boredom drives piglets to bite the tails of other piglets, and drives hens to peck other hens. This can cause serious problems if the wounds get infected.

Farmers deal with this problem not by solving the underlying causes of aggressive behavior, but by mutilating animals so that they are unable to injure each other. Hens commonly get their beaks cut with heated blades, while piglets get their teeth and tails clipped. This is also done to prevent piglets from biting their mothers' breasts. This can happen while they are feeding, as in farrowing cages the sows cannot move and are helpless.

Another mutilation procedure that is carried out to reduce conflict between animals is castration. Castration also makes animals grow faster, and makes them tamer when workers handle them, especially during their transport and killing. Steers are also mutilated, as they are dehorned to reduce the risk that they harm workers or other animals with their horns. This is done either by cutting their horns or by burning them off with caustic chemicals

These are extremely painful procedures, yet the animals aren't given any anesthetics or painkillers (since this would cost money without any increase in productivity). The result of this is that the animals suffer terribly. Just imagine what it would be like to get your own teeth cut with pliers or some other similar tool, or to get a bone or other parts of your body cut off without any painkiller. Moreover, these are not the only painful procedures they have to undergo. Mammals are also commonly branded with hot irons or by cutting small parts of their bodies or harming their bodies in other ways. Sometimes corrosive chemicals or freezing dry ice or liquid nitrogen is used to mark them. This, again, is done without any painkillers being given to them.

All these things affect animals of different species. Let's now look in more detail at the situation of the animals that are most commonly raised on farms today.

Pig farms

Pigs are usually kept in different kinds of facilities depending on what stage of the reproduction and life cycles they are in. During gestation, female pigs exploited for reproduction spend around four months confined in tiny metal crates with slatted floors. They are called gestation crates, and are only a bit bigger than their own bodies, so they can barely move. It's not only that they cannot walk, in fact they cannot even turn around, and it's only with great difficulty that they can manage to lie down or stand up.[23] We can imagine what it would be like to spend several months locked up like this. These animals suffer terribly physically, as their muscles and joints are severely harmed by these conditions. In addition to this, the sows also suffer psychologically from the extreme distress and boredom they have to endure. In other cases, sows are kept in groups but with very little room, so even though they don't suffer as much as in crates, they still endure lots of stress and, because of this, sometimes fight each other.

Before they give birth, they are carried out to other types of crates which are called farrowing crates, in which their piglets are born. These crates have some room for the piglets, but apart from that, they are similar to gestation crates. They are barely bigger than the sows themselves so the sows cannot move. This is so that the sows don't accidentally crush the piglets with their weight, given that they have so little room.[24]

When the piglets are weaned (which may be when they are over three weeks old), the sows are impregnated once again and the same cycle starts for them again, until they are around three years old and are sent to the slaughterhouse. For their part, the piglets are sent to pens that are usually crowded to gain weight.[25] Finally, they are killed when they are around four months old, unless their bodies are used to produce what is called "suckling pig meat," in which case they are killed when they are piglets (between one and a half months or three months). We must bear in mind that when pigs are not killed they can live up to 20 years or more. This is more than 30 times the time they actually live. This is what happens, by the way, in the case of those who have been rescued from farms and live in animal shelters or sanctuaries.

Cow and calf farms

Cows are exploited for several different purposes, including the production of milk, meat, and leather. Like all female mammals, cows only produce milk after giving birth (excluding the case of hormonal alterations), as their milk is meant to nourish their babies. For this reason, cows on dairy farms are continually made pregnant, often by artificial insemination. Of course, dairy farmers don't want the calves to drink the milk as that would lessen their profits. So, what happens to the babies? If they are female, they may be raised to produce milk for the dairy industry just as their mothers were. However, some females and all male calves face a different fate. They are taken away from their mothers shortly after being born. This is terribly traumatic for both the mother and her calf, who cry and call for each other for days.

Some calves used to produce "veal" are killed the same day they are born, sometimes just after birth. The rest are usually sent to tiny crates in which they have no room to move, and can't even turn around. Their necks are sometimes chained or tied, or their heads immobilized. This is done so that they can't exercise their muscles. In this way, their flesh remains as tender as possible. For the same reason, they are fed with formulas that are low in iron and other nutrients. This makes them feel weak, and causes them pain due to digestive issues.[26] Sometimes they are so weak that they aren't even able to walk properly when they are sent to be killed.

Other calves aren't used to produce "veal" but are raised longer to produce larger amounts of "beef." These animals aren't kept in crates, and live for several months longer, in some cases one or two years, until they grow large enough and are slaughtered.

For their part, cows used for milk production are milked for around 10 months after they are separated from their calves. Afterwards, they are made pregnant again and the same process is repeated. This goes on several times until the cows are exhausted and, like their calves before them, they are killed and transformed into meat. This happens when they are very young. Cows used to produce milk rarely live more than 5 or 6 years, and some are killed at 3. If they weren't slaughtered, they could live for another 15 years or more (even more than 20 according to some estimates).[27]

The repeated loss of their babies and their early deaths are terrible harms inflicted on these animals, but they are not the only ones. Cows often spend much if not all of their time indoors, in uncomfortable and boring environments. Their health is severely affected by the lives they are forced to live, and because of the hormones they are regularly administered to increase their milk production. This can cause them to suffer from painful conditions as well as infections in their legs and udders. Some people worry that this may not be healthy for milk consumers. But, most of all, it's terribly unhealthy for the cows themselves.

Chicken and hen farms

Around five out of every six animals killed in slaughterhouses are chickens. Most of them spend their lives in overcrowded indoor spaces, in which there's nothing but concrete, metal, and hundreds or thousands of other confined chickens. The industrial units in which they live don't contain individual feeders, so they may have to compete for food. Some animals aren't able to make it and starve or die of dehydration, but, since they are a minority, it's worth it for farmers to use this system, as it means less work for them and therefore lower cost per chicken.

Chickens grown for meat have been genetically selected to grow very quickly, and this causes many health problems for them.[28] Their legs are not sufficiently developed to hold their weight, which leads to injuries and pain. Some chickens can't even stand for this reason. In addition, their quick growth and high weight can lead them to suffer from heart diseases even if they are only some weeks old.[29] Some chickens could live for more than 10 years and even reach the age of 15, but they are killed when they are only a few weeks old. In open range farms, they are killed when they are a bit older, though the difference isn't that much, as they are slaughtered when they are around three months old.

Hens that are used to lay eggs don't do any better. In many farms around the world, they live in overcrowded battery cages. They have no room to move, as they live in a space about as large as a sheet of paper. If you have a piece of paper close to you right now you can imagine how little room these hens have and[30] what it means to live like this.

Hens in such environments suffer from high levels of stress, and this often drives them to peck other hens. Sometimes they die and their corpses remain in the cage until the other hens are gathered to be slaughtered. They also suffer a variety of physical harms: they are continuously losing feathers and getting skin abrasions by chafing against other hens or the metal of the cages, and standing on the wire of their cages often harms them. In some cases, their feet become embedded in the metal mesh, and so when they are taken out of the cages to be sent to the slaughterhouse their legs break and a part of them remains stuck to the cage.

In other cases, hens are kept in bigger cages or live similarly to chickens raised to be eaten. That is, in crowded conditions in industrial units, without being able to go outside. In these cases too, there are many who don't survive.

Like chickens raised for meat, they have been genetically selected, not for rapid growth, but to lay as many eggs as possible. This makes them vulnerable to disease, as laying so many eggs makes them likely to suffer from osteoporosis and other conditions. Finally, when their production decreases below the levels considered optimal, they are killed. This happens when they are quite young, rarely beyond the age of 2, often when they are just one and a half years old. The same happens to those hens that are kept as so-called "free range" hens. They usually live a bit longer, but they too are killed much younger than they could have otherwise lived.

Finally, since the sex ratio is approximately 50:50, for every hen hatched, there is also a male chick. As we have seen, these animals have been genetically selected, and the varieties used for producing meat are different from the ones selected to lay eggs. For this reason, the male chicks of laying hens aren't grown to be eaten, as they wouldn't grow as fast as the ones selected for that purpose. Since they can't lay eggs, and it isn't profitable to raise them for meat, the male chicks are disposable—just after they hatch from their eggs, they are separated from the females and killed. Sometimes they are thrown into a grinding machine. In many other cases, they are simply thrown into a bin,[31] where they die of suffocation or from being crushed by the weight of all the other male chicks thrown on top of them.

Fish farming

While the vast majority of the animals raised in land farms are chickens, the number of animals raised and killed in aquatic farms is even higher. Different types of fishes, including especially carps, tilapias, sturgeons, and salmons, are grown in them. It has been estimated that the number of them killed every year could be between 51 and 167 billion.[32] The number of crustaceans such as decapods (in particular shrimps and prawns) killed in aquatic farms is even higher. In addition, other animals are also raised and killed in aquatic farms, including frogs, turtles, and octopuses.[33]

Fish farms can consist of enclosures located within rivers, lakes, or the sea, such as cages from which the animals can't escape, or tanks where they are intensively raised. The conditions in these aquatic farms are similarly bad as those in factory farms on land. Fish farms apply industrial methods similar to the ones land farms apply. In these farms, animals live in crowded conditions.[34] This is very stressful for them, both because of the lack of room and because there are so many other animals around. In some cases, this can lead to fights and even cannibalism.[35] Sometimes this causes animals to suffer wounds and abrasions which can eventually become infected, as they collide and scrape their bodies against each other or the tanks or cages. Furthermore, when conditions become too crowded, aquatic animals can suffocate, as the water doesn't contain enough oxygen. Overcrowding also causes competition for food, as a result of which some animals may lack proper access to it. This is harmful for their health, and means they suffer due to the hunger they endure.

In these respects, their situation resembles that of animals in land farms. But there are also other reasons why animals suffer in these farms. The water is of poor quality, and contains chemicals that can hurt the animals (especially their skin and eyes). Artificial lights are sometimes used so they grow faster, and this also distresses the animals.

Because of all this, the health of the animals is very poor, and they often get sick. In addition, overcrowding causes disease to spread very quickly, leading easily to epidemics. To prevent this, huge amounts of antibiotics are thrown into the waters in which they are grown.[36] This heavy medication can have side effects on their health (in fact, other animals living around the farm are also affected by this, as the drugs, together with the waste of the fish farms, overflow into the surrounding areas).

As a result, death rates in fish farms at different stages of the growth of the animals are high. Still, even those who survive are eventually killed, just like mammals and birds in land farms: that's the whole point of breeding them.

Moreover, the animals that are grown in factory farms are often fed other animals, mainly aquatic ones. In some cases, these animals they are fed are also raised in farms, though they are often animals captured in fisheries. In this way, eating a fish raised in a fish farm means not only the death of the animal that is directly eaten but also that of many others that are killed to fatten that animal. In addition, many of the animals raised in fish farms, as well as other aquatic animals that are fished, are also used to feed animals kept in other farms. Their bodies are ground up to produce what is known as "fish flour," which is fed to all kinds of animals, including pigs and cows.

Killing animals

We have seen the way animals live, and we've found that their lives consist of constant suffering. This, unfortunately, continues until the end of their days. There's no rest for them, and certainly not at the moment of their deaths. They die as they live: without any consideration being given to them. They are killed in ways that cause them to endure extreme pain and anguish. This is, of course, in addition to the fact that at the end of the day, each of these animals is deprived of her or his life, the only one that each animal has.

Let's consider, first, the way animals are killed in fish farms.[37] Often they simply die of suffocation as they are taken out of the water. This is similar to what it would be like for us to die by drowning. In other cases, their bodies are cut so they bleed to death. This means they suffer the agony of their deaths while fully conscious. In other cases, they are killed by blows to the head, by electrocution, or by hypothermia (by introducing them to very cold water). All these methods of killing are very painful. In some cases, they are killed by carbon dioxide poisoning, or, in the case of large types of fishes, by shooting them in the head.

Land animals don't do any better. The suffering they endure in farms, though terrible, is made even worse during their trip to the slaughterhouse and their deaths. This starts with the process of loading them onto the trucks they are transported in. Many animals such as pigs are really distressed by being loaded and unloaded, and resist it. For this reason, they are often hit so that they get onto the trucks, or they are loaded in other brutal ways. This may be done using sticks, pricks, electric prods, or hammers. Birds are loaded as if they were things, often by holding them by their legs and throwing them into the crates. As a result, they often get their legs and other bones broken. They must make their journey with those injuries, and the hardships of travel increase the suffering they are forced to endure.[38]

Once on the trucks, the overcrowding may be even worse than in the farms. Animals have very little room, often little more than the size of their own bodies. Birds are carried out in piled crates which means that they get very little ventilation, particularly those in the lower crates, and this means that they may not get adequate oxygen, and may even suffocate.

Some of them, such as cows and calves, have to remain standing for long periods of time, which increases their exhaustion, sometimes causing them to fall on top of other animals. They may be injured because of sudden movements of the trucks, from falls, or collisions with other animals or crates, and can end up with broken bones. Certain parts of their bodies such as their hips or knees are particularly vulnerable to injury during transport. The conditions in which they have lived make them especially vulnerable to these injuries, since they haven't been able to move around and consequently their bones and muscles are extremely weak (remember that in farms many of them lack the room to move or walk).

Animals can feel sick because of the movement of the trucks, especially on curves, roundabouts, and turns. In addition, they suffer from the weather, sometimes enduring extreme heat or cold, wind, and rain blown into the trailer by strong winds. Moreover, they are not provided with any food or water. That would not be profitable, as they can survive without them until they are killed, and there would be no time for it to be converted in the animals' bodies into more meat to be sold. This means they also suffer from hunger and thirst, which adds to their exhaustion. And, again, since their health is in a terribly poor state due to their lives in farms, their capacity to withstand this is very low. Some animals die before they reach their destination, showing just how much these animals have to suffer.[39] Stress and fear can cause the animals to fight, and some may suffer severe wounds.

Once they arrive at the slaughterhouse, the misery of the animals is increased even further, perhaps reaching the highest levels it's possible for an animal to suffer. Slaughterhouses are all about ending lives, as many and as quickly as possible. That alone would make slaughterhouses terrible places for the animals that go there even if they felt no suffering at all. But in addition, they also suffer terrible pain and distress there.

When they get there, the animals are scared, as they are in a hostile and unfamiliar environment. They arrive hungry and thirsty after their journey from the farm. They are sometimes hit with spiked sticks to move them down through the slaughterhouse lines. Because of the life they've had, and because they're exhausted after their dreadful trip to the slaughterhouse, they may not be able to walk. Sometimes they collapse and can't make it through the line. Some even have heart attacks. In those cases, the slaughterhouse workers may drag the animals with hooks pierced through different parts of their bodies. Sometimes this rips apart the animal's body. We can imagine the pain and fear this causes them. On top of that, as they approach their deaths they can see and hear other animals being killed and can smell their blood. All this terrifies them.

In many countries (though not all), animals are meant to be stunned before they are killed. There are different methods of stunning. Pigs, for instance, are often stunned with what is called "electronarcosis," which consists in putting electric pliers on their heads and applying an electric charge that is meant to render them unconscious. This method causes them pain before they lose consciousness (as those who have suffered an electric shock will well know). In other cases, animals are stunned with gas, for which carbon dioxide is often used (this gas is sometimes used to kill them, but it's more often applied to render them unconscious). Again, during the time it takes for them to lose consciousness (which may be longer than half a minute), they can be very distressed (and sometimes feel pain, as the gas irritates their respiratory tracts). Cows (as well as bulls and calves) are usually stunned with captive bolt pistols. These are pistols that insert a bolt into their brain, or make a hole in it with compressed air.

As animals on the slaughterhouse lines are moving fast, this process is done very quickly. As a result of this, it's not uncommon that animals are not really stunned, and are fully conscious when they are killed. Moreover, sometimes this means that they are not stabbed in a way that kills them, and they can be quartered and skinned or boiled while fully conscious.

As we saw already, most animals killed in slaughterhouses are hens and chickens. In slaughterhouses, they are often killed by an automatic blade which cuts their throat while they are hanging upside down from the conveyor belt. This happens after their heads pass through the electrified stunning tanks. They are then moved to scalding tanks filled with boiling water where they will be defeathered.

However, on the conveyor belt, these animals are in a very uncomfortable and stressful situation from which they want to escape. So they are struggling and moving their wings and heads. For this reason, they sometimes pass over the electrified tanks with their heads raised above the water and therefore they never lose consciousness. As a result, they may still be moving when they reach the automatic blade, and so the blade may not cut their throat. The blade may not touch the animal, or instead cut another part of her or his body, such as the wings, face, or beak. The slaughterhouse workers may then manually decapitate these animals. However, they can miss many animals, as the conveyor belt runs quickly and doesn't stop. This means they will reach the scalding tanks fully conscious, where they are boiled alive.[40]

Something similar sometimes happens to pigs. After they are stunned, they are shackled by their legs and raised off the ground (which sometimes breaks their legs). They are killed afterwards by having their throats cut. If they are still conscious, as is sometimes the case, this causes them great pain and distress. Moreover, the time they spend on the line after having their throats cut but before they are thrown into the scalding tanks is shorter than the time it takes them to bleed to death. This means that those who aren't properly stunned are boiled alive while fully conscious. There are appalling reports from slaughterhouse workers which describe this graphically:

> These hogs get up to the scalding tank, hit the water and start screaming and kicking. Sometimes they thrash so much they kick water out of the tank... Sooner or later they drown. There's a rotating arm that pushes them under, no chance for them to get out. I'm not sure if they burn to death before they drown, but it takes them a couple of minutes to stop thrashing.[41]

Cows and calves also suffer a terrifying fate. After stunning, they are, like pigs, hung upside down and their throats are cut. But they are often not really stunned, and they are sometimes fully conscious when they are cut into pieces and skinned. Another worker in a slaughterhouse reported that he had seen many cases in which this happens. He said:

> The head moves, the eyes are wide and looking around... They die piece by piece.[42]

We can imagine the unbearable pain and horror that being quartered and skinned alive causes them. It sounds so horrifying that we may be tempted to doubt that it really happens. But it does, this is completely real, and it happens all the time in slaughterhouses all around the world. There is no incentive for slaughterhouses to prevent these things from happening, as doing so would mean significantly reducing the speed at which the animals are killed, thus reducing profits. Note also that given the huge numbers of animals killed every day, the number of animals who suffer this fate is enormous. This is something that happens routinely every day, and will go on happening indefinitely, day by day, as long as meat products are consumed.

In addition, we must bear in mind what happens if the slaughterhouse workers are stressed, if they get angry at some animal or if they just want to have fun torturing animals. There's really nothing to prevent them from causing extra harm to the animals if they want to. The animals are powerless in their hands, and if they choose to make them suffer even more, there is nothing to stop them. Another testimonial of a slaughterhouse worker describes this clearly and terribly:

> You're already going to kill the hog, but that's not enough. It has to suffer... you don't just kill it, you go in hard, push hard, blow the windpipe, make it drown in its own blood. Split its nose. A live hog would be running around the pit. It would just be looking up at me and I'd be sticking, and I would just take my knife and—eerk—cut its eye out while it was just sitting there. And this hog would just scream. One time I took my knife— it's sharp enough—and I sliced off the end of a hog's nose, just like a piece of bologna. The hog went crazy for a few seconds. Then it just sat there looking kind of stupid. So I took a handful of salt brine and ground it into his nose. Now that hog really went nuts, pushing its nose all over the place. I still had a bunch of salt in my hand—I was wearing a rubber glove—and I stuck the salt right up the hog's ass. The poor hog didn't know whether to shit or go blind... But I wasn't the only guy doing this kind of stuff... One guy I work with actually chases hogs into the scalding tank.[43]

Such cases may be a minority, but since so many animals are killed in slaughterhouses, there ends up being a huge number of victims of this kind of cruelty. Besides this, we mustn't forget that the other animals also suffer enormously during their slaughter.[44]

It's important to note that this fate awaits all animals raised for food, regardless of whether they have been raised in factory farms (as the overwhelming majority are) or on free range farms.

Fishing

The number of animals that are fished is so high that they are not measured in terms of individuals, but in tons. This makes it difficult to know how many animals are killed in this way. However, some estimates have been made, considering the average weight of different fish species. In this way, it has been calculated that between almost one trillion and more than two trillion fish(es) are caught annually by commercial fishers.[45] This figure sets aside other animals that are also fished, including mollusks such as cephalopods (including octopuses and squids), turtles, marine mammals, and others. In particular, the number of crustaceans that are fished (including crabs, lobsters, prawns, and shrimps) is very difficult to assess, but, because of their small size, it could even be much higher than that of all other aquatic animals that are captured.

Some fishing boats use nets while others use baits. Among the former, some use the method of trawling, which consists in releasing nets and pulling them to catch everything that falls into them. The animals that are caught this way may be dragged long distances. During that time, their bodies are in contact with the net mesh or with other animals, bumping and chafing against them. In addition, as they are dragged they are hit by other trapped animals or by obstacles in the net's path. Other boats use huge nets, several hundred meters long, that are left to drift freely. These nets are made so that aquatic animals can't see or smell them. As a result, they often get caught in them as their bodies get hooked in them. When this happens, they can spend days trapped in this way, until they starve or are captured and killed. Yet other boats target specific fish schools and surround them with nets until these animals have no way out. When this happens and the net is tightened, the animals are often crushed against each other, and can suffer severe injuries. They desperately try to escape and their struggle continues when they are raised out of the water. But there is no way to escape.

Among the boats using baits, some of them cast a very long fishing line, which may have thousands of baited hooks. A fish caught this way may bleed to death or die because of the injuries caused by the hooks while struggling to be free. This pain and distress lasts for a significant time, as once they bite the bait these animals can be dragged along with severe injuries for a very long time. Baits are also used to attract animals of large fish species such as tunas. When they are sufficiently close to the fishers, they are caught and pulled into the boat. To do so, fishers often pierce their bodies using spears or large hooks. Then, they stab them to death. In addition to all this, of course, the animals that are used as bait are also made to suffer and die.

In other cases, fishing is done not with boats, but with traps, in which the animals remain until they are brought to the surface. They can feel hunger as well as stress as they are unable to escape. Different types of fishes are also sometimes caught by using explosives that are thrown into the sea. The explosives can kill the animals or stun them, so they are easy to catch. Sometimes they make their swim bladder explode, killing them. Many animals that aren't deliberately fished are nevertheless killed in this way.

We can thus see that each of the different forms of fishing entails suffering. And there are also different ways in which they can die. Aquatic animals raised from the sea depths sometimes die because their internal organs explode due to decompression (that is, due to the change of pressure between the sea depths and the surface). Many others die of suffocation when they are taken out of the water. They may also die because, when they are raised with the nets or piled in boats, the weight of the other animals over them crushes their bodies. Others are frozen to death in ships' freezers. They may also be stabbed or beaten to death. Others have even worse deaths: they may be cooked or even eaten alive.[46] As we saw previously, all types of fishes, like other vertebrates, can feel suffering. And we also saw that many invertebrates appear to be sentient too, including certainly octopuses and other cephalopods such as squids, but also crustaceans such as lobsters, crabs, and others.

In light of this, considering the huge numbers of animals that are fished and what happens to them, we can imagine the appalling amount of suffering that fishing produces. Moreover, this practice doesn't only affect the targeted animals. Many other animals are killed by fishers too. All kinds of sentient beings can end up caught in fishing nets or bite the bait, including seabirds and marine mammals such as dolphins. Lost or abandoned fishing nets go on killing animals indefinitely. In some cases, they can inflict physical harms on them (for instance, by cutting their bodies or suffocating them), in others they just trap them until they starve in distress.

Environmentalists often claim that fishing is a problem due to the overfishing of seas and lakes. The suffering and death of the animals involved, though, is just the same in all cases, whether or not they are "overfished." So, from a point of view that considers the wellbeing of individual animals, we have no reason to think that fishing becomes acceptable when it's considered sustainable or environmentally friendly. As far as the animals are concerned, all fishing is overfishing.

Animals exploited for clothing

Many of the animals killed in farms to produce food products are also skinned, plucked, and exploited in other ways for the production of leather, feathers, or wool. This makes it more profitable to raise and kill the animals and thus helps sustain these exploitative practices.

Leather is taken from the animals once they are dead (though, as we have seen, in slaughterhouses, some animals are skinned while alive and fully conscious). Other products may be extracted from them regularly while they are alive. Consider for instance the case of geese that are currently farmed both for meat, foie gras, and for their feathers. Many of the feathers used for making pillows, duvet covers, coats, etc. are taken from farmed and killed birds once they are dead. Some are also collected when they fall from the birds. But many others are taken from them while they are still alive, by plucking them. We must note that feather follicles are linked to sensitive pain receptors. This makes this process terribly painful and distressing to birds, as it would be for us if someone pulled our hair out while we were fully conscious.[47] Moreover, this pain is increased by the fact that feathers are in many cases pulled from birds by using electrical machines which can also inflict wounds on them. When this happens, the pain these birds suffer may last for several days. But the suffering of animals is not considered important, so this process is repeated several times during a goose's life.

Other animals that are exploited both for their meat (and also their milk) and for clothing are sheep—or actually, maybe it would be more adequate to start calling them sheep*s*, as a way of stressing that they are individuals instead of an uncountable mass.[48] In any case, the exploitation these animals suffer causes them other harms in addition to the ones they undergo by being farmed as other animals are. Once they are adults, they are shorn every year until they are sent to the slaughterhouse. This is commonly done with powered shears that work similarly to clippers, and often very quickly. As a result, it often happens that a sheep undergoing this process gets cut. This can cause them much pain, and make the whole shearing process very stressful for them.[49]

In addition, these animals often suffer from a worm-caused infection called *fly-strike*. To prevent it, it's common to subject them to the practice called "mulesing," which consists in tearing strips of flesh from their buttocks to prevent infections.[50] We can imagine how painful it is.

Lambs are killed to be eaten when they are very young. In addition to depriving them of their lives, this is extremely distressing for their mothers from whom they are separated (as we saw above the same thing happens to cows and their calves). We may think that this is unrelated to the use of these animals for wool. But this isn't so. Both forms of exploitation (wool production and the killing of lambs) are connected, as they make each other more profitable, thus reinforcing each other.

Finally, other animals are exploited exclusively for the production of clothing. This happens in the case of those used to produce fur. To make a single fur coat, dozens of minks, foxes, or beavers and up to several hundreds of squirrels and chinchillas are killed. Most of the animals used for this purpose spend their whole lives in tiny cages on fur farms until they are killed. They live in conditions similar to the ones in which other animals such as pigs or hens live. Because of their fur, they can suffer a lot due to hot temperatures in the summer. Finally, when they are only a few months old, they are gassed or electrocuted, or get their necks broken. Many are skinned alive while fully conscious, as in the case of cows and calves in slaughterhouses.[51]

Other animals used for fur are killed in the wild. This happens in the case of seals that are slaughtered in raids by having their heads bashed in with clubs or by being shot.[52] But most animals killed for their fur in the wild are captured with traps. This causes the trapped animals not only significant pain but also terrible anxiety and distress. Animals can spend days caught in traps, during which they also suffer from hunger, thirst, and cold, and may be attacked by other animals as they can't escape. Sometimes, the animals harm their jaws severely by biting the metal traps. In other cases, they bite their own trapped limbs, in an attempt to bite them off in order to escape (sometimes they manage to do this). This can give us an idea of how desperate they are. Traps can be underwater, and then the animals die in terrible distress by drowning while they try desperately to escape for many minutes. Moreover, very often the animals that are caught in traps are not the ones the trappers aimed to capture, but others such as birds, dogs, or horses.[53]

In recent decades, the breeding and killing of animals for fur has faced increasing opposition. Many people are outraged by the fur industry, yet they see no problem with using animals in other ways. However, we must remember what we have seen in previous sections: this practice is not inherently worse for animals than breeding and killing them for food production.

Furthermore, the number of animals killed for food is much larger than the number killed for their fur: for each animal killed for the production of fur thousands can be killed in fish farms and slaughterhouses, and more than 40,000 in fishing nets. In any case, the forms of exploitation that affect fewer animals still add to the total suffering and death inflicted by humans on other animals. Moreover, if we oppose them, we also have reasons to object to the ones that affect more animals. We will see more about this in the next chapter.

Exploiting small animals

Finally, we need to consider those forms of exploitation which, though they kill large numbers of animals, are generally ignored because of the small size of the animals involved. These consist of the use of very small animals to obtain food, textiles, and other products.

An example of this is the use of bees. Many die each year in the production of honey, as well as other products such as pollen, royal jelly, propolis, and wax. It may seem that this should not matter much, as they are such small animals, but the truth is that, as we saw in the previous chapter, there are strong reasons to believe that they can suffer.

Bees produce honey from the nectar they extract from flowers, which they ingest and then regurgitate. The resulting vomit is the honey, which they keep in combs for later consumption. When this is removed from the hives, the bees are given water with sugar as a substitute, which is much worse for their health. And the removal of the honey from the hives is often done in ways that are harmful to the bees. It is not uncommon for some bees to be crushed or mutilated in the process. It is normal that the hives are filled with smoke so that the bees do not disturb the people who remove the combs. In other cases, they may heat them up to high temperatures so the bees escape and the combs are more easily removed.

Bee colonies are sometimes transported from one place to another, a process in which many bees die from heat, cold, or lack of ventilation, both during the journey and during the period they are stored. In addition, queen bees are often killed and replaced, and their wings are cut off so that they do not migrate. For reproduction, they are inseminated using syringes. The sperm used for this is often obtained by violently compressing the males, a process that often leads to their deaths.

Moreover, in many places, all the bees are left to die during the winter. Sometimes the hives are burned with the bees inside. This is done because it is cheaper to buy more bees the following year than to keep them alive through the winter. This happens often in cold climates where the bees may have problems surviving the winter.[54]

Although there is no census of the number of bees that die for this reason, their numbers are immense. In order to get a single spoonful of honey, a total of 12 bees need to work throughout their lives. This gives us an idea of the number of animals this involves. They could be up to a trillion or more.[55]

Another type of product obtained from the exploitation of small animals is silk. This is spun by the so-called "silk" worms that produce it to make cocoons for themselves. They do this to protect themselves when the time comes to transform themselves into butterflies. To obtain the silk, the cocoons are usually immersed in boiling water, or gassed. In this way, the worms die and the silk can be removed without breaking it. To get just two pounds (around a kilo) of silk, it may be necessary to kill several thousand worms,[56] so this is also a practice that kills a very large number of small animals which could be in the region of a billion. Other insects that are also used in the textile field are cochineals, which are bred and captured to produce red dye with their bodies. At least tens of billions of these animals (perhaps many more if we consider those that do not survive the breeding process) suffer this fate every year.[57]

Finally, in recent years, the use of insects as food has been increasingly promoted, which has led to the creation of insect farms. At present, for example, insect "hamburgers" are being produced using them, so that the material they are made of is less visible. Other products such as so-called "cricket flour" have also begun to be sold. The conditions in which these animals are kept are not very different from those of other animals kept on factory farms, though in the case of insect farming the overcrowding problem can be even worse. Furthermore, very few people know about the exploitation of insects.[58] There is a great danger that these farms will continue to grow, which will mean that a really huge number of these small animals will be raised and killed, in far greater numbers than other exploited animals.

According to some estimates,[59] the total number of invertebrates killed every year for the production of food might be between one and ten trillion, although this figure could be several times higher, especially due to the high numbers of crustaceans killed for food. Again, all this may seem trivial to some people. But if we consider the arguments that many invertebrates are capable of suffering, and remember the vast number of animals involved in these forms of exploitation, we can see that this is an important issue that shouldn't be disregarded.

When hell on Earth exists

Each of us is aware of only a tiny part of what happens in the world around us. This is especially so in the case of animal exploitation. Most people don't really know anything about the things we have looked at in this chapter. Some people know a little about some of the things animals are forced to endure. Others have a vague idea that animals often suffer. But few are aware of the true horror that is the daily reality of those animals exploited by human beings.

So, although most people consume animal products, very few of them have a clear idea of where those products come from. People don't usually know about what happens in farms and slaughterhouses on a daily basis. Most people simply ignore the ways in which animals are harmed. But when we take a look behind the curtain at what is really happening, even if it's a very brief and shallow one, we discover a world of true horror.

As mentioned before, these are not the only ways of exploiting animals that humans engage in. Nonhuman animals are exploited for many other purposes too. But what we have seen shows how much they suffer in the largest and most representative practices in which they are exploited. What we have seen is so terrible that we can safely conclude one thing: a truly huge number of animals endure hellish conditions at the hands of human beings. These are strong words. But in light of the many facts we have seen in this chapter about the situation of animals, it's hard to exaggerate how appalling their plight is.

For this reason, this issue is much more important than many people think. The question that thus arises is this: is there anything we can do about it? If so, then given what we have seen in this and in previous chapters, it appears that we should definitely do so. In the next chapter, we will assess what we can do.

Notes

1 Below in the following notes, there are links to different investigations by animal organizations which include footage at farms and slaughterhouses. In order

to show that they are representative of what happens globally, the investigations which have been linked to here have taken place in very different countries from Europe, South America, North America, Asia, and Oceania. In addition, the notes also include a long list of references from scientific publications, in particular from many publications which are not aimed at the general public but at those working for the animal exploitation industries.

2 More detailed information about this can be found in Animal Ethics (2016a) *Animal exploitation, Animal Ethics*, http://animal-ethics.org/animal-exploitation. Two selections of images of different forms of animal exploitation are McArthur, J.-A. & Wilson, K. (eds.) (2020) *Hidden: Animals in the anthropocene*, New York: Lantern and McArthur, J.-A. (2013) *We animals*, New York: Lantern. A few useful references about some of the ways animals are exploited or harmed which are not examined in this chapter are: van Hoek, C. S. & ten Cate, C. (1998) "Abnormal behavior in caged birds kept as pets", *Journal of Applied Animal Welfare Science*, 1, 51–64; Hignette, M. (1984) "Utilisation du cyanure pour la capture des poissons tropicaux marins destnes a l'aquariologie : methodes de diagnostic", *Oceanis*, 10, 585–591; Marsh, P. (2010) *Replacing myth with math: Using evidence-based programs to eradicate shelter overpopulation*, Concord: Town and Country, http://shelteroverpopulation.org/Books/Replacing_Myth_with_Math.pdf; Falvey, J. L. (1986) *An introduction to working animals*, Melbourne: MPW Australia; Taylor, K.; Gordon, N.; Langley, G. & Higgins, W. (2008) "Estimates for worldwide laboratory animal use in 2005", *Alternatives to Laboratory Animals*, 36, 327–342; LaFollette, H. & Shanks, N. (2016 [1996]) *Brute science: Dilemmas of animal experimentation*, New York: Routledge; Balcombe J. (2000) *The use of animals in higher education: Problems, alternatives, and recommendations*, Washington, D. C.: Humane Society Press; Jukes, N. & Chiuia, M. (2006 [1997]) *From guinea pig to computer mouse: Alternative methods for a progressive, humane education*, Leicester: InterNICHE, http://interniche.org/ru/system/files/public/Resources/Book/jukes_and_chiuia_-_2003_-_from_guinea_pig_to_computer_mouse_interniche_2nd_ed_en.pdf; George, I. & Jones, R. L. (2007) *Animals at war*, London: Usborne; Hediger, R. (ed.) (2012) *Animals and war: Studies of Europe and North America*, Leiden: Brill and Milburn, J. & Van Goozen, S. (2020) "Counting animals in war: First steps towards an inclusive just-war theory", *Social Theory and Practice*, 47, 657–685.

3 Animal Ethics (2016b) "Hunting", *Animal exploitation, Animal Ethics*, http://animal-ethics.org/hunting.

4 Cohn, P. (ed.) (1999) *Ethics and wildlife*, Lewiston: Edwin Mellen.

5 Bateson, P. & Bradshaw, E. L. (1997) "Physiological effects of hunting red deer (*Cervus elaphus*)", *Proceedings of the Royal Society B: Biological Sciences*, 264, 1707–1714.

6 Horta, O. (2010) "The ethics of the ecology of fear against the nonspeciesist paradigm: A shift in the aims of intervention in nature", *Between the Species*, 13/10, 163–187, http://digitalcommons.calpoly.edu/bts/vol13/iss10/10.

7 Cooke, S. J. & Cowx, I. G. (2004) "The role of recreational fisheries in global fish crises", *BioScience*, 54, 857–859.

8 Cooke, S. J. & Sneddon, L. U. (2007) "Animal welfare perspectives on recreational angling", *Applied Animal Behaviour Science*, 104, 176–198.

9 Cooke, S. J.; Schreer, J. F.; Wahl, D. H. & Philipp, D. P. (2002) "Physiological impacts of catch-and-release angling practices on largemouth bass and smallmouth bass", *American Fisheries Society Symposium*, 31, 489–512.

10 Barthel, B. L.; Cooke, S. J.; Suski, C. D. & Philipp, D. P. (2003) "Effects of landing net mesh type on injury and mortality in a freshwater recreational fishery", *Fisheries Research*, 63, 275–282.

11 Shelton, J.-A. (2004) "Killing animals that don't fit in: Moral dimensions of habitat restoration", *Between the Species*, 13/4, 1–21, http://digitalcommons.calpoly.edu/bts/vol13/iss4/3.

12 Friend, T. H. & Parker, M. L. (1999) "The effect of penning versus picketing on stereotypic behavior of circus elephants", *Applied Animal Behaviour Science*, 64, 213–225.

13 Dembiec, D. P.; Snider, R. J. & Zanella, A. J. (2004) "The effects of transport stress on tiger physiology and behavior", *Zoo Biology*, 23, 335–346.

14 CBS News (2009) "Circus defends use of hooks on elephants", *CBS*, March 3, http://cbsnews.com/news/circus-defends-use-of-hooks-on-elephants.

15 See Birke, L. (2002) "Effects of browse, human visitors and noise on the behaviour of captive orangutans", *Animal Welfare*, 11, 189–202 or Kiley-Worthington, M. (1990) *Animals in zoos and circuses: Chiron's world?*, Essex: Little Eco-Farms Publishing. For an introduction to the harms suffered by animals in circuses, see FIAPO—Federation of Indian Animal Protection Organisations (2017) *End circus suffering: An argument for the banning on the use of animals in circuses*, New Delhi: FIAPO, http://fiapo.org/fiaporg/wp-content/uploads/2017/Report_End_Circus_Suffering_Dossier_formatted.pdf.

16 Zamir, T. (2007) "The welfare-based defense of zoos", *Society and Animals*, 15, 191–201.

17 Davey, G. (2007) "Visitors' effects on the welfare of animals in the zoo: A review", *Journal of Applied Animal Welfare Science*, 10, 169–183.

18 See Norton, B. G. (1995) *Ethics on the ark: Zoos, animal welfare, and wildlife conservation*, Washington: Smithsonian Institution Press or Shani, A. & Pizam, A. (2010) "The role of animal-based attractions in ecological sustainability: Current issues and controversies", *Worldwide Hospitality and Tourism Themes*, 2, 281–298.

19 Cottle, L.; Tamir, D.; Hyseni, M.; Bühler, D. & Lindemann-Matthies, P. (2010) "Feeding live prey to zoo animals: Response of zoo visitors in Switzerland", *Zoo Biology*, 29, 344–350.

20 FAO—Food and Agriculture Organization of the United Nations (2018) "Livestock primary", *FAO Statistical Database*, http://faostat.fao.org/site/569/default.aspx#ancor. See also Šimčikas, S. (2020) "Estimates of global captive vertebrate numbers", *Rethink Priorities*, http://rethinkpriorities.org/publications/estimates-of-global-captive-vertebrate-numbers.

21 See for instance Radostits, O. M.; Gay, C. C.; Hinchcliff, K. W. & Constable, P. D. (2007 [1983]) *Veterinary medicine: A textbook of the diseases of cattle, horses, sheep, pigs and goats*, Philadelphia: Saunders or Swayne, D. E.; Glisson, J. R.; McDougald, L. R.; Nolan, L. K.; Suarez, D. L. & Nair, V. L. (2013) *Diseases of poultry*, New York: John Wiley and Sons; see also Van den Bogaard, A. E. & Stobberingh, E. E. (1999) "Antibiotic usage in animals", *Drugs*, 58, 589–607.

22 Gayle, D. (2013) "China boils baby chickens alive as country is engulfed by panic over continuing outbreak of new strain of bird flu", *Mail Online*, May 7, http://dailymail.co.uk/news/article-2320731/China-boils-baby-chickens-alive-country-engulfed-panic-continuing-outbreak-new-strain-bird-flu.html.

23 Marchant-Forde, J. N. (ed.) (2008) *The welfare of pigs*, Dordrecht: Springer.

24 This can be seen in this investigation carried out in New Zealand: Farmwatch (2014) "Farrowing crates—A life of torment for pigs", *Farmwatch, Vimeo*, http://vimeo.com/98829471, or in this 360° video: Animal Liberation Victoria (2016) "Pig truth 360°", *Animal Liberation Victoria*, http://alv.org.au/pig-truth/pig-truth-360. See also Marchant, J. N.; Rudd, A. R.; Mendl, M. T.; Broom, D. M.; Meredith, M. J.; Corning, S. & Simmins, P. H. (2000) "Timing and causes of piglet mortality in alternative and conventional farrowing systems", *Veterinary Record*, 147, 209–214. See also Tras los Muros (2020) *Factory:*

The industrial exploitation of pigs, Tras los Muros, http://traslosmuros.com/en/pig-factory-farm-investigation.

25 There are cases where these animals are raised in cages, as shown in this UK investigation: Viva!—Vegetarian International Voice for Animals (2015) "Scandal of Britain's battery piglets", *Viva UK, YouTube*, http://viva.org.uk/resources/video-library/scandal-britains-battery-piglets.

26 A video that clearly exposes the way this is done which was taken in an investigation in Chile is EligeVeganismo (2012) "Huérfanos de la leche: la industria de los lácteos en Chile", *EligeVeganismo, YouTube*, http://youtube.com/watch?v=jszYceaoA8o. Another video presenting how this is done in extensive farming is Sinergia Animal (2019) "Argentina: Investigación expone realidad de los tambos argentinos", *Sinergia Animal, YouTube*, http://youtube.com/watch?v=7VoV9dTT87c. See also Van Putten, G. (1982) "Welfare in veal calf units", *Veterinary Record*, 111, 437–440 or Le Neindre, P. (1993) "Evaluating housing systems for veal calves", *Journal of Animal Science*, 71, 1345–1354. Regarding the transport and death of these animals, see Animals Australia (2013) "Dairy calf cruelty investigation", *Investigations, Animals Australia*, http://animalsaustralia.org/investigations/dairy-calf-cruelty-investigation.

27 See Hemsworth, P. H.; Barnett, J. L.; Beveridge, L. & Matthews, L. R. (1995) "The welfare of extensively managed dairy cattle: A review", *Applied Animal Behaviour Science*, 42, 161–182 or Rushen, J. (2001) "Assessing the welfare of dairy cattle", *Journal of Applied Animal Welfare Science*, 4, 223–234.

28 About this, see for instance Weeks, C. A. & Butterworth, A. (2004) *Measuring and auditing broiler welfare*, Wallingford: CABI or Bessei, W. (2006) "Welfare of broilers: A review", *World's Poultry Science Journal*, 62, 455–466. The situation of these animals is exposed in this video with footage taken in Finland: Oikeutta Eläimille (2014) "Broilerihalli Isossakyrössä, toukokuu", *Oikeutta Eläimille, YouTube*, http://youtube.com/watch?v=F97UcIRCYTY.

29 About this, it's interesting to see Sethu, H. (2013) "A child raised to weigh 500 pounds by age 10?", *Counting Animals*, http://countinganimals.com/a-child-raised-to-weigh-five-hundred-pounds-by-age-ten. See also Morris, M. P. (1993) "National survey of leg problems", *Broiler Industry*, 56, 20–24 and Julian, R. J. (2005) "Production and growth related disorders and other metabolic diseases of poultry: A review", *The Veterinary Journal*, 169, 350–369. A more general study of how genetic selection for greater productivity impacts the health of animals is Rauw, W. M.; Kanis, E.; Noordhuizen-Stassen; E. N. & Grommers, F. J. (1998) "Undesirable side effects of selection for high production efficiency in farm animals: A review", *Livestock Production Science*, 56, 15–33.

30 Mercy for Animals (2017) "Battery Cages", *Mercy for Animals, YouTube*, https://www.youtube.com/watch?v=uFbFQ7pNZV4. See also Appleby, M. C. & Hughes, B. O. (1991) "Welfare of laying hens in cages and alternative systems: Environmental, physical and behavioral aspects", *World's Poultry Science Journal*, 47, 109–128 or European Food Safety Authority (2005) "Welfare aspects of various keeping systems for laying hens", *The EFSA Journal*, 197, 1–23, http://efsa.europa.eu/en/efsajournal/doc/197.pdf.

31 This can be seen here: Animals Australia (2015) "Brace yourself: The first day on Earth for chickens is terrifying", *Factory farming, Animals Australia*, http://animalsaustralia.org/features/meat-chicken-hatchery-investigation.php.

32 See FAO—Food and Agriculture Organization of the United Nations (2016) *The state of world fisheries and aquaculture*, Rome: FAO, http://fao.org/3/I9540EN/i9540en.pdf; Bollard, L. (2018) "Fish: The forgotten farm animal", *Open Philanthropy*, http://openphilanthropy.org/blog/fish-forgotten-farm-animal and Fishcount (2019a) "Numbers of farmed fish slaughtered each year", *Fishcount*.

org.uk, http://fishcount.org.uk/fish-count-estimates-2/numbers-of-farmed-fish-slaughtered-each-year. http://fao.org/3/I9540EN/i9540en.pdf.

33 Jacquet, J.; Franks, B.; Godfrey-Smith, P. & Sánchez-Suárez, W. (2019) "The case against octopus farming", *Issues in Science and Technology*, 35, 37–44.

34 See Essere Animali (2018) "Allevamenti intensivi di pesci: Prima indagine In Europa", *Essere Animali, YouTube*, http://youtube.com/watch?v=wImDWAA_ALc; Kirsch, J.-J. & Cerqueira, M. (2020) "Aquaculture in Asian countries", *Fish Welfare Initiative*, http://fishwelfareinitiative.org/aquaculture-in-asian-countries and FIAPO—Federation of Indian Animal Protection Organisations (2021) *Aquaculture: An investigation on trends and practices in India*, New Delhi: FIAPO, http://fiapo.org/fiaporg/wp-content/uploads/2020/aquaculture_investigation_report.pdf.

35 Katavić, I., Jug-dujaković, J. & Glamuzina, B. (1989) "Cannibalism as a factor affecting the survival of intensively cultured sea bass (*Dicentrarchus labrax*) fingerlings", *Aquaculture*, 77, 135–143.

36 See Parker, R. (2012 [1995]) *Aquaculture science*, Boston: Cengage Learning, cap. 11; Austin, B. (ed.) (2012) *Infectious disease in aquaculture: Prevention and control*, Philadelphia: Woodhead Publishing; see also Benbrook, C. M. (2002) "Antibiotic drug use in U.S. Aquaculture", *Institute for Agriculture and Trade Policy*, http://iatp.org/files/421_2_37397.pdf.

37 Robb, D. H. F. & Kestin, S. C. (2002) "Methods used to kill fish: Field observations and literature reviewed", *Animal Welfare*, 11, 269–282; Essere Animali, "Allevamenti intensivi di pesci".

38 This has been shown by these two investigations carried out in France: L214 (2010) "Elevage et ramassage des dindes", *L214*, http://l214.com/video/dindes-2010 and (2009) "Enquête sur les marchés aux bestiaux en France", *L214*, http://l214.com/video/marche-bestiaux-2009, as well as by this one carried out in the UK: Animal Aid (2014) "Catching chicken", *Undercover investigations, Animal Aid*, http://animalaid.org.uk/h/f/CAMPAIGNS/blog/ALL/4//?be_id=445.

39 This has been proved by studies measuring their stress hormone levels during transport, which has shown them to be extremely high. See Mitchell, M. (1992) "Indicators of physiological stress in broiler chickens during road transportation", *Animal Welfare*, 1, 91–103; Broom, D. M. (2003) "Transport stress in cattle and sheep with details of physiological, ethological and other indicators", *Deutsche Tierärztliche Wochenschrift*, 110, 83–89 or Averos, X.; Herranz, A.; Sanchez, R.; Comella, J. X. & Gosalvez, L. F. (2007) "Serum stress parameters in pigs transported to slaughter under commercial conditions in different seasons", *Veterinarni Medicina*, 52, 333–342. See also Appleby, M. C.; Cussen, V. A.; Garcés, L.; Lambert, L. A. & Turner, J. (2008) *Long distance transport and welfare of farm animals*, Wallingford: CABI.

40 Pitney, N. (2016) "Scientists believe the chickens we eat are being slaughtered while conscious", *The Huffington Post*, October 28, http://huffingtonpost.com/entry/chickens-slaughtered-conscious_us_580e3d35e4b000d0b157bf98.

41 Eisnitz, G. (1997) *Slaughterhouse: The shocking story of greed, neglect, and inhumane treatment inside the U.S. meat industry*, Amherst: Prometheus Books, p. 84.

42 Warrick, J. (2001) "They die piece by piece", *Washington Post*, April 10, A01.

43 Eisnitz, *Slaughterhouse*, pp. 92–93.

44 This can be seen in these videos from Spanish slaughterhouses: Igualdad Animal/Animal Equality (2008) "Matadero de cerdos", http://vimeo.com/1321076; (2009a) "Matadero de vacas y terneros", http://vimeo.com/4270529; (2009b) "Matadero de corderos", http://vimeo.com/5632402 and (2009c) "Matadero de conejos", http://vimeo.com/5632470, all them in *Igualdad Animal/Animal Equality, Vimeo*, as well as this one from the USA: Animal Outlook (2012) "30-

second clip: Chicken slaughter", *tryveg, YouTube,* http://youtube.com/watch?v=CHUfAMijzAA, and this one from Mexico: Tras los Muros (2018) "Slaughterhouse. What the meat industry hides", *Tras los Muros, YouTube,* http://youtube.com/watch?v=0VbTT5GUqBk.

45 Fishcount (2019b) "Numbers of fish caught from the wild each year", *Fishcount.org.uk,* http://fishcount.org.uk/fish-count-estimates-2/numbers-of-fish-caught-from-the-wild-each-year; see also FAO, *The state of world fisheries and aquaculture.*

46 Regarding this, see Robb and Kestin, "Methods used to kill fish", as well as this footage taken in Italy and the USA: Animal Equality (2012) *The killing of tuna, Animal Equality,* http://thekillingoftuna.org/; Mercy for Animals (2011) *Skinned alive—Cruel catfish slaughter exposed, Mercy for Animals,* http://fish.mercyforanimals.org or Essere Animali (2016) "La pesca dei polpi", *Investigazioni, Essere Animali,* http://essereanimali.org/pesca-dei-polpi.

47 Ostmann, O. W.; Ringer, R. K. & Tetzlaff, M. (1963) "The anatomy of the feather follicle and its immediate surroundings", *Poultry Science,* 42, 957–969.

48 This happens also with other terms such as "deer," or "fish" to name a group of animals (although the term "fishes" can be used to name different groups, as in "types of fishes", or "species of fishes", as it has been done here at different points).

49 See Farm Animal Welfare Council (FAWC) (1994) *Report on the welfare of sheep,* London: MAFF Publications or Fitzpatrick, J.; Scott, M. & Nolan, A. (2006) "Assessment of pain and welfare in sheep", *Small Ruminant Research,* 62, 55–61.

50 Lee, C. & Fisher, A. D. (2007) "Welfare consequences of mulesing of sheep", *Australian Veterinary Journal,* 85, 89–93. See also James, P. J. (2006) "Alternatives to mulesing and tail docking in sheep: A review", *Animal Production Science,* 46, 1–18.

51 Regarding this see Nimon, J. & Broom, M. (1999) "The welfare of farmed mink (*Mustela vison*) in relation to housing and management: A review", *Animal Welfare,* 8, 205–228; Hsieh-Yi; Yi-Chiao; Yu Fu; Maas, B. & Rissi, M. (2007) *Dying for fur: A report on the fur industry in China,* Basel: EAST International/SAP—Swiss Animal Protection, http:// animal-protection.net/furtrade/more/fur_report.pdf or Coalition to Abolish the Fur Trade—CAFT (2011) *The reality of commercial rabbit farming in Europe,* Manchester: Coalition to Abolish the Fur Trade, http://caft.org.uk/images/CAFT_Rabbit_Fur_Report.pdf.

52 Malouf A. & Sealing in Canada (1986) *Report of the Royal Commission on seals and the sealing industry in Canada,* Ottawa: Canadian Government Publishing Centre.

53 See Proulx, G. (ed.) (1999) *Mammal trapping,* Sherwood Park: Alpha Wildlife Research and Management or Fox, C. H. & Papouchis, C. M. (eds.) (2004) *Cull of the wild: A contemporary analysis of wildlife trapping in the United States,* Sacramento: Animal Protection Institute.

54 On the way bees are kept and the harms they suffer, see Root, A. I. (1980) *The ABC and XYZ of bee culture: An encyclopedia pertaining to scientific and practical culture of bees,* Medina: A. I. Root Company, p. 121; Graham, J. M. (ed.) (1992) *The hive and the honey bee,* Hamilton: Dadant and Sons; Garrido, C. & Nanetti, A. (2019) "Welfare of managed honey bees", in Carere C. & Mather J. (eds.) *The welfare of invertebrate animals,* Dordrecht: Springer, 69–104; Melicher, D., Wilson, E. S., Bowsher, J. H., Peterson, S. S.; Yocum, G. D. & Rinehart, J. P. (2019) "Long-distance transportation causes temperature stress in the honey bee, Apis mellifera (Hymenoptera: Apidae)", *Environmental Entomology,* 48, 691–701; Schukraft, J. "Managed honey bee welfare: Problems and potential interventions", *Rethink Priorities,* http://rethinkpriorities.org/blog/2019/11/11/managed-honey-bee-welfare-problems-and-potential-interventions-1. In addition to the harms mentioned above, it should be noted that bees are currently

dying massively due to the colony collapse disorder, which leads to the disbanding and mass death of bee colonies, for reasons that are not well understood yet but which seem to be caused by the way they are exploited. This is causing a very large increase in the already very high number of bees dying due to their use by humans. See VanEngelsdorp, D.; Evans, J. D.; Saegerman, C.; Mullin, C.; Haubruge, E.; Nguyen, B. K.; Frazier, M.; Cox-Foster, D.; Chen, Y; Underwood, R.; Tarpy, D. R.; Pettis, J. S. (2009) "Colony collapse disorder: A descriptive study", *PLoS One*, 4, e6481, 1–17.

55 See Root, *The ABC and XYZ of bee culture*; Schukraft, "Managed honey bee welfare".

56 Datta, R. K. & Nanavaty, M. (2005) *Global silk industry: A complete source book*, Boca Raton: Universal Publishers, cap. 4; This can also be seen in the following texts, which also examine other ways in which different insects are used: Tomasik, B. (2016) "Insect suffering from silk, shellac, carmine, and other insect products", *Essays on Reducing Suffering*, http://reducing-suffering.org/insect-suffering-silk-shellac-carmine-insect-products; Gildesgame, J. (2016) "Does insect suffering bug you?", *Blog, Faunalytics*, http://faunalytics.org/does-insect-suffering-bug-you.

57 See Rowe, A. (2017) *Global silkworm estimate*, http://getguesstimate.com/models/16701 and (2020) "Global cochineal production: Scale, welfare concerns, and potential interventions." *OSF Preprints*, http://osf.io/t57w2.

58 The growth of this industry can be seen in that there is even a specialized journal about it, the *Journal of Insects as Food and Feed*, http://wageningenacademic.com/loi/jiff. There is also beginning to be concern about the situation of animals used for this purpose, see Erens, J.; Es van, S.; Haverkort, F.; Kapsomenou, E. & Luijben, A. (2012) *A bug's life: Large-scale insect rearing in relation to animal welfare*, Wageningen: Wageningen University and Research. However, due to the lack of interest in animal suffering, this raises less concern than the impact of insects escaping from farms—particularly in the event that an accident or natural event breaches a farm, releasing millions of insects into a small area. Culbertson, A. (2018) "Six billion cockroaches bred for potions at AI-controlled farm in China", *Sky News*, April 19, http://news.sky.com/story/six-billion-cockroaches-bred-for-potions-at-ai-controlled-farm-in-china-11337785. In the next few years, the attention that this industry will receive can be expected to grow significantly.

59 See Rowe, A. (2020) "The scale of direct human impact on invertebrates", *OSF Preprints*, doi:10.31219/osf.io/psvk2; see also *Invertebrate Welfare* (2020) http://invertebratewelfare.org.

Chapter 4

Making the connection

The red button

Imagine that you live in a world in which there are many red buttons all around. These buttons are everywhere, and they can be pressed by anyone at any time. Each time you press one, two things happen: an animal, or several animals, suffers terribly and dies, and you feel a pleasurable sensation.

Imagine that most people push these buttons quite often. In fact, many people push them several times a day. Imagine that you too have pressed them many times, and have done so for as long as you can remember, even though you know there are some who refuse to do so. It turns out that it's possible to get a similar sensation to the one you obtain by pushing the red buttons by pushing blue buttons instead. These, when pressed, cause a pleasurable sensation very similar to that caused by the red buttons, but they do not cause any animals to suffer or die. However, those who press the red buttons say that the sensation caused by the blue ones, although pleasant, is not really the same as the one produced by the red buttons. For this reason, and also out of habit, you keep on pressing the red button that causes suffering and kills animals day after day.

What can we make of a situation like this? Would it be OK to push the red buttons?

Many people think it would not. What's more, they think this without having to reflect about it a lot. They find it obvious that pressing the red button while knowing its evil effects is the kind of thing a good person would never do.

Thinking this is comforting. If people really thought this way, the story of the button would be no more than that, a story. It would be a fictional example in the style of others we have seen before.

However, it may be worth giving this a second thought. Remember what we saw in the previous chapter. It's no fiction that animals suffer unspeakable agony at human hands. It's no fiction that they die for our pleasure. It is, in fact, something that happens every day. Such a horror should be shocking, as

DOI: 10.4324/9781003285922-5

shocking as the story of the red button. If we would be outraged that people pushed the button, shouldn't we also be outraged by what happens to animals in our farms and slaughterhouses?

In the story of the red button, animals suffer and die for a pretty trivial purpose—a pleasurable sensation that is more or less the same as the one produced by the harmless blue button. What is the reason they suffer and die in the real world? In the story of the red button there is a harmless alternative. Is there such an alternative to animal exploitation in the real world? In this chapter, we are going to try to answer these questions. In doing so, we will have the chance to revisit the red button world. But let's start from the beginning.

A double reality

This book started with the case of Teresa the cow. That was, fortunately, a story with a happy ending. The bad news is that her case was, unfortunately, an exception, as the previous chapter has sadly shown. Many other animals also try to escape from the places where they are suffering or where they fear they will be killed or harmed. Most of them, unfortunately, never make it. For instance, in December 2014, several cows escaped from a place called Anderson Custom Pack, a slaughterhouse in Idaho, after jumping over a six-foot fence. Two of them were shot to death and two others were quickly recaptured. The other two, however, managed to evade capture for several days. Eventually, however, they too ended up being captured. But, for some reason, this case didn't become as popular as Teresa's did. These cows never got any names. They were never rescued. Unlike Teresa, they were sent back to the slaughterhouse, where they were killed.

The truth is that this is a much more representative story than Teresa's. Moreover, as a matter of fact, the number of animals that are able to escape at all is completely insignificant, just a few among billions. Virtually all farmed animals end up dying in some fishing boat or slaughterhouse. We already know what happens there.

It's interesting that so many people are capable of feeling empathy for animals like Teresa, yet those same people do not manage to make the connection between their situation and that of the rest of the animals we exploit, including the cows that, like her, are raised to be taken to the slaughterhouse. It's as if all these animals we exploit for our benefit are in another kind of reality, as if they are not in the same world where we do recognize animals like Teresa. It seems that something prevents us from noticing the obvious fact that, in reality, these two separate worlds do not exist. Teresa is no different from the animals we kill. In the farms and slaughterhouses described in the previous chapter, the animals who die are the same as her.

This way of dividing reality in two is also evident in other cases. There are people who, knowing the terrible harms suffered by animals exploited by humans, react with indifference; they just don't care. But many other people think differently, and believe that things shouldn't be this way. However, even in such cases, it is common that these people do not feel responsible for what happens to animals. They see such violence against animals as something unrelated to them, which they have nothing to do with. Instead, they pass responsibility on to the people who are in direct contact with the animals, the ones working in the livestock industry. They conclude that these people are the ones who are acting badly by being cruel to animals.

However, the reality is somewhat different. It seems clear, in the light of what we have seen so far, that the animal exploitation industry does not care at all about the suffering of animals. There should be little doubt about this. But there is something else we need to bear in mind. We have to consider the reason why animals are exploited. It is not because there are people who, out of sadism, want to cause them harm.[1] What we saw in the previous chapter happens primarily because there is a demand for animal products and services. To put it more clearly, all the horrors we have just seen happen basically because people want to enjoy certain forms of entertainment, wear certain kinds of clothes, and eat certain types of food. Sometimes there are cases where someone tortures or kills an animal in their home out of sheer cruelty. But for every animal that suffers and dies in this way, there are millions who do so because of the demand for animal products. The only exception that could be made to this would be in the case of animals that die on farms and in slaughterhouses because of the cruelty of those who work there, which we have already seen. These cases are very numerous. But they are possible only because of the existence of such farms and slaughterhouses where millions of animals are killed, which, in turn, is due to the demand for animal products.

What happens is simply that the vast majority of people are unaware of what happens to animals. When people eat meat from animals such as pigs, chickens, fishes, cows…, what do they usually think about? The taste, whether it's cooked properly, etc. The same thing they think about if they eat anything else. They don't think about whether there might be something else behind that taste.

However, we have seen that for these products to reach the palates of those who consume them, the animals must suffer and die first. It is as if there were two parallel realities. One that we encounter when we have before us some product of animal exploitation. It is the one we see when we have not stopped to reflect on where these products come from. The other, the actual reality that hides behind that appearance, is the true story of animal suffering and death.

This double reality is present all the time. Think, for example, of what happens at a family dinner or a hamburger restaurant. The apparent reality, that which you see at first glance, is simply a relaxed and cordial situation, a nice, fun, happy scene, where someone is having a good time eating something tasty. That is the apparent reality, the one most people see. Meanwhile, beneath the surface, the true reality is very different from this. It's the one we saw in the previous chapter. It's what happens to animals so that we can consume them.

Another way things could be

The two sides of this double reality are closely connected. The hidden reality of the harms suffered by animals in farms and slaughterhouses takes place because of the visible reality of the consumption of animal products. This means that the appalling harms inflicted on animals described in the previous chapter could be avoided. Consider the use of animals for clothing. It's not difficult to avoid products such as fur, feathers, or wool. Leather is a far more common product that can be found in many pieces of clothing, especially shoes. However, today it's easy to find many of these products made with other materials. Some shops are specialized in them, but one can find many of these products in almost any regular store. Most sport shoe brands, for instance, including the most famous ones, have a great many products not made with animal materials in their catalogs.[2]

In fact, there are many textile products for whose production it's not necessary to harm animals, such as cotton, polyester, gore-tex, and others. So it's perfectly possible to wear clothes and shoes that aren't made with the feathers, hair, skin, or other products resulting from animal exploitation. If we reject such exploitation, this is the way to stop it.

What about the other ways animals are used? Consider the case of entertainment. It's clear that there are many ways to have fun without having to harm animals. In fact, most people never go hunting or fishing, just as they'd never attend bullfights or dog fights, for that matter. We don't need to attend circuses or other shows in which animals are exploited either. Many people agree with this. Doubts concerning what should be done arise more often, however, in the case of the eating of animals. What can be said about that?

Well, there are many people who have chosen not to eat animal products for health reasons (as they want to avoid heart disease, cancer, diabetes, or other conditions, or just want to improve their general fitness). Could there be other reasons to do this, reasons related to what happens to animals? To explore this issue, consider the following imaginary situation:

Strike at the slaughterhouse

Suppose you're planning your dinner for today. You haven't been able to go shopping yourself, but you've ordered what you need from your local store, and you're waiting for them to deliver it to you. You ordered some vegetables, rice, beans and pig meat. When they arrive, they bring you some unexpected news, though. There was a strike at the slaughterhouse, so they haven't been able to bring you the processed pig meat you ordered. Instead, they have brought you a baby piglet, who is licking the hand of the woman from the store, and trying to play with her while on her lap. They also brought a big knife and an apron. They tell you that if you want, you can just keep the vegetables. In this way, you'll be able to cook a meatless dinner. Otherwise, you can go to the kitchen sink (to avoid leaving bloodstains all around) and stab and kill the piglet yourself. The piglet will scream, cry, and try to escape while you're stabbing and bleeding her, but after a while she will be too weak to go on fighting for her life, and will eventually die. You'll then be ready to cook a meat dish as planned.

Picture yourself in that situation. Imagine you *really* are there and you really have to stab the piglet if you want to eat meat. What would you do?

Well, the fact is that in a situation such as this, many people would prefer not to kill the animal, even those who eat meat regularly. After all, we can eat something else. We can surely spare the piglet. But then, we may ask ourselves the following question: what is the difference between this case and buying a pack of processed meat at the store?

We may think that the difference is that if we kill the piglet ourselves, she will suffer a lot. But we have seen already that in slaughterhouses they are likely to suffer just as much, if not more, so this can't be the difference. The real reason is this: when we buy the meat at the store, it is someone else that has killed the animal we're having. But this doesn't seem relevant, as, aside from who does the killing, everything has happened to the animal in just the same way.

Let's consider another case that can help us to decide if animal exploitation is justified.

A different end for Teresa

Remember again the story of Teresa, the runaway cow. Now, imagine that this story takes a different course. It turns out that, after she is captured, some tests are done on her and it is established that she does not have brucellosis. However, the campaign to save her is unsuccessful. Therefore, it is finally decided to take her to the slaughterhouse. It happens that, for some reason, you are in that area at that time. You go to eat in a restaurant, and you are offered a specialty of the house: beef. And on their menu today they announce that they include precisely the meat of Teresa, the cow who tried to escape.

How would you respond to such an offer? To be sure, there are people who find Teresa's story simply anecdotal, curious, and who, when they read it, feel no special concern for her. Many of those people might have no problem eating Teresa's flesh later on, that is, Teresa's body parts. However, the question is addressed to you. What would you do? It's your decision, you have the possibility to choose what you want. Would you order the specialty of the house and eat Teresa, the cow that tried so hard to save herself but didn't succeed? Or would you prefer not to?

There are many people who would rather not eat Teresa. Now, if so, there's another question that immediately comes up. If we wouldn't eat Teresa, why would we eat other animals that feel and suffer just like her? The only difference is that they have been less lucky. But those other animals are really just like Teresa.

This is something that Mariella, a woman who was present when Teresa was captured, thought when that happened (this is a true story). After witnessing how Teresa tried in vain to run away again, she said that from that moment on she would not eat animals anymore.[3]

What's the difference?

There are many people who have made the same decision as Mariella. They have stopped consuming animal products not because they want to be healthier, but out of concern for the animals themselves. They've done it because they know the reality they face. They know the tremendous harms nonhuman animals suffer in order for us to eat them and wear them. And they have decided that they don't want to cause this to happen. So, they have started to live differently, and to eat and wear other products whose production doesn't entail harming animals.

This may seem quite counterintuitive at first. The use of these products is very common, so it's understandable that people rarely stop to think about this. It seems strange for us to consider that there may be something wrong about using animals, as it's something we've always done. For this reason, it's intuitive to most people that it's different to exploit animals for entertainment and for food. The problem, however, is that our intuitions aren't always reliable (remember that, in the past, many people had the intuition that certain practices that we now find outrageous were totally acceptable). So, we can't be sure that our intuitions aren't deceiving us here too. Moreover, we must be aware that these intuitions are very convenient ones for us to have, as they justify us in continuing to live just as we want to without having to change our behavior. So those intuitions may just be illusions we are deceiving ourselves with.

In addition, when we reflect on it, we can see that the rejection of animal exploitation is actually in line with what many of us think in other cases. Consider the case of dog fights, or of people who hurt nonhuman animals just for fun. Most people find this unacceptable. In fact, many oppose practices that make nonhuman animals suffer terribly and die in misery only for entertainment. But if this is so, maybe harming animals for other purposes should be rejected too. Perhaps it's better to examine this problem more closely. We need to know if there really is a relevant difference between the use of animals for entertainment and for food.

We might think that the difference lies in the degree of harm caused to the animals. But what we have seen about the lives and deaths of animals on farms and in slaughterhouses belies this. What happens in those places is just as bad as what happens in dog fights or bullfights, or even worse. In fact, it is interesting that, in countries where bullfighting exists, those who defend it often argue this point in an attempt to justify bullfights. They don't argue honestly, because those who make this argument don't really care about the animals who die in slaughterhouses either. But, despite this, what they say is true. However, this does not mean that bullfighting is a justifiable activity. On the contrary, what the argument shows is that the breeding and killing of animals for consumption is no less bad for the animals than bullfighting.

Considering this, we might think that perhaps the difference is in the motivation with which animals are harmed. Those who attend bullfights, dog fights, and other shows where animals are hurt, do so for pleasure. But, the argument goes, this is surely different from harming animals to eat them or to wear them. After all, we all need to eat and to be protected from cold weather. It's not just for pleasure, the argument goes, it's something necessary. For the animals involved it's all the same: they're going to suffer and die in the same way. But maybe we're more justified in causing this for food, given that we need to eat.

This argument is very intuitive. But let's examine it to see if it's sound too. The following example may be helpful for that. (It is an example that was presented some decades ago by a philosopher who wasn't trying to challenge speciesism and who actually ate animals, but wanted to examine if there is a justification for doing so.)[4]

Killing baseball

Suppose I want to exercise by swinging a baseball bat. It just so happens that I'm standing beside a cow and if I swing the bat, I will crush the poor cow's head and kill her. I may say that I need to exercise, as it's unhealthy not to do so. But then, there are many other ways I could exercise without doing this particular thing. However, I happen to enjoy swinging a bat more than exercising in other ways. Am I justified in swinging the bat and killing the cow?

If we think that the answer to this question is "No," then it seems we agree that our own pleasure doesn't justify killing an animal like a cow. I can't say I need to do so because it's necessary for me to exercise, as I can do that in other ways. But now suppose that what's at stake is not my need to exercise, but my need to nourish myself. It's certainly necessary to eat nutrients. But it's not necessary that those nutrients are obtained by eating animal products. It's possible to obtain them by eating other things that also include them. So, I can eat a dish without animal products, or I can have the cow killed and eat a steak. The vegetables are just as healthy, or maybe more so. But I just happen to enjoy eating steak more. Is it justified for me to kill the cow and eat the steak?

This case is just like the previous one. If our answer in the first case was "No," then it appears it that it should be so here too. The only difference between the cases is that we grew up in a society in which eating animals is considered acceptable. Still, in that same society, most people would claim that in the *Killing baseball* example we should say "No." Most people would reject the idea that killing a cow for pleasure is justified. But that's because they don't realize that the reason why we harm and kill animals in order to eat them is also our pleasure. When we think about it, we can easily see that these attitudes are clearly contradictory. This means that holding them together is mistaken, as those views contradict each other. The only way to avoid being mistaken is to abandon one of those two positions. We can reject either the idea that we shouldn't kill cows with bats for the pleasure of playing a certain game instead of another one, or the idea that it's acceptable to kill cows with knives for the pleasure of tasting a certain flavor instead of another one. If we think it's wrong to kill cows for fun, we must also think that it's wrong that they are killed to enjoy a certain flavor. This argument is very clear.

So, it turns out that people eat animals mainly because they enjoy it and because they're used to it. They like the way animal foods taste. So, surprising as it may be for some people, the ultimate reason we use animal products is not need but pleasure.

After reading what happens to animals exploited and killed for enter-tainment, we thought "that's terrible and unjustified, animals shouldn't be harmed like that for pleasure." But if that's so, then we would have to say the same thing in the case of those who are exploited and killed for food produc-tion. We can choose forms of leisure that do not harm animals. But we can also choose healthy and tasty ways of feeding ourselves that do not involve killing them and making them suffer.

Who pays the price of meat?

It is important to clarify that, despite what we have seen so far, those who consume animal products and services do not do so because they want ani-mals to suffer. Of course, there are people who do not care that animals suffer and die. But most of those who use animal products would prefer that this did not happen. It is just that they believe that their interest in using them justifies that suffering and death.

Can this be so? Is there such a justification? To answer this question, one has to compare what animal consumption means for the two parties involved. In other words, what is its price to those who consume them and to the an-imals themselves?

In shops and supermarkets, you can see the prices that different animal products have (the meat of different animals, such as cows, chickens, pigs or fish, as well as eggs, dairy products, etc.). The assumption, therefore, is that the price of these products is paid by those who buy and consume them. However, the reality is more complicated. Let's see this with the following concrete case:

The real cost of a chicken dish

Chickens raised for consumption spend their lives on farms where, as we have seen, they suffer dreadfully. As we have seen, the lives of these animals usually last about 6 or 7 weeks. Let us consider here the case of a chicken that has had a life span of 45 days.

By killing that chicken, you can perhaps obtain meat for five people to eat. With these figures, we can calculate the suffering time of the chicken that each person is responsible for. It will be 45 days divided by 5 people. That's nine days per person. This is the time that on average a chicken needs to suffer on a farm for a person to enjoy a single meal.

Besides the suffering endured by the animal, we must also take into account the damage caused by killing her and thus depriving her of the rest of her life. Having been killed to be eaten, the chicken will lose out on approximately ten years of life.

This means that each person who eats the chicken dish is responsible for approximately two years of the chicken's life being taken away. Let's assume that it took 15 minutes to eat that chicken dish. This means that, in exchange for 15 minutes of tasting this dish, this animal has had to suffer on a farm for approximately 9 days, and has been deprived of 2 years of life.

We can make this analysis even more detailed. It takes a few seconds to taste a bite of a dish. Let's assume that a portion of chicken is eaten in 24 bites. If, in order for us to eat such a portion, there is a chicken that has had to suffer 9 days, and has been deprived of 2 years of life, how much harm is inflicted on the chicken for each of those 24 bites? Doing the math, the result is as follows. In exchange for each brief moment of tasting its flesh, the chicken has had to suffer on average for about 9 hours on a farm. And it has been deprived of a month's life. That's just for every single bite. Every second of our taste pleasure is very expensive for the animal that is eaten.

With this simple calculation, we can see how much it costs to taste a mouthful of meat, in this case chicken. That is the real price of the meat. This cost is so high and so disproportionate to the benefit obtained by those who eat animal products that nobody would agree to pay the full cost in exchange for the enjoyment thus obtained.

That is, suppose that in order to savor a mouthful of chicken meat, we had to pay the price that animals pay for it ourselves. Or, put another way, that in order to taste a mouthful of chicken meat, we would have to suffer for nine hours and lose a month of life. It is obvious that no one would pay such a price. However, this is the true price of meat, the price of consuming animals for food. What you pay in the supermarket or in a restaurant is not the real cost of obtaining that product. It is only a minimal part of it. It does not include the cost to the animals. And, of course, this is not only the case for the price of chicken meat but also for other animal products.

Animals that aren't raised on factory farms suffer less, though as we have seen their suffering is very significant too, and they are equally deprived of their lives. So, by making calculations similar to the above, we can discover the true price of consuming other animal products too. The figures will vary for different animals, of course, depending on various factors, including their size. Some animals are very small (for example, some fish such as sardines, herrings, and anchovies, as well as invertebrates such as shrimps, crabs or small types of squid). Several of them can be consumed in one meal. So, in those cases, the price of a meal isn't paid by a single animal, but by several. In any case, even when large animals are killed, the price is so high that no one would willingly pay it in exchange for the pleasure of eating the meal. Moreover, as we have already seen, nowadays animals are often fed with other animals. This means that by consuming animal products we are not only eating the result of the suffering and death of the animals from which these products were obtained. We are also indirectly consuming all the other animals used to feed them. If we eat one fish that was fed 50 other animals, we are also paying for those 50 animals to suffer and die.

It bears repeating: most of the true price of meat is not the money we pay. Rather, it consists of the terrible harms done to the animals. They are the ones who actually pay the bill when we buy their meat.

Moreover, the benefit humans get from the suffering and death caused to the animals is far less significant than one would think. One might think this is due to health issues, because the consumption of animal products can be harmful. But there is another reason: the benefit someone can get from tasting a morsel of meat or another animal product instead of a vegetable meal is not the full enjoyment of that taste. It is the difference between the enjoyment of eating a mouthful of meat and the enjoyment of tasting a dish without animal products.[5] If we didn't eat animal products, we could eat other products of vegetable origin that would also taste good.

Likewise, the benefit obtained from wearing a fur garment would be the difference between the benefit obtained from it and the benefit that would be obtained from wearing another garment made without animal materials. The alternative to not using animals is not to go without clothes and to starve. It is simply to use other products that do not require animal exploitation.

Speciesism and the exploitation of animals

We can see this more clearly if we think about the matter from another perspective. Let us imagine that human beings were exploited by someone in the same way that we exploit animals. Such situations are common in fiction.

These scenarios are interesting, because they allow us to judge such exploitation from another perspective. Let's think about the following situation:

Changing roles

Imagine a science fiction or fantasy scenario, in a movie, in which some very powerful and intelligent beings appear who intend to use us as food. They could eat other things, but they like our taste. They feel some compassion for us, and they would prefer not to cause us any suffering, but beyond that they have no special sympathy for human beings.

In this scenario human beings are in the situation that nonhuman animals are in today. That is to say, they are in the place of the animals that they themselves exploit. And this happens, moreover, for the same reasons.

There are many such stories in popular culture. They involve beings like carnivorous aliens with advanced technologies, or superhuman vampires. They are a version, with a culinary twist, of the example we saw in Planet of the Apes. How do we usually react to these stories? The answer is very interesting. The truth is that most people think that the fictional beings that appear in them and exploit humans are not good people. We don't usually think they are acting in the right way. On the contrary, they are considered monsters, because of what they do to humans.

It's strange that we feel this way. It may seem normal, but it's actually quite contradictory. The reason is that anything we say about these cases could also be said about our consumption of animals. The situations are analogous. Humans exploit animals, and they say that this is justified because humans are more powerful. Or, because they are more intelligent. Or, because they have a more advanced culture. Or, because they have sympathy for other human beings, but not for other animals. But those other beings, whom people normally consider monstrous, are more powerful than humans. They are also more intelligent and advanced. And they have no sympathy for humans. On the contrary. They see us as food, as resources to be used. In other words, they see us just as we see nonhuman animals today.

Thus, the same reasons for claiming that the behavior of such beings is monstrous also call into question our own exploitation of nonhuman animals. If it is justified for humans to exploit and kill other animals for these reasons, then it should also be justified for other beings to do so to humans. It's a matter of simple logic. However, if it is not justified for humans to be exploited, then neither can animal exploitation be justified.

This is in line with what we already saw in Chapter 1, in rejecting that speciesism can be justified. We saw then that it is not acceptable to do to nonhuman animals what would never be done to human beings because of the species they belong to. But in our society, human beings would never be used for food, or to produce clothing from their skin. It is only considered conceivable and legitimate to do this in the case of animals of other species. The reason for this is clear: speciesism. But, if speciesism is unjustifiable, so too must be animal exploitation, which is one of its clearest hallmarks.

Discriminating against some animals in comparison to others

We have just seen that the consumption of animals as food is speciesist because it discriminates against nonhuman animals in favor of human beings. But there is another way in which animal consumption is speciesist. To see this, consider the following case:

Dog slaughterhouses

A large group of dogs are crowded together, with practically no space, inside a cage, on top of their own excrement. They haven't eaten or drunk for a long time, and they're scared to death. Finally, they are taken out of their cages, and beaten to death, without receiving any kind of consideration, suffering intensely from pain and terror all the time. When they stop moving, their skin is torn off. Some are still alive when this is done to them.

This is not a made-up story. Slaughterhouses for dogs and cats exist in different places, and many of the animals that die there suffer a fate like the one described here. Besides ending their lives, they are caused horrible suffering. They are raised in cages where they can hardly move, and are beaten to death, or boiled or skinned alive while fully conscious.[6] This practice is viewed with horror by many people, both in those same countries and elsewhere. This is understandable, for what is done to these animals is truly horrible. However, there is something odd here. In many cases, these same people who correctly criticize the consumption of dogs and cats have a different attitude when exactly the same thing is done to other animals. As we saw in the previous chapter, an immense number of pigs, calves, chickens, and fish all over the world endure the same things that are done to dogs and cats in certain countries. And the ability of a pig or a cow to suffer and enjoy things is no less than that of a dog or a cat. How can such a different attitude toward different animals be understood?

It should be made clear here that in countries where dogs and cats are not consumed for food, these animals are also attacked and harmed for various reasons. Many of them are bred and then killed or abandoned (which almost always means that they end up dying), suffering a lot because of it. However, other animals, such as pigs and chickens, are considered and treated even worse.

What is happening here is that some animals are discriminated against in favor of cats and dogs, simply because of the species they belong to. This is, then, another form of speciesism. So, we can see that there are several different types of speciesism. The most common is the one we have already seen, which discriminates against nonhuman animals for the benefit of human beings. But many other times some nonhuman animals are discriminated against in relation to others (like pigs in relation to dogs). This is as unjustifiable as any other form of speciesism.

Later on, we will see other examples of speciesism among different nonhuman animals. For the time being, what is important to note here is what follows if we oppose dog slaughterhouses. We have already seen that, not far from where we live, other animals (billions, in fact) are suffering just as those in dog slaughterhouses are. There is no reason to reject this only when the animals that are being harmed are dogs, and not when they are cows. Both cases are identical in all relevant respects.

This also shows that the attitude sometimes taken toward certain countries because of the way some animals are treated there is problematic. Some people in the West despise the consumption of dogs in certain Eastern countries (although dogs are also eaten in other places, such as parts of Switzerland). However, it should be noted that the consumption of animals other than dogs in Western countries has similar consequences. There are also people who, from abroad, criticize countries where there is a tradition of whaling, or bullfighting, for example. But in other countries, even if there are no such traditions, animals are also exploited in places like farms and slaughterhouses.

What's behind dairy products

At this point, we can understand why in order to stop causing animals to be harmed and killed we should not eat them or wear their skins. But, we may wonder, what about drinking milk and eating dairy products? Why should that be harmful to animals?

There are in fact several reasons why this is so, which we looked at in the previous chapter. Many cows are kept in factory farms today. They suffer in ways that are similar to the ones other animals suffer. But regardless of that, there are also other ways in which the consumption of milk and dairy products is harmful to them. As we saw already, cows are forced to get pregnant in order to produce milk, and their babies are killed afterwards too, once they have been terribly exploited to produce veal or beef meat.

Some may think that it would be possible to exploit them without killing the calves. Cows have been genetically selected to give as much milk as possible, so they could raise their calves and still have a significant amount of milk left over. But there's no reason for farmers to do this as their aim is to produce as much milk as possible, so calves are killed anyway. In any case, in those farms in which calves are left with their mothers, they are nevertheless killed after a few months when they have grown enough.

As we also saw, cows are forced to go through this process several times until they are killed, which is done as soon as their production decreases, even though they are still young.

All this is unnecessary, as we don't need to drink milk. Moreover, there are now many different vegetable drinks quite similar to milk, including soy, oat, rice, almond, or hazelnut drinks, among others. Soy drink in particular has become very popular in different countries. Other products such as vegetable yogurts and cheeses are produced today too. In light of this, we can conclude that what we saw in the case of the price of meat also applies to the price of dairy products paid by cows and calves.

The victims of egg production

Let's consider now the case of eggs. Some people may wonder why we shouldn't eat them. After all, unfertilized eggs are not sentient, so eggs themselves can't be harmed. However, eating eggs harms animals in very important ways, connected with what we have seen regarding the lives and deaths of laying hens and their sons, that is, their cockerels.

As we have seen, most eggs are produced in factory farms where hens suffer a great deal throughout their lives. In addition, regardless of whether the hens live in these farms or in other ones, once their production decreases, they are routinely killed and replaced with younger ones. They may still lay eggs, but as they lay fewer eggs than younger hens do, it's more profitable to kill them and replace them. Finally, as we have seen, for each laying hen, there's a male chicken that is killed just after hatching. This is intrinsic to the egg industry.

We must bear in mind that the last two things also happen on traditional, non-industrial farms. In addition, they need to have hens in the first place, and when they buy them they help finance the animal industry to go on breeding hens, exploiting female chickens and killing the males. Again, for each hen purchased, a male chicken is killed shortly after coming into existence.

These are very strong reasons to choose not to eat eggs. As in the case of meat and dairy products, we don't need to do this. We can just eat other things instead of eggs. So, again, the price of eggs paid by animals is extremely expensive.

Pushing the button that kills animals

Considering all this, the conclusion is clear. The consumption of a wide range of animal products is very common, there is no doubt about that. But it inflicts harms on nonhuman animals that we would never willingly suffer if we were in their place. Why, then, are animal products consumed, if no one would want to pay the true price for them? To answer this, let's consider one more case:

In the cell

Imagine that you are in a prison, inside a cell only a little bigger than your body, from which you have no way to escape. You suffer from injuries and illnesses, and you feel pain all over your body. The stench is also terrible. But the worst thing is the boredom and monotony of not being able to do anything but watch time go by.

Every day in the cell, the food you get is made with animal products. But today they offer you a choice. If you choose a dish without animal ingredients today, you'll be free from your prison. Otherwise, you will continue to suffer in your cell until, very soon, they end your life.

It's clear that in such a situation we would choose the dish without animal products, in order to free ourselves. No one in their right mind would argue with that. But consider a variant of the same case:

Suppose that in the same prison, in the next cell, there is another human being in exactly the same situation. Imagine that we have the possibility of saving that person with our decision. If one day we choose to eat a dish without animal products, that person will be set free.

Isn't it clear that that's what we should do? Now, let's consider one last variation of the case:

Suppose that in the next cell, instead of a human being, there is an animal of another species. It could be a calf, for example. Again, we can save that animal with our decision if we choose to eat a different dish today.

If speciesism is wrong, what reason do we have not to make that decision? These questions, especially the last one, show that the situation in this example is only partly fictitious. In fact, it well describes the decision we are faced with every day when choosing what to eat. Our situation in the cell is very similar to that suffered by many of the animals locked up on farms. And the decision that can save those animals is the same one that we can make in this case.[7] Therefore, if we do not make that decision, it is because it is the exploited animals that suffer and die, not the ones that consume them. It's because we are speciesists. But we have already seen that speciesism is not justified.

Thus, this case presents us with a situation similar to others we saw above. Consider the baseball case. We can either avoid killing the cow, or we can play with the bat. In the case of the cell, we can also save the animal from death, or we can eat a plate of animal products. The two situations are similar.

Both cases are also similar to the one we saw at the beginning of this chapter: the one with the red button. However, the case of the button describes reality even more accurately. This may seem surprising, but it is not so surprising in fact. As we can remember, what happens in this case is that people continually press a button that causes animals to suffer and die. The button is a symbol, a metaphor, but otherwise the example is totally true. It shows how the demand for animal exploitation works. This can be illustrated as follows:

The red button in reality

Animal exploitation works as if every place where meat and other animal products are sold had a button with this label: "Press me if you want animal exploitation to continue." Or, in other words: "Press me if you want animals to continue to suffer and be deprived of their lives (since that is the cost of animal products)". So, every time we buy one of those products, every time we take a tray of meat or a dozen eggs from the supermarket shelves and put them in our basket, we are pressing that button.

These buttons are placed in many places that are very visible everywhere, in places where anyone can press them. Every time someone presses one, it makes an animal, or several, suffer in terrible ways and die. But by pressing it, you can enjoy some animal product.

Most people press those buttons often. In fact, many people push them several times a day, although some refuse to do so. It would be possible to get a similar feeling if, instead of those products, they consumed others, although the sensation would not be exactly the same. Due to this, and because of habit, the button that kills and causes suffering to animals continues to be pressed day by day.

We continue to press that button every time we choose to consume a certain product. In this way, we demand that animals suffer and die, even if we don't like that this happens. As a result, as we have seen, this is what is happening to animals today. They are suffering such fates for a simple reason: because someone chose a certain product at the store.

However, we can also choose to consume other products, and by doing so, we will be pressing a very different button. That other button declares that we don't want any animals to be harmed for our benefit. In this way, we reject the exploitation and death of animals that we would otherwise condemn to suffer and die. Buttons of this kind are the real blue buttons of the story. We press them when we opt for products that are not of animal origin. And in doing so, we prevent more and more animals from entering the hell that is animal exploitation. Remember that several billion animals die every year in that hell. That means that, by taking this step, by pressing these blue buttons, we will be stopping the suffering and death of at least many hundreds of animals a year. Considering the annual numbers of animals killed for human consumption, we can avoid causing the death of tens of thousands of animals throughout our lives. In light of the figures presented in the previous chapter, we can estimate that two trillion vertebrates may be killed for this purpose each year. This means that over 73 years (which is approximately the average human life expectancy today), the number of vertebrates consumed may be about 146 trillion, or 146,000,000,000,000. 146 trillion among 7.9 billion humans (which is approximately the current human population) equals a total of 18,481, that is, almost 20,000 animals per person.[8] This is approximately the number of vertebrate animals that each human being could consume on average over a lifetime. If we consider invertebrates, the number of animals that are used goes way up. As we have seen, there are no very accurate estimations here, but we could be speaking about several trillion more animals per year (maybe even more). This includes especially crustaceans, as well as bees and other insects used as food (to which cochineals and silkworms, used in the textile industry, should be added).[9] Of course, the number of animals different people consume varies a lot, depending on what they eat and wear. Some people who eat invertebrates or animals that have been fed invertebrates may consume several hundred thousand animals during their lives.

The connection

There are certain moments in our lives when we make a connection between seemingly disparate facts, and realize something that until then was hidden from us. These are the moments when we manage to put together the clues that we already had but had not yet been able to recognize. When this happens, we have an initial feeling of surprise at what we have just understood, which is sometimes replaced later by one of astonishment at not having seen it before. It's not unusual, at that point, for us put our heads in our hands and think, "How could I not have seen this sooner, when all the evidence was there, in plain sight!"

In those moments, we mentally put the pieces of the puzzle together, and make the connection between them. And we move on to see things in a new way. This is what happens when we finally see the contradictions in things that, until now, had seemed normal to us, or when we realize that things that previously seemed unrelated are actually connected.

What we have seen in the previous sections has given us many clues to see the enormous contradictions in our attitudes toward animals,[10] and to see the similarities between the different ways in which we harm them.

To recap, we have seen all of the following contradictions in our attitudes toward nonhuman animals:

- When we hear the story of specific animals like Teresa, we feel sympathy for them, and we are happy that they survive. We don't want them to suffer and die. But we make many other animals like them suffer and die every day.
- We often feel bad about the terrible things done to exploited animals (such as when they put sows in cages where they cannot move for weeks,

when they separate calves from their mothers and confine them in solitude, or when they boil pigs and butcher cows alive). Yet, we continue to cause this through the consumption of animal products.

- Many people believe that harming and killing animals for fun, as in the case of dog fighting, or in the *Killing baseball* example, is unacceptable. But this is not really very different from killing animals in slaughterhouses.
- Similarly, many people are opposed to harming other individuals if it can be avoided, and believe that we should not do to others what we wouldn't want them to do to us. But, even so, we harm and kill an immense number of animals, even though we would oppose it if we were in their place.
- We think that reasons such as intelligence or power would not justify others in exploiting us, or other human beings. But we use those same reasons to try to justify our own exploitation of animals of other species.
- In addition, many people find it unacceptable to torment and kill dogs or cats to make food out of them. But we do it to animals that suffer the same way.

As we can see, our attitudes toward animal exploitation don't suffer from only a single contradiction; rather, they are riddled with them. We often fail to realize this. But once we put the pieces of the puzzle together and manage to see those contradictions, we can no longer unsee them.

For this reason, many people who initially considered animal consumption to be acceptable now no longer think so. Of course, there are also those who do not make the connection. They see the reasons for rejecting bullfighting or dog fighting, but don't realize that those same reasons also call into question other forms of animal exploitation. However, it is increasingly clear to more and more people that this is the case.

The same can be said of other ways of exploiting and harming animals, such as hunting, buying and selling animals, or using furs. Many people oppose these practices without questioning other forms of animal exploitation. But there's a growing number of people who see the parallels between the different ways in which animals are harmed for human benefit, and conclude that they are morally equivalent.

There are also people who come to this idea even without having previously been against some particular form of animal exploitation. There are those who have simply seen the reality that animals face, or have received information about it, and, in that moment, something has "clicked" in their heads. And there are others who have not been motivated by shocking images of animal exploitation, or by knowing the details of it. They have only read or heard the arguments against speciesism and animal exploitation, or for the consideration of sentient beings, and they have changed their way of seeing things.

All these people have reached this common point by different paths.[11] That makes perfect sense. There are actually many ways to make the connection, as many as there are contradictions in our attitudes toward animals of other species. But they can all lead to seeing things differently, and to acting accordingly.

Making it possible that animals are no longer harmed and killed

What we have just seen is the reason why more and more people have gone on to live without exploiting animals, which among other things means no longer eating the products of their exploitation. That is the first consequence of rejecting discrimination against animals. It is the step that allows us to stop causing enormous amounts of suffering and death.

Of course, as we have already seen, this step requires a little effort: to stop enjoying the use of animals. But in return it has a huge impact. That step has the power to prevent animal exploitation from happening anymore.

The name given to this step about two centuries ago is *vegetarianism*.[12] Today, however, other meanings have been attached to that word. For example, it is commonly used to refer to certain forms of meatless eating that do not exclude other products of animal exploitation (such as eggs and dairy products). Perhaps one could protest against this usage, since these products are not derived from plants, as the word "vegetarianism" suggests. In any case, to avoid confusion, there is another word, coined last century to refer to the position that refuses to exploit and attack animals. This word is *veganism*.

What is veganism?

Veganism is the position consisting in avoiding doing harm to animals, either directly (e.g., by hunting or fishing), or through the consumption of animal goods and services (e.g. by using animals as clothing or food).[13] In this way, veganism means not participating in practices that make animals suffer or die, such as shows where animals are attacked. Note, however, that many animals are exploited for other reasons. As we know, many are raised on farms and killed for their fur, hair or feathers to produce clothing. Even more are exploited for their meat, milk or eggs. In the face of this, veganism also means not taking part in any of these forms of exploitation, instead using clothing and food for which animals have not been killed or exploited.

The most visible aspect of veganism has to do with what we eat. It's also the one that avoids directly harming the largest number of animals. But veganism is not simply a way of eating. For instance, people who don't eat animal products but attend circuses with animals aren't vegan, as they are harming animals in another way.

Veganism has an impact on the demand for animal products, leading to fewer animals being bred, exploited, and killed because of us. Furthermore, by stopping their own use of animals, vegans send a message to other people. They make it visible that there are people who reject the exploitation of animals. This can foster more discussion of whether we should respect animals and question speciesism.

This is important. There are many bad things going on to which we would like to see an end. Human beings are exploited and discriminated against throughout the world. In many places, there are wars. We would like to be able to put an end to all this, although it is not easy. In the case of animal exploitation, however, our ability to act is clear and direct. To consume animals is to make that exploitation happen. But we can put a stop to that.

Who is responsible for animal exploitation?

At this point, some people may find the argument compelling, and yet think: "But, after all, why should I change my ways? I'm used to eating what I eat, and to wearing what I wear... If there are others who want to stop eating animals, then that's fine. Why should I be the one who changes while there are others who won't?"

There are different ways a position like this one can be defended. One is to say that if others are doing something that is wrong, then we are excused for doing it ourselves too. But this argument doesn't work. The first thing to note about this is that if you decide to stop contributing to animal exploitation, you won't be the only person doing so. Many other people all around the world are doing it too. Those who oppose speciesism are a very large group, though the community is not fully aware yet of how large it is and of how strong it's becoming. But even this is changing, as awareness of the importance of the defense of animals is growing.

Furthermore, the fact that something is approved of or rejected by the majority is not a valid reason to agree with it. This was discussed in Chapter 1, when we saw that tradition does not justify speciesism, with examples such as the widely accepted injustices of the past. Do we reject those unjust situations where many people suffered? If so, it means that the fact that many people agree with a certain injustice does not make it acceptable. So, even if other people press the button that causes animals to suffer, our reasons not to press it remain as strong as ever. We should not make any more animals victims of these awful buttons. Instead, what we should do is try to persuade others to stop pressing them.

In the face of this, there is another way in which some people argue that, since there are other people who use animals, we shouldn't have to stop doing so. We may think that even if we stop harming nonhuman animals, there will be other people who will continue to do so. So, while we may manage to save some animals, that will not end animal exploitation. This means there's no point in doing it. It's a lost cause.

The answer to this is that, even if the exploitation of nonhuman animals continues, when we manage to prevent some animals from suffering and dying, we achieve something very important. What? Well, that's just it: sparing those animals a terrible fate. That is a huge achievement. Perhaps it will be possible, one day, to end all exploitation of animals, even if that seems difficult from our current position. But the point is to try to save as many animals as possible, even if we cannot save them all. The number of victims of animal exploitation is absolutely overwhelming, but it is very important that this does not lead to the conclusion that there is nothing to be done. We would be achieving something already even if we could only prevent a single animal from being exploited, for that would already mean everything for that animal. And the good news is that we can reasonably aim to prevent the exploitation of a very large number of animals by not consuming them. Even if many people continue to use animals, if a large number of people stop consuming them, a segment of animal exploitation will disappear.

There is nevertheless another way to question the impact of veganism. This argument points out that even if we don't eat animals, there are going to be other people who do. And, for this reason, animal exploitation will take place anyway, regardless of what you or I do. This is because what counts is not just that someone consumes animal products, but that many do. Not eating an animal one day won't save that animal automatically. Nor will it save another animal.[14]

We may think that would rid us of the guilt of that animal being exploited. However, the reality is that we are responsible for the exploitation of animals. What causes animals to be killed in higher or lower numbers is the combined demand of many people. By consuming animals, we contribute our part to the aggregate demand that causes them to be exploited. So perhaps one visible way to rebut the objection that as vegans we do not make a change would be to look at the products that are sold at supermarkets and other stores. In many countries, they include a variety of products labeled as vegan. One example may be that of vegan burgers that are similar to the ones made with animal products. Many people buy them, otherwise, they wouldn't be there. Just a few decades ago, however, they weren't there. People didn't buy them. Instead, they bought animal products. Suppose the situation were still the same today, and the people who buy those vegan burgers today bought meat instead. In that case, the production of those vegan burgers would be much smaller, or inexistent, and there would be a higher demand for more meat products to be sold. This would cause more animals to be harmed. The same happens with other products.

If our individual decisions consisting in not using animal products or services didn't make a difference to the exploitation of animals, this story would be impossible. However, the story is real. Suppose we stop buying a certain animal product in a supermarket that we had been consuming every week until then. Instead, we buy some vegan product. And let us also assume that this does not automatically prevent an animal from being killed. This change in demand, though small, accrues to other similar changes. So, for instance, if in a local supermarket a handful of regular customers stop purchasing animal products, the market managers will eventually notice that they have sold fewer of these products, and therefore order fewer of them. Distributors will receive fewer orders and so order less in turn. And, when those changes reach a certain point, they cause a reduction in the production of animal products. Eventually, this means that fewer animals end up being killed. Achieving this depends, therefore, on choosing not to consume animal products.

That said, it should also be noted that the killing of animals may also be due to reasons other than demand. For example, this is what happens when the farming industry receives subsidies because of the pressure of its lobby. These lead to the production of more animal products than demanded by consumers. In other words, many animals are being exploited and killed without any demand for this. One might think that in cases like this, giving up one's personal animal consumption is pointless, and that only political and legislative action to end subsidies can end their exploitation. However, it seems more appropriate to say that, in cases like this, the fight against these subsidies plays a role alongside the spread of veganism. The elimination of these subsidies can reduce animal exploitation, which is very positive. But it can only reduce it to the level of demand. To put it more clearly: as long as animal products are purchased, animal farming will normally continue even without subsidies. On the other hand, if animal consumption falls sharply, this means that, for the same number of animals to be killed, subsidies have to increase, something against which there is usually political resistance. Finally, it will be much easier to combat animal exploitation subsidies, if social awareness against it has been raised. And to achieve this, the spread of consideration for animals and veganism are key.

Finally, there is a slightly different way of defending animal consumption. We have seen that our individual actions cause animal exploitation when they occur in conjunction with those of other people. In light of this, some might think that our individual actions alone have no consequences, that they only do so when added to the actions of other people. According to this argument, even if we consume animal products, it is not really our responsibility that animals are exploited. For us to be truly responsible, our individual consumption of animal products would have to be necessary for the animals to be killed. But the animals would still die even if we did not eat them.

This reasoning is not correct either. Our individual actions do have consequences, when combined with those of other people. As we have seen, our actions are part of a collective action carried out by many people, and that collective action causes nonhuman animals to be exploited. This does not absolve us of our responsibility. It simply adds our responsibility to that of other people. We can see this with the following example (presented by a non-vegan philosopher seeking to clarify the issue of who can be responsible for collective actions).[15]

100 bandits

Imagine that in a certain village there are a hundred people whose only food is beans. Each person has a hundred beans to eat. A hundred bandits arrive in the village. Each one steals all the beans from one person in the village. As a result, all the villagers are left without food, and they starve to death. It's clear that each of the bandits is responsible for the death of one villager.

Suppose that, some time later, the bandits return to the village, where there are a hundred more people each with a hundred beans. But now the bandits change their ways. Each one no longer steals his hundred beans from one person. Instead, each bandit steals just one bean from each of the hundred villagers. The result is the same as before. Each bandit steals a hundred beans, and each person in the village is left with no beans, just like before. So, again, they all starve to death. But the difference is that no one bandit causes any particular person to die on his own. After all, no one dies from eating one less bean. In a case like this, would we say that the bandits aren't responsible for anyone's death?

Imagine that one of the bandits claimed that, even if he had not carried out the robbery, the people of the village would still have died (since no one survives by eating only one bean). The same could be said by each of the other bandits. If we accepted what they say, we would have to conclude that none of them is responsible for anyone's death. However, this is absurd. The bandits are indeed responsible for the deaths of these people, but responsibility is joint. In other words, now they are no longer each responsible for the death of a particular villager, as they used to be. Now, they are all jointly responsible for the death of all 100 villagers. Their action remains essentially the same. After all, they each used to steal 100 beans from the village, and now they still do. And the effect of stealing 100 beans is that one person dies. There are several ways to explain this. We can say that for every 100 beans stolen in the village, one person dies, so that if someone steals 100 beans, he is responsible for one death. We can also say that since each bandit steals 1% of the beans from each person, he is responsible for 1% of the death of each person. If we add his 1% to the responsibility in the death of each of the 100 people, we could conclude that his responsibility would be equivalent to that of the death of one person. In short, the responsibility of the bandits remains the same, whether they are individually or jointly responsible.

This is also the case for animal products. Those who consume them demand that the animals be exploited, and they do so collectively. Each person who uses such products is thus responsible for a part of the exploitation of many animals. Which ones? All the animals who were exploited to obtain the products that person has consumed. Thus, each person is responsible for his or her share of the suffering and death of those animals.

Achieving collective change

In this way, we can see that we are responsible for the exploitation of animals, and that veganism helps animals by reducing the demand for animal products, thus causing fewer of them to die from exploitation at human hands. But it also has other very important effects.

Those who live without exploiting animals inspire others by the force of their example. Other people see what they do. Thus, more people become familiar with veganism. Over time, this is seen as an increasingly normal attitude, and this encourages more people to consider becoming vegan too. So, someone who becomes vegan, in addition to not contributing to animal exploitation, also encourages other people to do so. Furthermore, as more people do this, it helps to create a more favorable social environment for nonhuman animals to be taken into account. The more people who commit themselves to not exploiting animals, the more the rest of society will see those who act this way as a part of society whose arguments deserve to be taken seriously. In this way, veganism also helps us to achieve a major long-term change in the fight against speciesism.

Custom is no substitute for arguments

Everything we have seen so far, both in the previous chapters and in this one, gives us very strong reasons in favor of veganism. In light of this, it seems that we really should consider stopping the exploitation of animals. We have already seen that our preference for the taste of certain animal products is a very weak reason to reject veganism. But, besides taste, there is also habit. From infancy, we are raised to believe that using animals is something totally normal. This is another reason why so many people continue to contribute to animal exploitation—our education and socialization have conditioned us to do so. We grow up taking speciesism for granted. However, as we saw in Chapter 1, that is an idea that we should abandon. Fortunately, there are people who reflect on what they see, and do not accept that what is considered normal is necessarily what we ought to do. This encourages societies to move forward and improve, and it also helps veganism to spread.

No doubt there are still those who find veganism somewhat shocking. This is helped by the fact that there is a widespread lack of knowledge about speciesism and the arguments against it. This situation will change with time, as more information on the subject becomes available to the general public. Our social conditioning into the ideology of speciesism is very strong. However, although the ideology we are raised with imprisons us to a certain extent, it doesn't do so completely; we still have freedom of choice. And there are many people who do wonder whether they should accept what they have been taught. This explains why more and more people are rejecting speciesism.

Finally, there is something more difficult to overcome than mere learned ideas about how things should be. The behavior we get used to is related to our way of seeing the world. When you've been doing something all your life, you tend to keep doing it. And there is also social pressure to keep doing it. So it's easy to continue to collaborate with animal exploitation.[16] But, despite all this, we have the chance to do what we think is right. We must reject the idea that we are slaves of habit or social pressure. It's always in our hands to make a change for the better.

Obstacles can be overcome

Reasons like the ones we have seen convince many people. Yet, even if the arguments convince them, some lack the necessary willpower. If you're one of these people, you would like to stop using animals, but doing so seems too difficult. In view of this, it's important to remember something we've already seen. What to us is simply a difference in taste, to the exploited animals is the difference between life and death. This is actually a very strong motivation to put an end to our participation in their exploitation. Thinking about it can give us the courage to take the step.

In addition, when someone finds it difficult to stop exploiting animals there are various ways to make the transition easier. Here are some suggestions:

Ideas to help leave animal exploitation behind

Try it for a while. One option is to simply try living vegan for a certain period of time, like a couple of weeks, or a month, and see how it goes. If you've managed to make it, you'll probably be able to continue.

Start at home. Another option is to stop consuming animal products at home first, and then avoid them elsewhere too.

Start when you cook. You can also start by eating vegan every time you prepare your own food, and then take the step to do it in all other situations.

One vegan day a week, and then two, and three… You can choose to have one day a week without animal products. The next step is to have two days a week without animal products, then three, and so on. You can continue until you get to seven days a week without using animals; in other words: until you're actually living as a vegan. People whose willpower fails them the most can make their transition over a longer period of time, but this is a process that can be done quickly. If you take one step each week, in less than two months you'll be living without using animals.

One vegan meal a day, then another… Another way to do this is to start by having a vegan meal every day (for example, for dinner). Then, you can move on to doing that at breakfast as well. And finally you can do that with all your meals. Of course, you can also do this by starting with another of your daily meals.

These are all options that can work well for you. All you need to do is take them seriously, so once you start, you stick to the purpose you've set for yourself. It's a bad idea, however, to make exceptions to the rule you've decided to follow—for example, if one day you feel like consuming an animal product. To do this is partly to cheat yourself, although it is the animals that are most affected by it. In the end, it wouldn't be surprising that these exceptions lead to continuing as usual, without making a real change. A real commitment needs to be made. The options listed above are designed to help you take the initial step. But, in any case, it is clear that the best option for the animals is to do it as quickly as possible. That is why the best alternative is simply to stop contributing to animal exploitation right away. And if that process slows down at any point, you can start again right away. In practice, many people who have done this have ended up being vegan. Perhaps they thought at first that they would have a weak will that would not allow them to achieve their goal of stopping exploiting animals. But they eventually discovered that this was not the case. Once we take the initial step, one thing that helps us continue is to be aware of what it means for the animals that we consume as food. If we have the determination to end that, we will certainly succeed in doing so.

So, we can do it today, at this very moment. If you do it, you're unlikely to regret it. One day, when you remember the moment you made that decision, you'll think it was one of the best decisions you ever made. And you may be surprised that you hesitated to make it.

Cutting the cake fairly

We have just seen that the move to veganism is easier than it seems, although it may require a certain amount of willpower. But the same is true of many things that really matter. No major change in history has come automatically. They all required considerable effort. In this chapter, we have seen that the benefits we gain from harming animals are really trivial compared to the harm we cause them. In view of this, we can conclude that, if we consider the importance of what is at stake, the effort required not to eat animals is surely not so great after all. In the next chapter, we will see in more detail why this is so.

Notes

1 Many people have hostile attitudes toward at least some nonhuman animals. But it seems that in most cases people are speciesist toward nonhuman animals

without necessarily having an attitude of hatred toward them. This is why a distinction has been made between speciesism and another concept, "misothery," which names hatred for nonhuman animals. See Mason, J. (2009 [1998]) "Misothery", in Bekoff, M. (ed.) *Encyclopedia of animal rights and animal welfare*, Santa Barbara: Greenwood, 383; the concept is also mentioned in Stallwood, K. (2013) "The politics of animal rights advocacy", *Relations: Beyond Anthropocentrism*, 1, 47–56.

2 Just by doing an internet search of terms like "vegan shoes," you can find different brands specialized in these products. But in any shop when you see a product that suits you, you can also easily check the materials it is made of.

3 Redazione, GeaPress (2011) "La mucca a nuoto nello Stretto di Messina. La storia di Mariella, da quel giorno diventata vegetariana", *Gea Press*, May 11, http://geapress.org/animali-in-emergenza/la-mucca-a-nuoto-nello-stretto-di-messina-foto-della-cattura-in-spiaggia/15951.

4 This thought experiment appears in Nozick, R. (1974) *Anarchy, state and utopia*. New York: Basil Blackwell, p. 37.

5 See McMahan, "Eating animals the nice way".

6 Animal Equality (2015) *Voiceless friends: The dog meat trade exposed*, http://voicelessfriends.org. See also Batchelor, T. (2015) "Animal rights campaigners blast last Western country to allow cats and dogs to be eaten", *Express*, November 3, http://express.co.uk/news/world/616467/Eating-cats-dogs-should-be-banned-Switzerland-animal-rights-campaigners.

7 The only difference is that in this case, we save an animal that already exists and is already suffering, and in the real world, we stop making animals suffer. But this difference, in practice, is not relevant to the parallel between the two cases.

8 See Worldometer (2021) "World population", *Population, Worldometer*, http://worldometers.info and "Life expectancy of the world population", *Demographics, Worldometer*, http://worldometers.info/demographics/life-expectancy. In the future, more precise estimates of the number of small invertebrates exploited may bring us closer to a more accurate overall estimate of the total number of animals killed for use by humans. It should also be noted that the number of exploited animals has been growing over the years and may continue to increase. But to avoid speculating about this, we can simply extrapolate the current annual figure.

9 See *Invertebrate Welfare*.

10 In the introduction to this book, we saw a survey that suggested that there is significant concern for animals, which is at odds with the reality of animal exploitation. An even more recent survey, also conducted in the United States, yielded even more remarkable results. Forty-nine percent of those questioned were in favor of abolishing factory farms, 47% in favor of abolishing slaughterhouses and even 33% in favor of abolishing animal farming. Of course, such results contrast with the fact that the vast majority of the population are consumers of products from factory farming and slaughterhouses. This suggests that, deep down, many people suspect that there is something wrong with harming animals, as when they are killed for us to use. See Reese Anthis, J. (2017) "Survey of US attitudes toward animal farming and animal-free food", *Research Publications, Sentience Institute*, http://sentienceinstitute.org/animal-farming-attitudes-survey-2017. Of course, this is by no means something that can be generalized, many other people are indifferent to the issue. But it's nonetheless a fact that deserves to be highlighted. See also regarding this Weathers, S. T.; Caviola, L.; Scherer, L.; Pfister, S.; Fischer, B.; Bump, J. B. & Jaacks, L. M. (2020) "Quantifying the valuation of animal welfare among Americans", *Journal of Agricultural and Environmental Ethics*, 33, 261–282.

11 More in-depth statistical studies on the number of people who have given up animal consumption, and more scientific research and publications on the subject are needed. There are, however, a number of journalistic publications based on small-scale studies that consistently indicate that the number of people taking this step is growing steadily in different countries. See just a few examples from different countries (there are many more): Sareen, A. (2013) "Interest in vegan diets on the rise: Google Trends notes public's increased curiosity in veganism", *The Huffington Post*, April 3, http://huffingtonpost.com/2013/04/02/interest-in-vegan-diets-on-the-rise_n_3003221.html; Stevens, K. (2014) "No lie can live forever: Predicting a vegan America by 2050", *The Huffington Post*, October 3, http://huffingtonpost.com/kathy-stevens/predicting-a-vegan-america_b_4905691.html; MINTEL—Market Intelligence Agency (2015) "Young consumers are hungry for meat alternatives in Germany", *MINTEL*, June 15, http://mintel.com/press-centre/food-and-drink/young-consumers-are-hungry-for-meat-alternatives-in-germany; Animal Libre (2016) "El aumento de vegetarianos salvó a dos millones de animales en Chile", *Noticias*, http://animallibre.org/vidasalvadas; Vegan Trade Journal (2018) "Almost half of UK vegans made the change in the last year, according to new data", *Vegan Trade Journal*, https://www.vegantradejournal.com/almost-half-of-uk-vegans-made-the-change-in-the-last-year-according-to-new-data; Animals Australia (2020) "Surge in Aussies eating vegetarian continues", *Compassionate living, Animals Australia*, http://animalsaustralia.org/features/study-shows-surge-in-Aussies-eating-veg.php; Bielinska, K.; Rehder, L. & Trautmann, W. (2020) *Germany is leading a vegalution—vegan revolution in Europe*, United States Department of Agriculture, Foreign Agricultural Service, https://www.fas.usda.gov/data/germany-germany-leading-vegalution-vegan-revolution-europe; Unión Vegana Argentina (2020) *Población vegana y vegetariana*, Unión Vegana Argentina, http://www.unionvegana.org/poblacion-vegana-y-vegetariana-2020; Sentient Media (2021) "Veganism is more than just a fad", *Sentient Media*, https://sentientmedia.org/increase-in-veganism. All this setting aside the case of India, where according to official records up to 30% of people don't eat animals, the highest percentage worldwide, see Office of the Registrar General & Census Commissioner, India (2014) *Sample registration system: Baseline survey 2014*, New Delhi: Ministry of Home Affairs.

12 Since some people consider themselves vegetarians and eat some animal products such as dairy products or eggs, attempts have been made to deny that the origin of the word "vegetarianism" comes from "vegetable." It has been argued that the term comes from a Latin term, "vegetus," which would mean "healthy and fit." Historical evidence shows, however, that this is not correct, and that the word "vegetarianism" comes from "vegetable" (this makes sense, otherwise it seems that the term would have to be "vegetusism," or some other similar one). See Davis, J. (2011) "The vegetus myth", *VegSource.com*, 1 de junio, http://vegsource.com/john-davis/the-vegetus-myth.html and Davis, J. et al. (2011) "Extracts from some journals 1842–48: The earliest known uses of the word 'vegetarian'", *International Vegetarian Union*, http://ivu.org/history/vegetarian.html.

13 The British Vegan Society, the first of its kind to be created worldwide, defines veganism as "a way of living which seeks to exclude, as far as is possible and practicable, all forms of exploitation of, and cruelty to, animals for food, clothing or any other purpose", The Vegan Society (2016) "Definition of veganism", *Go vegan, The Vegan Society*, http://vegansociety.com/go-vegan/definition-veganism.

 The rejection of the consumption of animals has been addressed in some texts already cited above, such as Gompertz, *Moral inquiries on the situation of man and of brutes*; Salt, *Animals' rights* and Singer, *Animal liberation*, as well as in Regan, T. (1975) "The moral basis of vegetarianism", *Canadian Journal of Philosophy*, 5, 181–214; Davis, W. H. (1976) "Man-eating aliens", *Journal of Value Inquiry*, 10, 178–185; Adams, C. J. (2015 [1991]) *The sexual politics of meat: A feminist-vegetarian critical theory*, New York: Bloomsbury; Norcross, A. (2004) "Puppies, pigs, and people: Eating meat and marginal cases", *Philosophical Perspectives*, 18, 229–245; Sapontzis, S. F. (ed.) (2004) *Food for thought: The debate over eating meat*, Amherst: Prometheus Books; Francione, G. L. (2000) *Introduction to animal rights: Your child or the dog?*, Philadelphia: Temple University Press and (2008) *Animals as persons: Essays on the abolition of animal exploitation*, New York: Columbia University Press; McPherson, T. (2014) "A case for ethical veganism: Intuitive and methodological considerations", *Journal of Moral Philosophy*, 11, 677–703; Hooley, D. & Nobis, N. (2015) "A moral argument for veganism", in Chignell, A.; Cuneo, T. & Halteman, M. C. (eds.) *Philosophy comes to dinner: Arguments about the ethics of eating*, London: Routledge, 92–108; Bruers, S. (2015) "The core argument for veganism", *Philosophia*, 43, 271–290; Engel Jr., M. (2019) "Fishy reasoning and the ethics of eating", *Between the Species*, 23, 52–103; Huemer, M. (2019) *Dialogues on ethical vegetarianism*, New York: Routledge; Andrew, J. P. (2020) "The insignificance of taste: Why gustatory pleasure is never a morally sufficient reason to cause harm", *Southwest Philosophy Review*, 36, 153–160; Dhont, K. & Hodson, G. (2020) *Why we love and exploit animals: Bridging insights from academia and advocacy*, New York: Routledge and Rowley, J. K. (2020) *Towards a vegan jurisprudence: The need for a reorientation of human rights*, London: Lexington Books.

14 This claim is presented in Fischer, B. (2019) *The ethics of eating animals: Usually bad, sometimes wrong, often permissible*, New York: Routledge. For a different view see Killoren, D. (2021) "Causal impotence and veganism: Recent developments and possible ways forward", in Wright, L. (ed.) *The Routledge handbook of vegan studies*, New York: Routledge, 111–121; see also Nefsky, J. (2018) "Consumer choice and collective impact", in Barnhill, A.; Doggett, T. & Budolfson, M. (eds.) (2018) *The Oxford handbook of food ethics*, Oxford: Oxford University Press, 267–286.

15 This thought experiment appears in Glover, J. (1988) "It makes no difference whether or not I do it", in Singer, P. (ed.) *Applied ethics*, Oxford: Oxford University Press, 125–144, pp. 128–129.

16 This was pointed out already in Singer, *Animal Liberation*; it is examined in more detail in Joy, M. (2009) *Why we love dogs, eat pigs, and wear cows: An introduction to carnism*, Newburyport: Conari Press; see also Bastian et al. "Don't mind meat?".

Chapter 5

Living without exploiting animals

Questions and answers

Three stories

The introduction to this book pointed out that from the 1970s on there was a spectacular growth of the movement for animals and against speciesism. But what happened before? Let's go back a few decades, to the middle of the 20th century. We find a woman, Eva Batt, who is struggling to spread veganism, at a time when veganism is still practically unknown. But Eva is a pioneer, and spends many years engaged in activism to spread respect for animals. She strives to let others know the reasons for not eating animals, and disseminates recipes without animal products to encourage people to take a similar stand.[1]

In the times when she lived, it wasn't as easy for Eva to be vegan as it is for us today. But nevertheless, she did it. She fought for what she believed in, and her work bore fruit. Eva made a key contribution to spreading respect for animals. Without the work of pioneering people like her, who knows what the state of the defense of animals would be today.

Now let's move back further in time. We're now in the early 19th century, more than a century before the word "veganism" even existed. Here we find Lewis Gompertz, who is thinking about the ethical way to act toward other animals. He decides he will no longer eat animal products, because producing them harms animals. He lives accordingly, and becomes extremely active in the first organizations for the defense of animals in Europe, which he helps to found. He writes some pioneering essays about this issue.[2] Lewis is also an inventor. There were no automobiles back then, and horses were exploited in terrible ways for transport. Many were beaten and forced to work till they died of exhaustion. Lewis helps to develop bicycles, so people can use them instead of exploiting horses. Again, it's definitely easier to live vegan today than in Lewis Gompertz's time. Yet he did it. He fought for animals and made a difference for them.

Let's move back in time again, this time not just a few decades or centuries. Let's move back a whole millennium. We're in what is now Syria in the 11th century. A blind poet named Abul Al Ma'arri speaks out for

DOI: 10.4324/9781003285922-6

animals and decides to stop consuming animals to avoid harming them. He writes, "I wish that I perceived my way before my hair went gray."[3] We can imagine what his attitude meant in that time. It's definitely easier to live without using animals today. Yet he did it, many centuries before the word "veganism" even existed.

All three of these stories are true. It's inspiring to think of them if at some point we consider being vegan difficult. In fact, it's not that tough. It might have been hard for Eva, Lewis, and Abul at first. After some time, it just became a part of their everyday lives. This happens too, most of the time, for everyone else who becomes vegan.

After you decide to stop harming animals, at some point, you just stop seeing animals as something edible. It's similar to how we look at human beings. We don't see other humans as food we should refrain from eating. It's not that we think "I could eat a nice human burger today, but that would be unethical, so I'll refrain from doing it." In fact, we don't think of other humans as food, because we recognize them as individuals like us. That's why it's not difficult not to eat human beings. It's not a huge sacrifice not to eat what you don't see as food. For this reason, it's easier to abstain from eating other sentient animals too when you recognize them as individuals and not as food. To be sure, you could eat animals, just as you could eat human meat, but it's something that eventually seems strange and not something you feel like doing at all.

In previous chapters, we have seen the reasons for not treating animals as food. The reasons are strong and relatively simple. Nonetheless, they may rebut some common ideas, as most people have eaten animals all their lives. So, it's understandable that we may have all sorts of doubts about whether we should actually stop using animals. In this chapter, we're going to take a look at some of them.

It's a healthy option

We've already seen that mere taste is not a very sound basis for harming nonhuman animals. However, perhaps we might think that there's another question we haven't examined in enough detail: is it necessary to exploit animals? There are people who have doubts about whether a diet without animal products can be fully healthy. This is understandable, since in our society the idea that we need to eat animals is quite widespread.

In fact, this opinion persists even though it clashes with another idea that is widespread today. Health authorities continually point out that the diets of most people in many countries are unhealthy because of the amount of animal products they contain. It is currently well known that many people have health issues because they are eating too many animal products, not because of a lack of them.

However, veganism is becoming more well known. For this reason, more people know that a vegan diet is not only not harmful to health but can also actually have positive effects. Numerous studies on the subject make this clear, and statements have been made about this by the most influential professional organizations of dieticians and nutritionists around the world. This includes one of the most important organizations worldwide in this field, whose position is the following:

The position of the Academy of Nutrition and Dietetics on vegan diets

In its study of animal-free diets, the Academy of Nutrition and Dietetics (previously known as the American Dietetic Association) came to a very clear conclusion. It has stated conclusively that not eating animal products doesn't need to pose any kind of health risk at any stage of life. In fact, it can have advantages in comparison to diets including animal products. This statement is very clear:

> Appropriately planned vegetarian diets, including total vegetarian or vegan diets, are healthful, nutritionally adequate, and may provide health benefits in the prevention and treatment of certain diseases. Well-planned vegetarian diets are appropriate for individuals during all stages of the life cycle, including pregnancy, lactation, infancy, childhood, and adolescence, and for athletes.[4]

Other respected organizations from different parts of the world have backed this position, or adopted similar ones. These include, for example, the UK National Health Service, the Dietitians Association of Australia, Dietitians of Canada, the Irish Nutrition & Dietetic Institute, the Spanish Association of Dietitians & Nutritionists, the Argentine Society of Nutrition, the Directorate-General of Health of Portugal, the Italian Society of Human Nutrition and, in its nutritional recommendations document, the Nordic Council, which includes Denmark, Finland, Iceland, Norway, and Sweden.[5]

It's worth noting that these nutritionist organizations have no interest in defending animals (in fact, in other studies they usually speak about the consumption of animal products). Their judgment on the complete adequacy of diets free of animal products is based solely on the evidence.

We can see some of this evidence for ourselves. There have already been several generations of people who have lived without eating animal products and have reached old age in a healthy state. Millions of vegans, including some who have been vegan for decades, are perfectly healthy. This includes people who were raised vegan and have been vegan for their whole lives.

Of course, like those who are not vegan, not all vegans eat well. All diets must be balanced, and the vegan diet is no exception. If someone only eats French fries, she may be vegan, but she has a very bad diet. But it isn't only vegans who may have an unhealthy diet; the same is true of those who consume animal products. If someone eats only fried eggs, she also has a very bad diet. Those who only eat potatoes will have many deficiencies, for example, vitamin A. But those who eat only fried eggs will also have many deficiencies, for example, vitamin C (in fact, such a diet would lead to death by scurvy).

A false idea that is sometimes heard is that, in order to carry out demanding physical activity, it is necessary to consume animal protein.[6] In fact, in order to have energy, what we need are sufficient calories, which we can find in many foods even if they are low in protein. Protein is required for the growth and maintenance of our bodies.

Another incorrect belief is that plant-based proteins are not suitable for adequate nutrition and so animal proteins are indispensable. In fact, we don't need proteins of any given kind as such. Proteins are made up of amino acids, and it is those amino acids that we need. When we eat protein our body breaks it down into the amino acids it's made from and then, from these amino acids, it makes the proteins that we need. The amino acids are the building blocks we need to make our own protein. And these amino acids are present in both animal proteins and in plant-based ones. Therefore, it's simply not true that we need to eat animal protein.[7] There are plant foods which are very rich in protein, such as legumes and nuts. Grains also provide protein. A diet that includes these foods will have no problem regarding protein intake. In fact, today in many countries people who eat animal products probably consume not too little, but too much protein.

The same is true of the minerals our bodies need, which are found in many vegetable foods.[8] Iron, for instance, is present in a variety of foods including legumes, nuts, and leafy green vegetables such as spinach. Calcium can be obtained from many sources, for example kale, broccoli, and other leafy green vegetables, nuts, and seeds, and it is also present in some fruits such as oranges, as well as in many fortified foods (such as breakfast cereals and plant milks). As for omega-3 fatty acids, they can be obtained by eating foods like nuts and seeds of different types.[9] There's another nutrient, vitamin D, of which deficiencies are common among the general population who consume animal products. Consequently, many foods are fortified with it—although this vitamin can also be obtained by spending time in the sun. With respect to vitamin B_{12}, there has been some controversy as to whether it can be obtained from vegetable sources such as algae. It seems that it can't, or that it is present in only very small amounts, but in any case, there are multiple foods fortified with this vitamin. There are also many supplements that contain it (that are not produced from animal products, but from bacteria). Therefore, if we consume these products or supplements, we shouldn't have any problem with B_{12}.[10] Note also that those who consume animal products also take some form of supplemental vitamin B_{12}. Some people need to take these supplements directly because they don't assimilate adequate amounts of this vitamin from their food. But almost everyone who consumes animal products from current farming practices also consumes supplemental B_{12} indirectly, because it is given to animals. Due to the poor-quality food given to animals on farms today, it is common for farmed animals to be deficient in B_{12}. For this reason, it is common practice to supplement their feed with vitamin B_{12}, or, in the case of ruminants, with cobalt (which they use to synthesize the vitamin).[11] So a person who consumes animals is also getting their B_{12} through supplementation, that is, through the supplementation given to the animals they eat.

In addition, we should not only think about what nutrients may not be in non-animal products. It is also interesting to note that, for their part, animal products contain no fiber and are low in nutrients such as vitamin C and beta-carotene.

Due to all of this, there's no reason to believe that those who don't eat animal products and have a well-balanced diet will have nutritional issues. It's the same with those who do consume animal products. It's worth emphasizing that this has been shown in studies produced by the most important nutrition organizations in the world. In addition, it may be pointed out too that even if these studies hadn't been done, the fact that there have been generations of vegans who have enjoyed good health indicates that a vegan diet is healthy.

In spite of this evidence, it is still possible to find nutritionists who believe that a vegan diet cannot be healthy. There are also medical doctors who still think this, although in their case, it is more understandable, as nutrition is not usually studied in medical school. But in light of what we have seen so far, what this shows is that while these nutritionists and doctors may be excellent professionals in other respects, they are not very well informed on this topic.

Despite the evidence that vegan diets are healthy, there are still biases against them. Suppose, for instance, that someone who is not vegan suffers an ankle sprain in an accident. No one will think that has anything to do with what this person eats. Everyone will understand that it's due to the accident. The same is true in the case of vegans, of course. However, when something like that happens to vegans, some people argue that maybe veganism had something to do with it, because it may have somehow weakened that person (this is not a purely hypothetical example; it is something the author of this book has been told in such a situation). This happens despite the fact that in an accident anyone can suffer a sprain, regardless of their diet.

The same is true of health problems that have a more obvious relationship with nutrition. Imagine that someone who is not vegan and has a very bad diet (for instance, one containing mostly sweets) has some health problem related to poor nutrition such as, say, anemia. People would understand that the cause of anemia is that very bad diet. Now, suppose this person is vegan. There would be people who say that the cause is not that this person eats so poorly, but that she is a vegan. But this would not be correct—the real cause would be her poor diet. If she had a balanced vegan diet, she wouldn't have had that problem. This is true of both vegans and non-vegans. The relevant point here is how good or bad someone's nutrition is. And this is independent of whether someone's diet is vegan or not.

Sometimes we hear about vegans with nutritional deficiencies, and this might make us think that there is a problem with vegan diets, but this just isn't true. Of course, there are vegans with nutrition problems, just as there are people who eat animal products who have such problems. But, as we have just seen, the reason for these problems is not that these people are vegans, but that they don't follow an adequate diet, although they could easily do so on a vegan diet. Consider the case of people who consume animal products and have problems with anemia. It would seem to many people that the most reasonable explanation for their problem is not that they aren't vegans, but that they don't eat well. The same is true for vegans.

Therefore, these criticisms of vegan nutrition are unfounded. Even so, they have the consequence that many people, when they move toward veganism, become interested in learning more about nutrition. This is not always the case, of course, but it's something that happens sometimes. Many people, when they begin to learn about veganism and still don't know much about it may fear that the warnings of those who criticize vegan diets may be at least partly right, and so they think they need to learn more about nutrition. As we have seen, these warnings are often unfounded, but they end up having that effect anyway. In addition, vegans often notice that those who speak ill of veganism are looking for reasons to criticize it. Therefore, being healthy is a way to refute all these unfounded criticisms.

Some people, having learned about nutrition for the reasons mentioned above, continue to have an interest in the topic as they become aware of the importance of good nutrition. Consequently, the health benefits of animal-free diets have become better known than before. It's now well known that on a vegan diet you'll consume less saturated fat and no dietary cholesterol. You'll also avoid the consumption of the hormones and antibiotics routinely given to animals on farms. Furthermore, you'll typically increase your intake of fiber and nutrients such as vitamin C, beta-carotene, folic acid, and potassium, among others. Eating vegan tends to reduce your blood pressure and to reduce the risk of diabetes and cardiovascular issues, especially heart disease. It's also been pointed out that it may help prevent several forms of cancer. Overall, the available evidence suggests that a balanced vegan diet can lead to a longer, healthier life.[12]

It's certainly a good thing that a diet free from animal products has these health benefits. However, this argument is by no means necessary to defend veganism, whose point is simply to avoid harming those who can feel and suffer. Other than that, when considering transitioning to a vegan diet what we need to know is that a vegan diet can be perfectly healthy, and free from nutritional deficiencies.

A variety of options

One might also wonder whether giving up animal products is too demanding. In fact, while taking that step can certainly require some effort, it will probably be much less difficult than it might seem at first. Giving up animal products doesn't mean giving up on the pleasures of eating—there are a huge number of vegan dishes just as tasty as those containing animal products.

There are plenty of different vegan things we can eat. The variety of plant-based products is huge. In a supermarket or farmer's market, we can find a great assortment of fruits, greens, and other vegetables. We can also consume many other foods such as cereals, legumes, pasta, mushrooms, and nuts.[13] There are many common dishes in the traditional cuisine of many countries that are made from these products, and many others that can be made vegan easily just by changing an ingredient. And it's never been easier to learn how to prepare plenty of delicious vegan dishes. There are hundreds of websites, blogs, videos, and cookbooks explaining how to make many different kinds of vegan dishes. Those who have little time to cook can find vegan food in supermarkets that is quick and easy to prepare.[14]

Thus, a vegan diet does not have to be monotonous or difficult. In fact, lots of people have discovered many new dishes as a result of becoming vegan. As a result, many people find that when they begin to eat vegan, their diet becomes more varied. This may seem striking at first glance, but the fact is that in practice it often happens, given the wide variety of tasty vegan dishes.

Some people may miss the flavors of certain animal products. This is perfectly normal, but it usually happens only at the beginning. After some time without eating such products, that desire usually fades away. In any case, nowadays there are a large number of vegan products with a taste very similar to that of animal products, such as hamburgers, sausages, cheeses, yogurts, and plant milks. It's even possible to prepare them at home, for which, again, there's a huge assortment of recipes available on the internet.

In many places, eating out as a vegan is also easier than ever before. The number of vegan restaurants has grown massively in many countries. Furthermore, there are many restaurants that, while not vegan, have many vegan options on their menus. This is especially true of restaurants that have cuisine from different countries. For instance, Italian restaurants have pasta and pizza that can be made without using animal products. Chinese, Vietnamese, and Thai restaurants usually offer dishes made exclusively with vegetables, including rice and noodle dishes, as well as with other products such as mushrooms and soy products. Mexican restaurants often offer vegan options made with corn and beans. Arab, Turkish, and Greek restaurants include some delicious dishes with hummus, falafel, and vegetables. Indian and Pakistani restaurants commonly offer many stews and curry dishes made with vegetables alone. And there are many other restaurants where you can find options without animal products including Japanese, Caribbean, and Ethiopian ones, just to name a few. Note also that today it's easy to find places to eat or to order vegan food online.

One might worry that this will make eating more expensive, but this need not be so. In fact, in supermarkets, vegetables are usually less expensive than meat products. Some people may get the wrong impression because some products such as vegan burgers, cheeses, or yogurts can be more expensive than those made from animal products. In fact, most vegans do not commonly consume those products. But even if you pay more for those substitutes than for the animal products you used to buy, you are likely to pay less for the rest of your shopping and that will more than make up for the difference.

As meat products are offered in many places, and at different prices, eating vegan when you are out may sometimes be more expensive if you don't live near an inexpensive restaurant with vegan options. But even if this is so, since it's likely that you'll pay less at the supermarket, the total amount of money that you spend on food annually shouldn't be higher than what you used to spend buying animal products.

This is not to deny that, if you're used to eating animal products, you may have to make an effort to go vegan. Maybe you're worried about this right now. But what we have seen so far suggests that the effort will be much less than you might initially think.

Why not avoid only some animal products?

In the previous chapter, we saw that, even if we want to stop harming animals, at first we might lack the willpower to stop eating them. An alternative that is sometimes proposed is to stop eating only some animal products. For instance, some people do not eat mammals and birds, but eat fish products, in the belief that a fish doesn't suffer as much. As we saw in Chapter 2, this assumption, though intuitive, isn't established. But even if it were, that need not make a difference here. Whether a fish may suffer less than a mammal or a bird is a question different from whether the fish is able to suffer. And in order to be harmed by our actions, the latter is enough. As long as a fish can suffer, we can harm that animal with our actions, regardless of whether other animals can suffer more. We might think that if they did not suffer so much, it would be less bad to eat them rather than other animals. But the decision needn't be between severely harming one animal and harming another even more—rather we can decide not to harm either of them. What's more, one has to take into account the size of the average fish that is eaten, which is much smaller than that of the mammals that are usually killed for food. For this reason, choosing to eat fish products to avoid eating the meat of mammals usually means that even more animals suffer and die. Mammals and birds live terrible lives on farms, but in fish farms, the situation is no better.

Sometimes it is argued that we should give up the consumption of animal flesh, while continuing to eat other products such as eggs or milk. However, these products have severe consequences for cows, calves, and chickens. If we want to have the best possible impact, avoiding all products resulting from harming animals is better than avoiding only some of them. So, the best option available is not to use animal products at all, rather than using only some animal products. If we avoid pushing the red button every time, that will be much better than if we press it only every now and then.

It's much better to completely avoid pressing the red button instead of pressing it only in some cases. If you feel like you lack the willpower to make the transition, just remember that there are easy ways to do so, like those proposed at the end of the previous chapter. You can also reach out to other vegans for advice or help. And of course, you can also bear in mind the impact that your choice has for the animals.

Aren't animals already protected by law? Could we solve the problem by treating exploited animals better?

Many people, when they first learn how dreadful the situation of animals is, wonder: is this legal? People often think there must be a lot of animal protection laws that are systematically being broken.

However, things are a bit more complex. Almost everything we saw in Chapter 3 about how animals suffer and die is completely legal. And, when it's not (as in the cases we have already seen of slaughterhouse workers torturing animals for fun), it's practically impossible to avoid. This may be surprising at first, but upon reflection it's easy to see that it's not so strange. The majority of people consume animal products, and because of this, the law allows virtually anything that is necessary in order to obtain those products. For this reason, the legal protection animals have today is minimal. The societies we live in are speciesist, and that includes their laws.

We might think the solution is to establish laws that ensure animals are well treated throughout their lives. However, this is not possible. There are many people who want to eat animal products on a daily basis. This demand can only be met by killing billions of mammals and birds, and trillions of aquatic animals every year. It wouldn't be possible to eat animals every day if so many of them weren't killed. And in order to raise and kill such large numbers of animals, it's necessary to do it the way it's currently being done in farms, slaughterhouses, fish farms, and with fishing nets.[15] If one wanted to raise animals in less brutal conditions, it would not be possible to raise so many.

We might think that the animal exploitation industry necessarily has to treat animals well, since otherwise the animals would be in poor health, and might even die, in which case worse quality products, and in smaller quantities, would be obtained from animal exploitation. Thus, the argument goes, their exploitation would not be profitable. At first glance, this argument seems reasonable, but in fact it's not correct. The truth is that many animals do become sick and die, and many more of them would do so if they were not taken to the slaughterhouse at such a young age. Moreover, since animals on farms are packed so closely together, disease spreads very easily. We have already seen that in order to avoid this, it's necessary to give them large quantities of antibiotics and other medicines.[16] But intensive animal exploitation is still profitable. In fact, it's very profitable. With thousands of animals on a farm, even though many die, the resulting quantity of animal products is of such magnitude that it outweighs those deaths by far.

In addition, we must remember that the vast majority of animals that are eaten (or consumed indirectly) are aquatic animals, including small fish species such as sardines, herrings, and anchovies, and other aquatic animals such as prawns and shrimps. We have already seen what happens to these animals when they are caught. Many die due to the explosion of their organs by decompression, are frozen alive, crushed by the weight of other animals, or cooked alive. All these forms of death are very painful. In addition, they also suffer in other ways by being dragged in nets, being pulled out of the water, and being handled. Because of this, it's almost impossible to consume these animals without causing them suffering.

Furthermore, we must not forget that mammals and birds are eventually sent to the slaughterhouse, and the same fate awaits those few animals raised in a situation of relative freedom, instead of in factory farms. In slaughterhouses, these animals endure the same suffering as those from industrial farms. So, even if they avoid some of the horrors of industrial farms during their lives, they don't escape the horrors of the slaughterhouse. Those that are killed outside of slaughterhouses are not free from suffering either. Pigs killed in a traditional way, for example, are tied up, stabbed, and bled alive while they are fully conscious, causing them terrible fear and pain.

Finally, we must also bear in mind that there are other practices that cause terrible suffering to animals, such as the separation of calves from their mothers. And these practices occur on all farms, whether industrial or not. Thus, even if a cow has plenty of outdoor space, she'll still suffer horribly when her calves are taken from her to be killed.

In any case, suppose this were not so. Would that mean that no harm would be caused to animals used as food? To answer this, we can think about what we saw in Chapter 2 about the death of sentient beings. If death is a harm to human beings, then it's also a harm to other animals who are also able to feel and to enjoy their experiences. If a being could have good experiences in her life, by killing her we deprive her of them, and that will be bad for her. This means that we harm animals not only when we cause them suffering, but when we kill them too. This is true even if we do it painlessly.[17] And it's something that can't be avoided if we eat animals.

We can also remember what we saw in the previous chapter. Suppose that in order to taste a piece of meat, one had to suffer a harm like that caused to animals when they're killed. No one would accept it. Therefore, it cannot be fair to kill animals in order to eat them, even if it's done painlessly. This is regardless of the fact that, as we have seen, in practice, people don't eat animals that have been killed painlessly, but animals that have suffered a great deal.

What if killing animals were necessary?

There is another way the arguments in defense of animals are challenged. Sometimes people appeal to hypothetical scenarios, asking questions like these: "What if you were alone on a desert island where you had nothing to eat except an animal, wouldn't you eat that animal?" Or: "What if you were attacked by a tiger or another animal who would inevitably kill you unless you killed that animal?"

These hypothetical questions would be relevant if they had relevant points in common with our actual situation. Asking far-fetched questions in ethics is not a bad way of thinking; on the contrary, it's actually a very useful method which can allow us to better understand the problems we face. Moreover, using our imagination can help us to overcome some biases we may have. What this method requires is that there is some relevant similarity between the hypothetical case and our actual situation.

Is this the case in scenarios in which our survival depends on the death of an animal? Well, it could be pointed out, first, that in the present situation our lives are not being threatened by a tiger or any other animal. To be sure, the lives of some human beings may be threatened by some large predators, but the question here is: is that *your* situation? The answer to this question is probably no. Still, the reason to challenge the validity of these scenarios is different—when we choose whether or not to eat animals, we're not choosing between killing animals or dying. After all, there are other things we can eat. So, given that this is the case, we can choose to live vegan, and there are strong reasons to do so. Therefore, our responses to those hypothetical cases aren't relevant here. Some people may say that even in a case in which they were attacked by animals they wouldn't kill the animals. Many others say they would kill them. But they would probably also be in favor of self-defense when attacked by humans, in a case where they had to choose between being killed or killing the person who's trying to murder them.[18] This doesn't justify going around murdering people, though, and there's no difference when it comes to other animals. In the same way, we can't justify animal exploitation, given that animal exploitation isn't about a choice between our lives and those of animals. It's not necessary in any way to kill them in order to protect our own wellbeing.

Why care about other animals if they don't care about us?

Some may respond to this by claiming that the example of the tiger actually shows us something important, which is that nonhuman animals don't care about human beings. Animals such as tigers, sharks, or snakes have no qualms about killing us. So, the argument would go, it seems that there's no reason why we should care about them, given that there's no reciprocity on their side. That is, since nonhuman animals don't care about us, we shouldn't care about them.

One response to this argument is that the vast majority of nonhuman animals have no interest in killing us. Only a tiny minority are big predators who could kill us in a situation such as the one described above. However, let's suppose the argument worked. Would that mean that we're justified in acting toward nonhuman animals as we do today? Not at all. Animals such as pigs, hens, cows, goats, or horses are not interested in killing us and eating us. Neither are any crustaceans, octopus, or fish, with the exception of predators such as sharks. So, if the argument worked, we would not be justified in harming them and killing them to eat them. We would only be justified in eating animals such as tigers, snakes, lions, and other big carnivores (which, incidentally, are not the animals people usually eat).

However, the main reasons why this argument doesn't work are different. They are the ones we've seen already in Chapter 1. There we saw several arguments for the conclusion that we shouldn't disregard the interests of sentient beings. This is true regardless of whether they have the capacity to understand that other individuals have interests too or to respect those interests. This is why we should care about babies, for instance, or about those humans who don't have complex intellectual capacities.

Some people may think that by saying this we're claiming that humans are superior to nonhuman animals at least in one respect: we can respect nonhuman animals but they can't respect us. This claim is confusing however, because it mixes two different things. It's true that we can respect other beings because we have some capacities that other animals don't possess. But that doesn't imply any kind of superiority in the sense that we deserve more respect. It's one thing to need respect and another to be able to respect others. These are two different things, and they shouldn't be lumped together. Consider the following case:

The speciesist doctor

Imagine that, while traveling, you have an accident. You decide to visit a nearby doctor to get medical attention. But when you knock on the doctor's office door, he asks whether you are also a medical practitioner. You say you're not, puzzled by such a strange question. "In that case," the doctor responds "I can't see you."

"Why is that?"

"Well, for a simple reason," the doctor says. "I've been reading about the arguments in support of speciesism, and have been convinced by the idea that you should only respect someone if she can reciprocate by respecting you. "So," the doctor continues, "I'm applying this argument to other situations too. If reciprocity is all that matters, then in order to receive medical attention it's necessary to also be a doctor of medicine."

Would anyone think that what the doctor says is convincing? Hardly so. One doesn't need to be a doctor in order to receive medical attention. These are two totally different things. The same would happen if instead of a doctor we considered the case of a speciesist baker who sold delicious breads and cakes, but only to those who were also bakers themselves.

Are nonhuman animals there for us to use?

The arguments we have just seen are not complex ones. But there are claims that are even more straightforward and simple. One such claim is that we're justified in using other animals simply because that's the role nonhuman animals have in the world:[19] to be used by humans for food and other purposes.

Those who make this claim seem to assume that our roles as exploiters or as those who are exploited are somehow assigned to us at birth. But this is absurd. Being born in a family or a country that is rich or poor is just a matter of luck. The same is true of species. No one is born to be a servant to others—what really happens is that we assign them such a role because it's convenient for us to do so. But the fact that something is convenient for us doesn't make it right. Having an interest in exploiting someone unfairly doesn't make it legitimate.

It is sometimes claimed that nonhuman animals have the role of serving human beings because humans are at the apex among animals because of our greater abilities. But we already know that this argument doesn't work. If you need a refresher, this was discussed in Chapter 1.

What it means to say humans are omnivores

In other cases, it's claimed that humans are omnivores, and for this reason, we should not try to avoid harming animals. This argument assumes that there is something like a human nature of which being omnivorous is part, and that this determines how we should behave.

This claim is misguided, though. Humans being omnivores doesn't mean that humans have to eat both vegetables and meat products. Rather, it means that they usually eat both plant and animal products. It does not mean that we can't have a healthy diet without animal products. We couldn't be healthy, however, on a diet that only included animal products: we'd die, in fact. It's sometimes argued that some peoples who have traditionally lived in the Arctic only ate animals. In fact, this is not so. They also ate some vegetables such as algae, wild berries, roots, and certain grains that grow in that area.

Even so, their life expectancy was very short, to which their heavily meat-based diet particularly contributed.[20] In any case, nowadays these people no longer eat the same way, because today they have supermarkets where they can buy other products that they need, and restaurants that offer other assortments of foods.

We now know that we don't need to eat animal products to survive. So, being omnivores, we can choose to eat animal products or not to eat them. It's our choice, and we have very good reasons for not including them in our diet.

The meaning of the term "omnivorism" is sometimes not well understood, and it is believed that saying that humans are "omnivores" means stating that humans *have to* eat both vegetables and animal products. But this is not correct. If saying we're omnivores meant we have to eat animals, then the claim that we're omnivores would simply be wrong. Anyway, as we've seen, this is not so. This is not really the meaning of the word "omnivorism," and, for the reasons we already know, we don't need to eat animal products.

Is what humans ate thousands of years ago relevant?

Another argument is that humans evolved into today's *Homo sapiens* because, during that evolutionary process, they ate meat. Some may say that this is controversial, or that there have also been different species of hominids that ate meat and have not survived to the present day, or that through a longer period our ancestors ate plants. But the diets of our distant ancestors are irrelevant to the choices facing us today. Today, we can live healthily on a vegan diet. That, and not what happened tens or hundreds of thousands of years ago, is what matters for this decision.

The claim that eating other animals is fine because other animals do it too

This is a very common argument, which suggests that we should imitate nonhuman animals. But this is a self-contradictory suggestion. This is because, as mentioned above, not all animals behave in the same ways. Some animals eat other animals, but many others don't. Why should we imitate the former instead of the latter?

Furthermore, many animals do a lot of things we don't want to imitate. Some of them kill their mothers after coming out of their eggs. Some male animals kill the cubs of other males to mate with their mothers. Moreover, these animals don't read, listen to music, watch shows, go to the doctor, live in houses, or brush their teeth. If we don't imitate these animals in so many things, why should we imitate them in a practice that all the available arguments show us to be morally questionable?

Once again, the appeal to what is considered natural

Other people say that it's simply natural for us to eat animals, and that is why we have done so throughout history. But we have already seen the reasons why this doesn't matter when it comes to choosing how to act. To start with, it's actually very difficult to know precisely what it means to say that doing something is natural. Does it mean that it was done by the animals we descended from, our ancestors? Or that there is some way our genes move us to do it? Or what, exactly? We might say that whatever isn't the result of technology and culture is natural (although many nonhuman animals have cultures of their own which are often considered natural). At any rate, if we accept this, we can say, more to the point and in line with what we have already seen, that whether something is natural is totally irrelevant to whether it is right or wrong. There are many natural things that are bad such as disease, premature death, and all the suffering that comes from the difficulties imposed on us by survival. Conversely, there are many things that aren't natural that are very good, such as clothes, medicines, comfortable homes, and books, for example. No one complains that having long lives free from suffering is not natural. What's natural is only appealed to when a justification is sought for something that someone wants to do which can't be justified otherwise. But we already know that appealing to what's natural does not justify anything.

The idea that the stronger does the right thing by exploiting the weaker

According to this argument, humans kill and eat other animals because we're stronger. It is in this way that we put ourselves at the top of the trophic chain. That's the way things work in nature—our right to do it is entailed by our power to do it.

This idea is somewhat odd. There is a difference between something existing and something being justified. Many unjust situations exist. People often harm each other in ways most of us see as unjustified. In fact, on reflection, most of us wouldn't think that the mere fact that one is willing to eat another and has the capacity to do so makes it OK to do so. Consider the following case:

Cannibal billionaire

Imagine the case of a very powerful and intelligent billionaire, who enjoys eating other human beings, and does so every now and then. His intelligence, and his ample resources, make it possible for him to do so with impunity.

This person has both the desire and the power to eat other human beings. Therefore, the argument that we have seen before appealing to the food chain would be perfectly applicable here as well. However, most people would deny that it is right for this billionaire to kill innocent humans. If so, then we cannot accept that the mere capacity and desire to eat someone makes it justified. Therefore, this argument can't justify eating animals.

Can we all live without harming animals?

In the previous pages, we've been looking at different arguments trying to show that we have no reason to respect animals' interests in not being exploited. But there are other ways in which animal exploitation has been defended. According to one of them, if we all stopped eating animals, we would not have enough vegetables to feed everyone. If this were right, then veganism might not be a feasible option, no matter how much we wanted to respect animals.

This argument is unsuccessful because one of its assumptions is false. In fact, just the opposite is true. Animals raised to be eaten must be fed. However, only a part of the food used to feed them is used by the animals to grow. The rest will be used by their bodies to perform the functions required for the animal to live. This means that many more people can be fed by directly consuming a certain amount of legumes, grains, or other vegetables than by killing and eating animals that have been raised with that same amount of plant foods.[21] Thus, if we eat meat products, we need to use more vegetables, or else to kill other animals to feed them to the animals we raise. In fact, this is what happens in the case of fished animals: a large number of them are used to feed to animals on farms, especially other fish in fish farms.[22] So, what this argument claims is wrong.

What will happen when we stop eating animals?

There is another argument that also appeals to some alleged catastrophic consequences that might occur if we all became vegan. It's sometimes claimed that if we didn't eat animals, they would overpopulate the land and eventually leave no room for us to live.

This argument wouldn't apply in the case of the majority of the animals killed to be eaten. This is because, as humans don't live in the water, the argument cannot give those taking it seriously any reason to eat any type of fish, crustacean, or other aquatic animals. More to the point, as with the previous objection, this argument doesn't work because it presupposes something that is not really going to happen. The argument assumes that the animals we raise on farms would go on existing and continually multiplying. But the animals people eat are there because humans bring them into existence by breeding them. If the defense of animals is successful, then human beings will progressively cease exploiting animals and, as a result, there will be fewer animals brought into existence to be slaughtered. This will not happen suddenly; it will take time, though for the sake of animals, it would be best if it happened sooner rather than later. So there's not going to be an overpopulation of chickens, pigs, and cows because we suddenly stop killing them.

Is it right to exploit and kill animals because we brought them into existence?

Once we recognize the fact that animals on farms only exist because we eat them, a different argument can be presented. It's sometimes claimed that although there are several ways in which exploiting animals is harmful for them, it also benefits them overall. The reason to argue for this is related to what we saw in the previous argument. The animals we exploit exist only because we bring them into existence. If we didn't eat them or use them for other purposes, they wouldn't exist at all. So, according to this claim, if their lives are sufficiently good, then we shouldn't regret killing them.

There are several things to be said about this. The first is that this argument can't apply to the animals that are fished. Remember that several trillions of these animals are captured and killed every year: they are many more than the animals killed in slaughterhouses. What about the animals raised on farms? The vast majority live in industrial farms, where we know already how much they suffer. Therefore, we can conclude that many, if not most, of these animals have lives that contain more suffering than happiness. This means that for them, having been brought into existence was something negative for them. It has been quite harmful, actually. So, we can conclude that for almost all the animals eaten today this argument doesn't apply.

What about the other animals? If this argument really worked, it would have consequences most people find very hard to accept. The premise of the argument is that if we bring someone into existence who has lived a good life, then we are entitled to kill that being. This is controversial, though. To see this, consider the next case, which like the others seen before was presented in a movie:

The Island

In this story, hundreds of human beings are kept in isolation from the outer world, living relatively happy lives, and they are told that one day they're going to go live on a beautiful island. This makes them very happy. When the time comes for them to go to "the island," they are taken away and killed, for their organs or for other purposes. They don't know they are going to be killed. If they weren't going to be killed for those purposes they would never have existed.

Many people think that what goes on in *The Island* is wrong. But there is only one sound way to defend this objection. That is, to reject the notion that we can kill someone if we have caused her or him to exist with the purpose of killing that individual and her life has been good enough. But even if we accepted that argument, then animal exploitation still couldn't be justified for this reason because the lives of exploited animals are terrible.[23]

At any rate, I'm not going to argue here that what happens in *The Island* is wrong. My intention here is just to point out that the only difference between *The Island* and animal exploitation is the species to which those who are killed belong. But we have seen that a mere difference in species is irrelevant. So, if we think that what happens in *The Island* is wrong, we have to reject the killing of animals whose lives contain more happiness than suffering and are brought into existence by someone who had the purpose of killing them. If, instead, we accept the killing of those animals, we have to accept what happens in *The Island* too.

The claim that those employed in animal exploitation industries need to make a living too

Another argument claims that what is at stake in animal exploitation is not just our own pleasure in tasting animal products or our convenience in using animals in other ways. Animal exploitation companies are businesses that employ people. If we stop using the products they produce, those people will be unemployed. So, the argument goes, veganism is not an acceptable position after all.

Some might reply that this argument seems to ignore the fact that the production of vegetables and other vegan products also employs people. Or that, because ending the use of animals will be a gradual process, it will also mean a step-by-step change in the economy that will not bring about a sudden crisis for all the people working in activities related to animal exploitation. But those reasons would be beside the point. The main point here is that this defense of animal exploitation is possible only if we already accept a speciesist view. It assumes that our interests can justify harming animals in appalling ways. Losing a job is a serious setback, no doubt, and in certain cases, it can be a disaster if one doesn't have any other source of income and can't get hired elsewhere. But being kept your whole life in a crate just slightly bigger than your body just to be killed in agony—maybe by being boiled or dismembered while you're still conscious—is not just a serious setback. It's absolutely terrifying, not only in some cases, but always. This indicates that it's not justified to do to animals all the horrible things that animals are forced to suffer, whether or not this allows certain jobs to exist. We can only accept this argument if we think animals count for nothing, or virtually nothing, which is blatantly speciesist.

Throughout history, there have been multiple examples of human beings benefiting from causing terrible harm to others. Often, in order to do this on a massive scale, they have hired other people to help them do so, and this has provided jobs to many people. But that doesn't justify such practices. If someone works as a torturer, for example, we understand that keeping his job does not justify the harm caused by what he does. If we think, however, that it does justify institutions that harm animals, we may need to go again through the arguments about speciesism we saw in Chapter 1.

The claim that vegans also cause animals to die

Finally, another objection that is sometimes raised is that the consumption of vegan products also negatively affects animals. For example, it is argued that crop cultivation also leads to many animals being killed, albeit accidentally. This especially affects small animals such as mice or invertebrates, who can be killed by harvesting machines, for example. Sometimes it's also argued that the transport of products, even if they are plant-based, is carried out in vehicles that run over animals (in some cases, vertebrates; in many others, small invertebrates). This is an argument that can be offered in good faith, with the intention of finding a way to save those animals. But in other cases, it's used to claim that we need not try to live vegan. The line of reasoning is that, because we kill animals no matter what we eat, we needn't try to stop consuming animal products.

This argument starts with something true, but derives a wrong conclusion from it. It's true that many activities run the risk of harming animals. For example, a truck carrying chairs can run over animals. However, that does not imply that veganism entails we shouldn't use chairs. And the same is true of any other product or service, even if in itself it has nothing to do with animal exploitation. In fact, something similar happens in cases of activities that harm humans. Every year there are traffic accidents all over the world, where many human beings die. However, the use of automobiles and other road vehicles is still acceptable. And we understand that this doesn't mean that we don't care that people die in accidents. Neither does this mean, of course, that we don't care that people die in other ways. Imagine that someone said that, because the use of automobiles means that some human beings will die in accidents, if we use automobiles we shouldn't mind killing human beings. We would think such a statement is absurd. The more deaths we avoid, the better. Of course, we should be aware that the use of cars ends up causing the deaths of human beings. But this doesn't mean that, because this happens, we can exploit and kill other human beings.

In the case of exploited animals, we can follow a similar line of reasoning. The fact that some animals are accidentally killed by cars doesn't justify exploiting and killing other animals. On the contrary, this means that we must take into account that animals die this way, and that we should support actions to prevent not only the deaths of exploited animals but also of those who die from these causes.

In light of this, we may think that we should redefine veganism as the position consisting in trying to avoid doing harm to animals. This makes sense, though on the other hand maybe this is too scrupulous a specification. We may just indicate that veganism means rejecting those practices that, in themselves, necessarily harm animals. However, we shouldn't forget that there are other practices that in themselves don't necessarily involve harming animals but that, depending on the circumstances, can imply harming animals. The transportation of vegetables or chairs is an example of this.

Respecting others

Despite all that has been said above, there is another argument sometimes used in favor of exploiting animals which claims that doing so is a matter of freedom. According to this argument, those who reject animal exploitation are free to do so, but they shouldn't object to other people engaging in it, as that would mean failing to respect their freedom. This is argued for in some cases by claiming that our behavior toward nonhuman animals is a matter of personal ethics, and that personal ethics are a matter of taste. According to this argument, we should just accept the views others have, and not tell them what to do. This is claimed despite the fact that in our societies, it is rather easy to use animals as we please.

This is confused in several ways. To start with, this argument itself is used to try to convince us of a certain view: that we should not try to convince others of what we think. That is, by using this argument, we do what according to the argument we shouldn't do.

Secondly, ethical issues are not just a matter of taste. They concern very serious questions that affect others and not only us. Moreover, even if we have very different ethical positions, that doesn't mean we can't evaluate each of those views, and judge whether they are adequate. Often they aren't. They can be contradictory, for example. Actually, this even applies to matters of taste too. For instance, I can't consistently say that I don't like chocolate and that I like all cocoa products. That's a contradiction, because chocolate is a cocoa product.

The same is true in ethics. You can say that only those with certain intellectual capacities should be respected. Or you can say all humans should be respected. But if you say both things together, that's a contradiction, because not all humans will have any particular intellectual capacities. Similarly, you can say that we should act impartially, or you can say, alternatively, that speciesism is correct. But if you say both things together, that's another contradiction. The same is true in the case of other arguments we saw above. Ethics can involve personal views up to a certain point. But it's restricted by the necessity to avoid contradictions, just like any other field. Logical consistency implies that we sometimes have to choose between different positions, even though both seem good to us, because they contradict each other. It also implies that sometimes we have to accept something that doesn't seem good to us, if the alternative is even worse.

So yes, we can certainly judge views in ethics. And we often do, actually! After all, most of us think we can discuss issues such as racism, sexism, or abuse of the vulnerable, and that we can present reasons to oppose them. It's not just that we dislike them—we can present arguments to show that they are unfair and arbitrary. And we can do the same in the case of speciesism.

Finally, the whole idea that our ethical views are personal and that we shouldn't want others to share them is very odd. This idea seems to completely miss what ethical views are about. Suppose that I claim to oppose murder, rape, and slavery. However, I make it clear that I just mean that *I* shouldn't murder, rape, or enslave, but I don't oppose others doing it. That would be a very odd view, no doubt. More to the point, we would say that if I had such a view, I wouldn't really be opposed to murder, rape, or slavery. What opposing those practices means is opposing that they take place at all, and not just refusing to participate in them oneself. The same is true when it comes to speciesism.

It can also be pointed out here that by expressing our disapproval of speciesism, we are not disrespecting those who endorse it. Disagreeing with someone is not the same as disrespecting them. In any case, there is a deeper problem with the argument we are examining here. The argument states that we should respect others. However, we fail to respect animals by discriminating against and harming them. Therefore, the argument is attempting to defend a contradictory position—that disrespect must be respected.

The contradiction arises because the argument claims that we should respect "others" while at the same time assuming that "the others" are only human beings, not nonhuman animals. But we have already seen that this is a form of discrimination.

What really matters is what reasons there are to respect animals

Some people attack veganism by saying that some vegans have attitudes that are disagreeable. The underlying assumption is that, because the attitude of these people is objectionable, so is veganism. Perhaps it could be said that the objectionable attitudes displayed by some vegans may be due to fatigue, due to the disrespectful treatment those who defend animals are sometimes subjected to. In any case, there is something more important to say here.

The fact that there are some vegans with bad attitudes doesn't mean that veganism is objectionable. Whether a view is correct depends on the reasons for and against it, not on whether those who defend it are nice or not. This is just common sense. Newton, so it is said, was an arrogant and insufferable person. But whether Newtonian physics is right or wrong does not depend on that. In the same way, some of those who eat animals behave impolitely. But this is not the reason to consider whether to stop eating animals; the harm caused to animals is.

Also, we should bear in mind that supporters of veganism are a very diverse group. Although there are vegans with attitudes we don't like, this can't be generalized to all of them. There are also vegans who play chess, but this doesn't mean that all of them do! The same is true of the characteristics of those who consume animal products.

In fact, it's totally normal that among those who defend veganism, there are people of all kinds. And this is a positive thing. At first glance, this may surprise some people, but in reality it's quite logical. Vegans are normal people, with all their defects and virtues, not perfect ones. This is good not because those defects are good, since they aren't, and they have negative consequences. Rather, it's positive for a very different reason.

If all vegans were perfect

Imagine that all vegans were perfect, without flaws. Suppose all of them were intelligent, pleasant, and very understanding people. We might think that this would be good for veganism. But, in fact, it would be very worrying. It would suggest that veganism is not an option for everyone, but only for a part of the population. And, unfortunately, a lot of people are not like that. Most of us are normal people who could be better in many respects. So it's good that anyone can be vegan, regardless of their personality. Thus, the fact that there are not only friendly vegans but also people with many flaws, shows that it's perfectly possible for veganism to end up becoming the norm in our society.

This being said, it would clearly be better to avoid hostile and unpleasant attitudes, as they don't help to spread respect for animals. This is true even if the fact that animal exploitation is reprehensible is totally independent of the character traits of vegans.

At any rate, we can also say that vegans, with all their flaws and mistakes, do at least one very positive thing, in that they avoid harming animals. This is something everyone can do.

There is another very different way of arguing against veganism that is also based on the conduct of some people, or, more specifically, of one person in particular. This is an argument that can be particularly surprising. In any case, since there are people who have used it, let's see what it says. To assess it, consider this hypothetical argument in favor of veganism:

An example of a bad argument

Imagine that someone used the following argument to defend veganism: "Hitler was not a vegan; he used leather and ate animal products. His followers said that he avoided meat to create the legend that he was a healthy spartan, but while he might have avoided some meat products, he ate others, and never stopped using other animal products. He was also, of course, the highest authority in a country where animal exploitation took place. He also closed down some vegetarian societies. So if Hitler wasn't a vegan perhaps there's something wrong with not being vegan."

Is this argument sound? No. It's ridiculous. Whatever Hitler did is irrelevant to whether it's right or wrong to harm animals for our own benefit. Otherwise, if the argument were acceptable, we would have to accept that, because Hitler had a mustache, then having a mustache is immoral. Actually, we could come up with a long list of cruel dictators, perpetrators of genocide, serial killers, and other horrible people who ate meat. But proponents of veganism don't argue that people who eat animals share any other characteristics with these people. That would be an absurd argument.

However, a similar argument has sometimes been used to defend eating animals, by claiming that Hitler was a vegetarian. This is a strange argument, not because Hitler did eat animal products, but for the reason we have just seen.[24]

Finally, some people defend animal exploitation by claiming that vegans believe themselves to be superior to everyone else. The same arguments that we have seen above in this section apply here. But another point can also be made. Regardless of the personality any individual may have, veganism itself doesn't imply the belief that one is superior to others. If anything, it implies just the opposite. Animal exploitation is defended by claiming that human beings are superior or that we count more than animals of other species. The consumption of animals thus puts our enjoyment above not causing their suffering. In other words, consuming animals implies that they are inferior because they are not members of our species.

What happens, instead, if we oppose speciesism? We will be rejecting this idea that we are superior. We won't believe ourselves to be better or more important than other animals. And, for that reason, we will choose to oppose their exploitation, and we'll stop participating in it.

Reactions to veganism that indicate it's moving in the right direction

So far we have seen a long list of objections against veganism. As we can see, none of them works. In some cases, they are based on assumptions that aren't true. In others, there are very conclusive arguments against them.

However, sometimes there is another obstacle to stopping the consumption of animals—though it's usually not the most important one[25]—which is hostile reactions from non-vegans. These are not very common. But sometimes, when people find out that someone doesn't eat animals, even if that person hasn't said anything about the matter, they start criticizing vegans and defending the use of animals.

What could explain these reactions? It may be the fact that a person who chooses not to exploit animals shows that it's possible to live that way.

This is very positive, as it encourages many other people to question animal exploitation, seeing that they could do the same. It makes people think about it. This is why, upon discovering someone who is vegan, people who are not vegan will ask questions and be interested in talking about it. But for the same reason, there are people who react rudely, because they dislike the idea of questioning the use of animals. Interestingly, they don't criticize people who don't consume animals because of a health problem.

The reason for this is easy to understand, as it often happens that we don't want to reflect on what we think or the way we act. We dislike the idea that we may be doing something wrong. However, on reflection, it makes more sense to think about this than to try to dismiss such questions. We must also note that trying to ridicule someone does not amount to challenging their reasons. It's more reasonable to think about whether those reasons make sense.

Why are animals being harmed?

There are various doubts that may confront us when we first think about the reasons to oppose animal exploitation. In this chapter, we have seen responses to some of them.

There are some decisions in our lives that we can avoid. But others are unavoidable. In every person's life, there come moments in which we must face difficult decisions because of the consequences our actions could have. Those are important moments in our lives. They are the moments when we have to ask ourselves if we're really doing what it would be fair and reasonable to expect from us, or if we're failing in that task.

We like to think that the problem with the harms suffered by animals is really just a problem with the way the animal exploitation industry currently acts. The truth, however, is that all the horrible things that happen to animals because of their exploitation happen because we live in a society that accepts such things, and because consumers pay for them to happen. People who use animal products have a desire to go on using these products, but not an equally strong desire to know the reality of what obtaining these products involves. And the way in which animal products are packaged and sold is designed to prevent that reality from being visible. In this way, it could be argued that animal exploitation industries are doing the dirty work in two ways: first, by directly inflicting the actual harm on animals that the public (albeit inadvertently) demands to be done and second, by hiding those harms from the public view, so they don't have to think about the harm the use of animals causes to them. But such harm is still taking place, and it's very real. This is something we have to face and reject. The next chapter will finish the presentation of what this means, in addition to explaining what else we can do for animals.

At the beginning of this chapter, we saw the story of three pioneers: Eva Batt, Lewis Gompertz, and Abul Al Ma'arri. This chapter will conclude it with some more words by Abul, the blind vegan poet of medieval times. In another poem, he wrote:

A perpetual loss I feel if, knowing[ly],
I believe a falsehood or deny the truth.[26]

At this point, we already know the truth behind the use of animals. We also know some of the falsehoods behind the idea that we shouldn't respect animals of species other than our own.

Notes

1 Eva belonged to an association that was small in her day, but eventually grew much larger, the *Vegan Society* of the United Kingdom, which was founded in 1944. On Eva's views, see Batt, E. (1993 [1964]) "Why veganism?", In Dinshah, H. J. (ed.) *Here's harmlessness: An anthology of ahimsa*, Malaga: American Vegan Society, 7–12.

2 Gompertz's work, *Moral inquiries on the situation of man and of brutes*, was already cited above twice, since, despite being written at the beginning of the 19th century, it remains an excellent book. In fact, no book or piece about animals and ethics written before the late 20th century compares to it.

3 Al Ma'arri, A. A. (2000 [ca. 10th–11th century]), in Pay, R. (comp.) *Humanistic texts*, http://humanistictexts.org/al_ma'arri.htm (see also Nicholson, R. A. [comp.] [1922] *Translations of Eastern poetry and prose*, Cambridge: Cambridge University Press).

4 Melina, V.; Craig, W. J. & Levin, S. (2016 [1987]) "Position of the Academy of Nutrition and Dietetics: Vegetarian diets", *Journal of the Academy of Nutrition and Dietetics*, 116, 1970–1980, http://andjrnl.org/article/S2212–2672(16)311 92-3/pdf.

5 National Health Service, United Kingdom (2015) "The vegan diet", *NHS Choices*, http://nhs.uk/Livewell/Vegetarianhealth/Pages/Vegandiets.aspx; Dietitians Association of Australia (2016) "Vegan diets", *Nutrition Information A-Z*, http://daa.asn.au/for-the-public/smart-eating-for-you/nutrition-a-z/vegan-diets; Dietitians of Canada (2014) "Healthy eating guidelines for vegans", *Your Health*, http://dietitians.ca/Your-Health/Nutrition-A-Z/Vegetarian-Diets/Eating-Guidelines-for-Vegans.aspx; Irish Nutrition and Dietetic Institute (2016) *Eating well on a vegetarian diet, factsheet*, Dublin: Irish Nutrition and Dietetic Institute; Asociación Española de Dietistas y Nutricionistas (2006) "La dieta vegetariana sí, pero bien planificada y con vitamina B$_{12}$", *Gaceta Médica*, 175, 20; Gallo, D.; Manuzza, M.; Echegaray, N; Montero, J.; Munner, M.; Rovirosa, A.; Sánchez, M. A. & Murria, R. S. (2013) "Alimentación vegetariana", *Sociedad Argentina de Nutrición*, http://sanutricion.org.ar/files/upload/files/Alimentacion_Vegetariana_Revision_final.pdf; Gomes Silva, S. C.; Pinho, J. P.; Borges, C.; Teixeira Santos, C.; Santos, A. & Graça, P. (2015) *Linhas de orientação para uma alimentação vegetariana saudável*, Programa Nacional para a Promoção da Alimentação Saudável, Direção-Geral da Saúde, http://nutrimento. pt/manuais-pnpas/linhas-de-orientacao-para-uma-alimentacao-vegetariana-saudavel; Agnoli, C.; Baroni, L.; Bertini, I.; Ciappellano, S.; Fabbri, A.; Papa,

M.; Pellegrini, N.; Sbarbati, R.; Scarino, M. L.; Siani, V. & Sieri, S. (2017) "Position paper on vegetarian diets from the working group of the Italian Society of Human Nutrition", *Nutrition, Metabolism and Cardiovascular Diseases*, 27, 1037–1052 and Nordic co-operation—Norden (2014) *Nordic nutrition recommendations 2012: Integrating nutrition and physical activity*, Copenhagen: Nordic Council of Ministers, http://norden.org/en/theme/nordic-nutrition-recommendation/nordic-nutrition-recommendations-2012.

6 Evidence shows that the consumption of animal products is unnecessary for the performance of demanding physical activity, including sports. This is already indicated by the position of the Academy of Nutrition and Dietetics cited above, and is also indicated in Nieman, D. C. (1988) "Vegetarian dietary practices and endurance performance", *American Journal of Clinical Nutrition*, 48, 754–761.

7 Young, V. R. & Pellett, P. L. (1994) "Plant proteins in relation to human protein and amino acid nutrition", *American Journal of Clinical Nutrition*, 59, 1203S–1212S; Marsh, K. A.; Munn, E. A. & Baines, S. K. (2012) "Protein and vegetarian diets", *Medical Journal of Australia*, 1, 7–10.

8 On how vegan people can have good levels of minerals, see Haddad, E. H.; Berk, L. S.; Kettering, J. D.; Hubbard, R. W. & Peters, W. R. (1999) "Dietary intake and biochemical, hematologic, and immune status of vegans compared with non-vegetarians", *American Journal of Clinical Nutrition*, 70, 586S–593S; Craig, W. J. (1994) "Iron status of vegetarians", *American Journal of Clinical Nutrition*, 59, 1233S–1237S or Weaver, C. M. & Plawecki, K. L. (1995) "Dietary calcium: Adequacy of a vegetarian diet", *American Journal of Clinical Nutrition*, 59, 1238S–S1241S; see also for a more general study Institute of Medicine (2001) *Dietary reference intakes for vitamin A, vitamin K, arsenic, boron, chromium, copper, iodine, iron, manganese, molybdenum, nickel, silicon, vanadium, and zinc*, Washington, DC: National Academy Press, http://nap.edu/read/10026/chapter/1.

9 On this, see Rosell, M. S.; Lloyd-Wright, Z.; Appleby, P. N.; Sanders, T. A.; Allen, N. E. & Key, T. J. (2005) "Long-chain n-3 polyunsaturated fatty acids in plasma in British meat-eating, vegetarian, and vegan men", *American Journal of Clinical Nutrition*, 82, 327–334 or Harris, W. S. (2014) "Achieving optimal n-3 fatty acid status: the vegetarian's challenge… or not", *American Journal of Clinical Nutrition*, 100, 449S–452S.

10 See Animal Ethics (2017) "Vegan nutrition", *Veganism, Animal Ethics*, http://animal-ethics.org/nutrition; see also Mangels, R.; Messina, V. & Messina, M. (2011) *The dietitian's guide to vegetarian diets*, Sudbury: Jones and Bartlett; Melina, V. & Davis, B. (2014) *Becoming vegan: The complete reference to plant-based nutrition*, comprehensive ed., Summertown: Book Publishing and Norris, J. & Messina, V. (2011) *Vegan for life: Everything you need to know to be healthy and fit on a plant-based diet*, Cambridge: Da Capo; Baroni, L.; Goggi, S.; Battaglino, R.; Berveglieri, M.; Fasan, I.; Filippin, D.; Griffith , P.; Rizzo, G.; Tomasini, C.; Tosatti, M. A. & Battino, M. A. (2019) "Vegan nutrition for mothers and children: Practical tools for healthcare providers", *Nutrients*, 11/1, a. 5; Koeder, C. (2020) *Vegan baby: A guide to complementary feeding: For vegans between the ages of 4 and 12 months*, International Vegetarian Union, http://ivu.org/nutrition/health-nutrition/vegan-baby/file.html. There is also much information available in Norris, J., Vegan Outreach (2016 [2003]) *VeganHealth.org: Nutrient recommendations and research*, http://veganhealth.org. The purpose of this book is not to provide extensive information about nutrition, but the above-mentioned studies, which are much more comprehensive, include broad guidelines on vegan nutrition.

11 EFSA FEEDAP—European Food Safety Authority Panel on Additives and Products or Substances used in Animal Feed (2012) "Scientific opinion on safety and efficacy of cobalt carbonate as feed additive for ruminants, horses and rabbits",

EFSA Journal, 10, 2727 and (2018) "Safety and efficacy of vitamin B_{12} (in the form of cyanocobalamin) produced by *Ensifer* spp. as a feed additive for all animal species based on a dossier submitted by VITAC EEIG", *EFSA Journal*, 16, 5336. It has been studied whether this can be problematic due to possible carcinogenic effects of cobalt.

12 On this, see Singh, P. N.; Sabaté, J. & Fraser, G. E. (2003) "Does low meat consumption increase life expectancy in humans?", *American Journal of Clinical Nutrition*, 78, 526S–532S; Fraser, G. E. (2009) "Vegetarian diets: What do we know of their effects on common chronic diseases?", *American Journal of Clinical Nutrition*, 89, 1607S–1612S; Ha, V. & de Souza, R. J. (2015). "Fleshing out" the benefits of adopting a vegetarian diet", *Journal of the American Heart Association*, 4, 1–3 or Appleby, P. N. & Key, T. J. (2016) "The long-term health of vegetarians and vegans", *Proceedings of the Nutrition Society*, 75, 287–293.

13 This objection also ignores the fact that animal products are not as varied as they may seem. Consider the terrestrial animals (mammals and birds) that are commonly eaten in many countries. The number of species is small. They include mainly cows, pigs, chickens, lambs, ducks, turkeys, and goats (although other animals are also killed and eaten in certain places). More types of animals are eaten in the case of aquatic animals, including fish species as well as invertebrate ones. But, in general, the animals that are usually eaten aren't members of a very large number of species. What makes animal products diverse is mainly the different ways they are prepared. However, there are also multiple ways to prepare very tasty dishes using only vegan ingredients. In fact, many people who consume animals eat relatively monotonously, eating very similar things every week. An animal-free diet needn't be as monotonous as this at all.

14 The packaging of some food products sometimes indicates that they may include traces of some animal ingredients. This shouldn't confuse us. What that means is not that such ingredients have been used in small proportions in the manufacture of those products. On the contrary, what it means is that these products, despite not including those ingredients in their preparation, can contain them in tiny quantities because they have been produced in facilities where those ingredients are used to make other products. This is relevant information for those who suffer allergies, since they could have health problems by consuming even minimal amounts of some ingredients. But by buying these products, we are not contributing to animal exploitation as we do when we buy products that do contain animal ingredients.

15 On this, it's interesting to see Sethu, H. (2014) "Do you know someone who buys meat only from a small local farm?", *Counting Animals*, http://countinganimals.com/do-you-know-someone-who-buys-meat-only-from-a-small-local-farm.

16 There are those who think that something like this should be reported by veterinary staff in charge of monitoring what happens on farms. This role is presented for instance in Rollin, B. E. (2013 [1996]) *An introduction to veterinary medical ethics: Theory and cases*, Ames: Blackwell. Unfortunately, in reality, the role such staff typically has is to collaborate so that the use of animals can continue to be carried out in the most profitable manner, see Sobbrio, P. & Pettorali, M. (2018) *Gli animali da produzione alimentare come esseri senzienti: Considerazioni giuridiche e veterinarie*, Milan: Key editore.

17 This point has been often made in the literature, see Salt, *Animals' rights*; Clark, *The moral status of animals*; Pluhar, *Beyond prejudice*; see especially Francione, G. L. (1995) *Animals, property and the law*, Philadelphia: Temple University Press; Delon, N. (2014) "La mort : un mal non nécessaire, surtout pour les animaux heureux !", *Revue Semestrielle de Droit Animalier*, 2, 247–276; Stanescu, V. (2014) "Crocodile tears, compassionate carnivores and the marketing of 'happy meat'",

in Sorenson, J. (ed.) *Critical animal studies: Thinking the unthinkable*, Toronto: Canadian Scholars Press, 216–233; Bernstein, *The moral equality of humans and animals*; Wrenn, C. (2015) *A rational approach to animal rights: Extensions in abolitionist theory*, Basingstoke: Palgrave Macmillan, p. 69 and López, F. F. (2019) "Moral risk and humane farming", *Utilitas*, 31, 463–476. See also Haynes, R. P. (2008) *Animal welfare: Competing conceptions and their ethical implications*, Dordrecht: Springer. Laws prescribing the reduction of harm to exploited animals have been described as charitable though nevertheless unjust in Stallwood, K. (2014) *Growl: Life lessons, hard truths, and bold strategies from an animal advocate*, New York: Lantern Books, p. 210.

18 On this issue, see Abbate, C. E. (2015) "The search for liability in the defensive killing of nonhuman animals", *Social Theory and Practice*, 41, 106–130.

19 See Aristotle (1998 [ca. 4th century a.c.) *Politics*, Oxford: Oxford University Press, 1256b.

20 Bennett, J. & Rowley, S. (eds.) (2004) *Uqalurait: An oral history of Nunavut*, Montreal: McGill-Queen's University Press, cap. 5. These peoples have also traditionally consumed raw meat, which has given them certain nutrients that are not obtained in processed and cooked meat. The price, however, often consists in contracting parasites, which cause trichinosis and other diseases. There is a myth according to which the diet of these peoples didn't pose problems of cardiovascular diseases, but it has been proven that this is not so, but just the other way around. Bjerregaard, P.; Young, T. K. & Hegele, R. A. (2003) "Low incidence of cardiovascular disease among the Inuit—what is the evidence?", *Atherosclerosis*, 166, 351–357. Plus, in addition to such disease risks, this diet also involves problems related to the consumption of few plants, such as constipation.

21 Deckers, J. (2011) "Does the consumption of farmed animal products cause human hunger?", *Journal of Hunger & Environmental Nutrition*, 6, 353–377.

22 Mood, A. & Brooke, P. (2012) "Estimating the number of farmed fish killed in global aquaculture each year", *Fishcount.org.uk*, http://fishcount.org.uk/published/std/fishcountstudy2.pdf.

23 There is an argument in support of this claim, which goes as follows. Suppose we're deciding whether it would be good if someone who doesn't exist yet lived a happy life, even if it were a short one. Some might conclude that would be good, or that at least it wouldn't be bad. We might think that that would allow us to cause the existence of this individual with the plan of killing him or her afterwards. But once that individual already exists and can live a future with positive things, it would not be right to kill him or her. Doing so would deprive that individual of their future. Many also have the intuition that it would be better if that individual wasn't brought into existence for that purpose, although that is a separate question.

24 See Patterson, C. (2008) *Eternal Treblinka: Our treatment of animals and the Holocaust*, New York: Lantern Books, 2002.

25 A study showed that the most commonly mentioned reason for not giving up the use of animals is the attachment to certain dishes, and that social pressure would play a very minor role, as would tradition and price. Unfortunately, lack of knowledge about nutritional issues such as those explained above is another reason why people continue to eat animal products. See Humane League Labs (2014) "Diet change and demographic characteristics of vegans, vegetarians, semi-vegetarians, and omnivores", *The Humane League*, http://humaneleague-labs.org/static/reports/2014/04/diet-change-and-demographic-characteristics1.pdf, pp. 13–14.

26 Al Ma'arri, in *Humanistic texts*.

Chapter 6

In defense of animals!

Running late...

Imagine the following scenario. A group of people are talking. Someone in the group mentions a news item: there has been a murder. The victim was drowned, and the killer has already been arrested. On hearing the news, one member of the group expresses his indignation, claiming that killing is an absolutely despicable act. He then tells us, in passing, that he has just seen another person drown. Shocked by this, we ask him what happened. He explains that he saw a person drown in a pool. He tells us that there were many life buoys by the pool, but that unfortunately there was no one to throw one. When we hear that, we ask him how come he didn't do anything without waiting for someone else to do it? Why didn't he throw a buoy, or try to rescue the person in some other way? He replies that he had no time to do so, as he was late for an appointment. Hearing this, we become indignant. We reproach him for not preventing a death when he could have. He responds that our outrage is improper, since he didn't murder the person in question. He just didn't help that person.

Most of us believe that someone who behaved like this would be acting very wrongly. It would be deeply inconsistent of us to condemn those who actively harm others while also being unwilling to help prevent others from suffering equally serious harms. For this reason, almost everyone agrees that, in addition to not exploiting others, we should also give them our help whenever they need it and we are able to do so. This is so even if we haven't caused their situation. If someone needs help because other people are abusing her, most people think we should come to her defense. And if someone needs help because of an accident or illness, or some other natural cause, we also think that it's right to help her. This attitude is almost always held when the victims are human beings. If the same attitude isn't held when the victims are non-human animals, then the reason for this is clear. You guessed it: speciesism.

In the previous chapters, we saw that humans do terrible things to other animals. We also saw what is required for this to end: that we stop contributing

DOI: 10.4324/9781003285922-7

to animal exploitation. In addition, we saw that by publicly showing that we live our lives without consuming animals, we also encourage others to do the same. This is because we not only stop contributing to the demand for the products of animal exploitation and killing but we also set an example. By acting in this way, we make it visible that it's perfectly possible to live without exploiting animals, and to give them the consideration that we would like to receive if we were in their place.

However, as we'll see next, there's much more that we can do for animals.

The claim that, even if we respect other animals, humans should be our priority

Even if we stop exploiting animals, there will be other people who continue to do so. As long as this happens, the exploited animals will need our help. Without it, their exploitation will never end. Therefore, we need to work to make people aware of the consequences of speciesism. We can use our time, or part of it, to help more people side with the animals. This is what millions have already done around the world, who have come to defend animals. We will see later on how this can be done. But first let us consider some of the objections that are sometimes presented against those who defend animals.

There are people with speciesist attitudes who don't like that there are others who care about nonhuman animals. For this reason, they reproach them for helping nonhuman animals instead of humans. This is interesting, as these people would not receive such criticism if instead of dedicating their time and effort to helping animals they just spent their time having fun or doing things for their own benefit.[1]

One simple answer to this is that defending animals isn't incompatible with defending humans. Even if someone uses her time to help human beings, this doesn't mean that they can't stop exploiting animals.[2] Nothing forces human rights activists to eat animals.

This answer is correct. But it already concedes a lot to speciesism. Why is it necessary to give such an explanation? Let's consider the case of those who defend, for example, women who are the victims of violence, or children, or human beings who suffer from famine in faraway places. Do these people have to spend their time defending adult men living in their own country for their behavior to be legitimate? Obviously not. Claiming this would be a form of discrimination. It would mean assuming that what happens to women, children, and people living elsewhere matters less than what happens to adult men living near us. This is clearly unacceptable.

Why is such a justification required of those who defend animals? Because it is being assumed in the first place that animals count for less. By stating that those who defend animals of other species should spend their time defending human beings instead, a speciesist attitude is being expressed. Those who defend animals do not have to justify themselves, but rather explain the arguments for rejecting speciesism. Therefore, defending nonhuman animals is not merely acceptable. It is also the right thing to do. It is not something for which an apology should be made. On the contrary, it is speciesism that is unacceptable.

In addition, there are also others who are altruistic toward human beings, but indifferent toward other animals. This is common, given what we have seen before. Speciesism is strongly embedded in our minds. Many people are completely unaware of the reasons we should reject this form of discrimination. But we shouldn't give up for that reason. Rather, this shows that we must continue to work for animals, so more people reject speciesism. Although there may be people who won't abandon their prejudices, more and more will do so.

Moreover, since speciesism is so widespread, there are many people with speciesist attitudes even among people who sympathize with the defense of animals. To understand this, we just need to bear in mind that discriminating against someone doesn't always mean causing them harm, or having no respect for them. It only means treating them worse than other individuals, for unjustified reasons. In fact, those who are discriminated against are often given some amount of respect, but less than those who don't suffer such discrimination. For example, a racist can respect African people to some extent, but less than Europeans. That is racism all the same. But that person, despite being a racist, may think that the racist slavery of past centuries was a horrible thing. This explains why, when racist slavery was abolished, it did not mean the end of blatant forms of racism. In fact, segregation laws continued to exist in several countries, even though human slavery was already illegal there. Likewise, many sexist people nevertheless reject feminicide.

Similarly, there are vegans who nevertheless believe that humans always come first. We can see this in the case of vegans who get involved in causes helping certain human beings because they believe they are important causes, but do nothing (or do much less) to defend nonhuman animals, just because they give more importance to human interests because they are human. This is an example of a vegan, but speciesist, attitude. This can be understood by considering the following. Suppose we considered it legitimate to treat animals of other species worse than human beings. Even so, animal exploitation is something so brutal that we could very well continue to oppose it. The same is true of the racists who reject slavery. One can be against participating in the exploitation of animals, but continue to discriminate against them in other ways.

Given the terrible situation of animals, the emphasis is sometimes only on the need to stop exploiting them. This means that the question of the worse consideration nonhuman animals receive is set aside. But we have already seen that speciesism is not an acceptable view. All beings that feel and suffer matter, and species isn't a relevant difference. This means that the defense of animals is not something secondary. We do not have to set it aside, nor subordinate it in comparison to concern for human beings.

The reality of speciesism: the misfortune of not being born human

It is sometimes claimed that those who defend nonhuman animals are being speciesist against human beings. According to this argument, animal defenders give humans less attention than other animals, despite the fact that humans need it so much. In relation to this, it is also often said that many human beings are treated "worse than animals." There is no shortage of occasions for such claims. After all, human beings often commit many atrocities against other human beings.

What can be said about this? There is no doubt that many human beings are exploited, discriminated against, and abused in horrible ways. However, there are many cases in which people who say that some human beings are treated worse than other animals, are not saying it metaphorically. They're not just using a set phrase. This statement is often made in the belief that it is literally true. That is, some people actually believe that the situation of nonhuman animals is better than that of many human beings.

The reason why some people think this is very simple: they are not really familiar with what the situation of nonhuman animals is like. When they think of animals, what comes to their mind is animals kept as companions, such as dogs, and they think of these animals as being in comfortable homes where they are well taken care of. None of this is realistic. To start with, the overall situation of dogs really is terrible. Some enjoy happy lives, but they are a minority. Many of them are abandoned and die, suffering a lot in the process, often not long after birth. Others are raised in puppy mills which are similar to factory farms. Others are kept in appalling conditions, tied all their life to a short rope, enjoying no company, locked down in tiny places, sometimes suffering from hunger or being beaten up every now and then. In addition, the vast majority of animals kept by humans aren't dogs, but animals raised in factory farms to be eaten, that undergo gigantic amounts of suffering. Remember what we saw in Chapter 3, when we examined what animal exploitation means for its trillions of victims. After having seen there what the situation of animals is like, we can understand that to say that nonhuman animals are treated better than human beings is to fail to understand reality. The exceptions there may be to the general way humans act toward other animals shouldn't hide the overwhelming reality of animal exploitation, in which animals suffer and die every day in numbers many times greater than the total number of human beings who live in the world.

The contrast between the attitude toward human beings and other animals when it comes to giving them help is also crystal clear. All around the world, there are many political and social organizations, nonprofit entities, and other movements whose goal is to defend human beings. They face great difficulties, and they still have an immense amount of work ahead. But millions of people are involved in them, and they have large amounts of resources to achieve their goals. In contrast, the organizations dedicated to the defense of animals involve a considerably smaller number of people, and have far fewer resources.

This is the situation not only with regard to animals harmed by humans. In the next section, we will see some examples of how many animals living in the wild can be helped. But such cases are currently very few. Animals of other species often die in massive numbers from hunger, disease, cold, etc., with almost no help provided. The attention they receive is insignificant in comparison to what they would be given if they were human beings. To be sure, there are many humans in such situations that receive very little help. But the attention nonhuman animals receive is even smaller—in fact, in most cases it's completely nonexistent.

In light of all this, the claim that those who defend animals are discriminating against human beings because the latter need our help more has no basis in reality. All the evidence conclusively shows that it is the other way around. It is clearly not the case that nonhuman animals are treated better than humans. They suffer terrible harms, and the attention they receive is much less than what is given to humans. Therefore, we have conclusive reasons to defend animals and to help them when they are in need. Doing so is not a speciesist behavior that discriminates against human beings. In fact, if this seems wrong to some people, it is because they are the ones who have a speciesist attitude against nonhuman animals. What is speciesist is to think that animals of other species don't matter because they are not human.

Helping those in need: the case of animals in the wild

We can therefore conclude that once we reject speciesism, we not only stop harming animals but we stop discriminating against them in general. And, as we have already seen, this also means giving them our help when they need it, in those situations where we would certainly do so if they were human beings.[3] There are many cases in which this is possible. In this way, the rejection of speciesism goes beyond the rejection of animal exploitation.

This happens in many cases when wild animals are rescued in situations where otherwise they would suffer significantly and die. This is the case, for example, when animals trapped in pools, quicksand, or frozen lakes, or marine animals stranded on the coast, are saved. There are many examples of such rescues, which appear in the media from time to time. There are also different examples of animals being helped during natural disasters, when floods, fires, earthquakes, etc. occur. In many of these situations, the animals would die if they were not helped. Sometimes initiatives are carried out to help animals continuously over time: for instance, in shelters, orphanages, and medical centers where help is given to orphaned, injured, or sick animals.[4]

Consider the following example where aid has been given to animals in need in the wild.

Saved Apes

Apes have a much higher chance of surviving to adulthood than the vast majority of animals living in the wild (since in nature the most common fate is to die shortly after birth). Despite this, throughout their lives, they face many dangers and difficulties. One cause of their suffering and death is violence from other animals of their own group or from neighboring groups. Stronger apes sometimes attack weaker ones, particularly in the case of young apes. Another cause of death and suffering is disease. Sometimes disease kills animals indirectly by disabling them and making it impossible for them to feed themselves, as in the case of polio for example. This disease leaves animals unable to move their arms and legs normally, to the point where they cannot even take food and put it in their mouths.

There have been cases in which primatologists have reacted by helping these animals. Sometimes they have done so by feeding those who could not feed themselves. In other cases they have provided them with polio vaccines (by introducing the vaccine into fruit given to the animals).

There have been also cases where they've protected the weakest animals in the group from being killed by other primates.[5]

Some in the scientific community have opposed these actions. They've claimed that interventions of this kind, done to help animals, break the supposed scientific ideal of noninterference. According to this, primatologists shouldn't interact with animals beyond what is strictly necessary to obtain the information required for their studies. For the most part, they should let animals' lives run their course as much as possible, as they would have had humans not appeared. This implies that they should let the animals suffer and die.[6] But is this right?

To answer this question, it is useful to follow the same method we have used before. Consider what we would think if the victims weren't chimpanzees, but human beings. Suppose that the primatologists had chosen to become anthropologists, and they were investigating a community of human beings living in an isolated tribe in the Amazon or in Papua New Guinea. And suppose further that some people of this tribe were starving because of the effects of polio, and that it was perfectly possible for the team to provide them with food and a vaccine for their disease. Imagine, too, that some of the adult human beings in this community were violent and abusive and intended to kill tribal children.

What should anthropologists do? Refrain from interfering, and let all those horrible deaths take place? Or, on the contrary, intervene by helping potential victims, saving them from certain death?

Most people believe that the right thing to do in cases like this would be to help the victims. Why is a different attitude maintained when the victims are not human, but of other species?

If we reject speciesism, we must not deny help to nonhuman animals in situations where we would help them if only they were human. If we say that we must not interfere, we fail to show these animals the consideration they require. They do not need us to watch them suffer and die, but to help them, just as anyone in their position would.

Let us now consider another case with a much greater impact. Often, action is taken in ways that are very positive for the animals, even when the purpose of such actions is not to aid those animals. A very clear example is the following:

Saving animals from dying from diseases

We have already seen that many animals suffer and die from diseases. For many of these diseases there are vaccines that could save the animals from dying in this way. And for decades many of them have been saved, because they have been given those vaccines. This is done so that the animals do not get diseases that can spread to humans, or to the animals they exploit, such as those raised for food. This has been done in the case of fatal diseases such as rabies, Ebola, hepatitis, swine flu, tuberculosis, etc. Many of these diseases cause great suffering and death to the animals that contract them. The main way in which animals are immunized is by introducing the vaccine in small doses into little pieces of food with a smell that is attractive to the animals. These are spread over large areas of land. When the animals eat them, they are immunized against the disease. This method has been successfully applied in many countries. In this way, diseases such as rabies have been completely eradicated in large areas of Europe and North America.[7]

Although this measure is carried out because of its usefulness to humans, it shows that it is perfectly possible to help animals in need. If there is no problem in implementing such measures to benefit humans, there should be no problem in implementing them to benefit the animals themselves.

In fact, there are other similar examples. Consider what happens to animals in danger of death due to lack of food or water. There are areas where certain animals live that attract tourists, such as many national parks. Sometimes, when there are droughts or harsh winters in these places, food is provided to the animals to prevent them from starving to death.[8] It is important that these kinds of actions do not lead to a growing population of animals that have high mortality rates shortly after birth, as this causes more animals to die in the end, and more suffering than that which these actions directly prevent.

In fact, these measures are done to keep tourists coming to these areas to see them, but they in any case benefit the animals very much. Moreover, they show that we already have the capacity to help a large number of animals, as we have been doing for decades. Similarly, we could do so in the interest of the animals themselves even if no benefit to humans were at stake.

All these actions helping wild animals are much more important than we may think at first. Some people believe that when they are not exploited by humans, animals enjoy wonderful lives. But the reality is that they suffer and die from a whole range of causes: disease, hunger and thirst, adverse weather conditions, accidents, parasites, natural disasters, and so on. This comes as a surprise to some people, but when we think about it, we can see right away that it makes sense. We know very well that things like cold, hunger, and disease harm human beings. How could they not harm other animals as well? Of course they do, and on a massive scale. These things affect animals much more than we commonly imagine. In fact, many of the animals that are born in the wild do not even reach adulthood. Many live lives with enormous amounts of suffering, greater even than the enjoyment they may have in their short lives.[9] In some of these situations, it is within our power to help them—should we do so, or should we turn our backs on them and leave them to their fate?

Helping animals in need is very good for them. Among the best things we can do for someone, whether they are human beings or animals of other species, is to save their life or prevent them from suffering. However, there are certain views according to which humans should be helped, but not other sentient animals. These positions reject the latter on the grounds that doing so is unnatural, or goes against what certain environmentalist views would prescribe.[10] According to these views, if it is natural for an animal to suffer terribly and die in nature, then this animal should suffer and die.

How can we think about whether this is right or not? Well, we can consider where we stand when it comes to human beings in similar circumstances. Most of us understand that helping human beings in need is the right thing to do. Whether something is natural is irrelevant, it is their situation of need that is important. But then, if we think this in the case for human beings, what nonspeciesist reason is there not to think the same in the case of other animals?[11] All this is in addition to the fact that, in many cases, there is no clear distinction between what is and what is not the result of human action. Many extreme weather events and wildfires, for instance, may be due, at least in part, to human impact on the climate. Due to this, there should be no reason to refrain from helping wild animals affected by weather events by claiming that we should let what is natural follow its course. Also, most ecosystems have been transformed by humans, so whatever happens in them is no longer fully natural. This happens most obviously in urban, suburban, industrial, and agricultural areas, but also in many other places, such as forests planted by humans.[12] Again, appealing to what is natural to avoid helping animals in need in those areas does not seem right.

It is true that there are many cases in which we cannot do anything about the harms animals suffer today. In some cases, our actions could have negative effects if they are not very well thought out. However, other cases are different. There are circumstances in which animals are already being helped successfully.

We can thus see the change of perspective that comes with abandoning speciesism. When we truly realize that there is no justification for speciesism, we have a very different attitude toward animals. This doesn't mean only respecting animals a little more than we do today (which, as we have seen, is very little, or little more than nothing). On the contrary, it means fundamentally changing the way we act toward them. Instead of harming animals of other species, we can act for their benefit, as we would like others to do for us if we were in their place.

All sentient animals matter, not just those that are exploited. We should also be concerned about what happens to those that live in the wild. We should also spread this idea so that, when it is possible to help animals, we do. This is very important, as it can save a large number of animals.[13]

Studying the best way to help animals that do not live in captivity

In addition to the examples we have just seen, there are many other ways to help animals living in the wild. It is therefore important that people become aware of this, so that when they are in a position to help an animal, they do so. But something else is needed to improve the situation of these animals on a larger scale. To be able to do this properly, we need to increase our knowledge about which factors harm and benefit animals, and how to act in a way that is positive for them. We might think that this is something that is already very well known, but in fact it's not. The studies that have been carried out so far have focused on the factors that are important for the conservation of animal populations or species, or the environments in which they live. But this is different from what affects them as sentient individuals, causing more or less suffering in their lives. The latter is something that has only recently been researched, combining the contributions made in different fields in the natural sciences, in particular biology and veterinary science. The progress made in this way will make it possible for interdisciplinary work in this field to be done, which will multiply the effectiveness of future work to help animals in the wild.[14] In this respect, the contributions that can be made by those who study or work in these scientific fields are very important. There are several ways to help animals about which it would be especially important to acquire more knowledge. These include the further development of wild animal vaccination, which was already mentioned above, as well as the rescue of animals affected by particularly harmful weather events or natural disasters, such as floods or droughts, or the construction of structures to provide shelter from the weather for animals. It may also be important to develop methods for studying the states of suffering and welfare experienced by animals in the wild (considering, among other factors, how they behave and what their physical condition is). Another promising area is the study of the situation of wild animals living in urban and agricultural environments, such as birds and other small animals. We can investigate ways in which their suffering can be increased or reduced. With all the knowledge that can be gained from these and other related studies, it will be possible to increase our capacity to help animals in the wild much more.[15]

In short, the reasons for defending animals in the wild are simple, and they are totally in line with the reasons to help other human beings. Moreover, it is not something utopian, but it is already being done today, and with further study, it can be done with even greater success. But let's look now at some of the objections to helping animals in the wild, and the responses that can be given to them.

Let's not discriminate against some animals in comparison to others

Some people say we should only care about domesticated animals, not about animals in the wild. Why do some people think this?

It is sometimes claimed that we have a special obligation toward certain animals because, as we use them for our benefit, we are indebted to them. According to the argument, this would mean that when we use them, we have a duty not to treat them harshly, and also that we have no duties toward those animals in the wild we don't use—just for that reason, because we don't use them. But in light of what we have seen in previous chapters, we have strong reasons to reject this argument. If all sentient beings deserve respect, then this applies to wild animals as much as to those that humans exploit. In fact, this is also the reason why animal exploitation is unjustified. Inflicting terrible harms on sentient animals (such as death and significant suffering) is not an acceptable practice just because we make some effort to make those harms less bad. This means there should be no "debt" to animals for exploiting them, because we shouldn't be exploiting them at all in the first place. It also means this is not a successful argument for not caring about helping wild animals.

There is another way to argue that we shouldn't care about animals in the wild that may seem more acceptable at first glance. It is to say that exploited animals are in such a bad situation that we should not worry about the rest. However, there is no reason to accept this. Exploited animals are in a terrible situation, and so we have reason to stop exploiting them and to speak out on their behalf, but, again, this doesn't mean that we should deny other animals help.

Previously, we saw that it is very common to treat some animals much worse than others. Pigs and chickens are treated worse than dogs and cats.

We saw that this is a form of speciesism, which does not favor humans over other animals, but favors certain nonhuman animals over others. The fact is that there are many other forms of speciesism which do the same thing. For example, a fish will typically receive far less consideration than another vertebrate, even though the fish can also feel suffering and enjoyment. In turn, many invertebrates, such as octopuses, can also suffer, but they are hardly considered compared to vertebrates. And small animals are often treated with much greater indifference than larger ones. For example, rabbits and mice may suffer and enjoy themselves as much as many larger animals, but they are usually given much less consideration. This is even more extreme in the case of smaller invertebrates that are also sentient.

For some people, it may be counterintuitive that these animals are also worth considering. But more and more people are opposed to speciesism, and are in favor of showing respect for all sentient beings, regardless of their size, or of whether they live in the wild or have been domesticated.[16]

A very important difference: the defense of animals and environmentalism

There is another objection that is sometimes raised against helping animals in the wild that was already mentioned above. This is the claim that we should let nature run its course without human interference. This claim is most often defended out of certain environmentalist views. At this point, it is important to clarify a point about which there is much confusion.

To this day, it is still common not to distinguish between two movements that defend different things and that are often in opposition: environmentalism and the defense of animals. This confusion occurs, among other reasons, because both have to do with animals living in the wild. This confusion is detrimental to the defense of animals, because, although it is growing very quickly, it's still less widespread than environmentalism. Due to this, sometimes people tend to see the defense of animals as if it were a form of environmentalism. But there are big differences between these two movements. Some of them were discussed in Chapter 3 when we examined conservationist defenses of hunting and zoos. We will see some other important differences now.

Environmental conservationism advocates the conservation of ecosystems, landscapes, and species. How does it consider animals? As a part of the natural environment that surrounds humans. Thus, when it defends the protection of animals, it's because they are in a certain ecosystem, or because they belong to a certain species.

This is a very different approach compared to the defense of animals. If we reject speciesism, we will no longer see animals as alien to the group we are part of. On the contrary, we will see them as part of this same group. That is, as part of the group of beings who can feel and suffer. Human beings belong to this group, but other sentient animals do too. Nonhuman animals are not part of the environment that surrounds the group we belong to, but are part of this group too. We all belong to the group of beings who can feel and suffer.

As we have seen, what's important for whether or not an animal is part of this group is not the species she belongs to, or that she lives in a certain ecosystem. The only thing that counts is that she is sentient. This is what distinguishes sentient animals from ecosystems, because the latter don't have the capacity to suffer and enjoy. Neither do species, which are not organisms with nervous systems of any kind, but only sets or classifications of individuals. Those who can suffer and enjoy are individual animals.

This difference between the defense of animals and environmentalism has very important practical consequences. Some have to do with their position concerning animal exploitation, others, with their position regarding the situation of animals in nature.

Let's consider first the consequences related to animal exploitation. We have already seen that if we reject speciesism, we will oppose this exploitation. Environmentalism, on the other hand, rejects it only if it has a negative environmental impact. Moreover, it can support it in certain cases, if it considers that it can help environmental conservation. Thereby, it advocates practices such as sustainable animal farming, in addition to others which we have seen, including support for certain kinds of hunting and the defense of zoos for conservationist purposes. Of course, many people may disagree with these practices and yet have an affinity with environmentalism. But what underlies this concern is not that they are environmentalists, but that, in addition to agreeing with certain environmental ideas, they also have other ideas that lead them to reject harming animals. Bear in mind also that the defense of entities such as ecosystems, landscapes, or species, which are conservationist ideals, is different from the defense of animals as individuals.

The second difference in practice between the defense of animals and environmentalism lies in their attitude toward animals that live in the wild. Environmental conservationism supports those interventions that favor the conservation of environmental values. But such measures may harm animals. Examples of this are the killings of animals that are believed not to belong in a certain area because they aren't native, or that are thought to affect the ecological balance or the conservation of some species.[17] We can see this in the following specific cases.

Killing wild ducks and horses for conservationist reasons

Ruddy ducks are animals originally from North America who were introduced to Europe last century. They have a black and white head. White-headed duck, originally from Europe, have, as their name suggests, totally white heads. Ruddy ducks now sometimes reproduce with white-headed ducks. As they have hybrid offspring, there are fewer ducks with totally white heads. To prevent this, a systematic slaughter of ruddy ducks is being carried out.

At the same time, a large number of wild horses have been captured and killed in North America. This has been done with the intention of recreating ecosystems that existed before European colonization. Prior to this, in pre-Columbian times, there were no horses anywhere in the Americas the wild horses of North America are descended from horses transported from Europe. But the reason for this is that the first human beings who came to the Americas, thousands of years before Europeans, exterminated the horses who lived there. There were horses before there were humans in the Americas.

These are two examples of interventions performed to conserve a certain species or to ensure that a certain ecosystem exists or is preserved. If we respect animals as sentient individuals, we will reject such interventions as harmful for them.[18] As discussed in Chapter 3, these measures are defended only when those that are harmed by them are nonhuman animals. This means that something is being done to animals that would never be done to humans, a clear instance of speciesism in action. People often think that environmentalist efforts are positive for animals living in a certain ecosystem. However, the examples we have just seen show that there are many cases in which measures to keep an ecosystem or a species intact are harmful to animals.

This raises eyebrows among some people, at least at first. We have already seen that there is a tendency to conflate the defense of animals with environmentalism. This mistake is encouraged by the fact that animals are living beings, just like other natural entities like plants, and that most of them live in the wild. But we have seen already that the reason to care about animals does not depend at all on this; quite the contrary, it is not because they are alive, but only because they can suffer and enjoy themselves. It is sentient beings that need respect, not because they are animals or biological organisms, but because they suffer. In fact, it was pointed out in Chapter 2 that if machines or programs were created which performed functions like those of central nervous systems, they could be sentient, and so we would have to take them into account as well, since what we did to them could be harmful to them.[19] We don't need to have the same attitude toward animals that are not sentient, such as sponges, because they don't feel anything, and thus cannot be harmed. Likewise, whether or not animals live in nature is also irrelevant in terms of whether they should be respected: both those exploited by humans and those in the wild need to be taken into account. And, as we have seen, the latter are not in a paradisiacal situation at all, quite the contrary.

In short, we can conclude that helping animals in need is not only perfectly legitimate but it's also the fairest thing to do. If we care about animals, we will try to act in favor of those living in the wild, since, as we have already seen, they are in a state of real need. In addition to this, we should not accept harming and killing animals in order to promote conservationist goals, as we would never do so if they were human beings.[20] In all cases, the idea is the same one we have already seen several times in this book: we can act toward animals as we would like others to act toward us if we were in their place. In other words: we can act without discriminating against anyone because of their species.

Taking action: reaching out to as many people as possible

In previous chapters, we saw the reasons not to exploit nonhuman animals, and we have just seen the reasons to care for other animals in need. So, once we have come this far, and with all that we already know, we can ask ourselves what we can each do on our own to improve the situation of animals. Many people spread the word about the defense of animals by talking about it with friends, relatives, and other people around them. By joining all the other people who do this, a large number of people can be reached. However, this course of action has a smaller impact than other forms of advocacy that are aimed at a larger audience. If we talk to those around us, we will reach some people. But if we engage in projects or organizations that address broad sectors of society, our transformational potential will be far greater. Obviously, there can be exceptions to this, for example, if we reach a particular person who is in a situation where they can have a great deal of influence. And often talking to those around us is something that requires very little extra time or effort, because we can do it while spending time with those people in a relaxed atmosphere. But if this is not the case, if it is something that requires a lot of time or energy on our part, then we are almost certainly going to have too small an impact for our efforts to have been worth it.

In addition, it's worth noting that those who try to convince the people around them sometimes succeed, but not always. There are times when, after explaining to people all the reasons for respecting animals, after describing to them the consequences that disregarding animals has for them, and after preparing for them a lot of delicious dishes without animal products, many find that such efforts are not successful. The people they have been encouraging to be concerned about animals continue to live as before, without changing their way of life and without doing anything for animals. There are those who, faced with this failure, then try to convince these people by appealing to their own self-interest, telling them that the consumption of animal products is bad for their health. But, with a few exceptions, it is rare that this changes their behavior very substantially.

Those who find themselves in this type of situation often ask themselves questions such as "what else could I say to this person that I haven't already said" or "what can I do to make them respect animals" and the answer to this question is very simple: possibly nothing. It's very likely that in a situation like this, there's nothing that can be done to change that person. It just so happens that there are people who are never going to give up speciesism, or stop using animal products and services. As we have already seen, this is not surprising, given how entrenched speciesism and the use of animals as resources are. But three things need to be said about this:

First of all, it should be borne in mind that when someone is adequately informed about the reasons for respecting animals, they may not stop using animals, but may change their opinion on the matter. This may have an effect on how these people act on a small scale (for example, it may lead them to express ideas favorable toward animals when they have conversations on the subject). When these changes in attitudes occur in many people, even if they are small, they can contribute to a collective shift in attitudes toward nonhuman animals. In this way, the antispeciesist message can also have a social impact when it reaches people who only partially accept it.

Second, people usually have limits on what they are willing to accept. So, if after much talking about respecting animals with someone, we find that they are not willing to change their position, stubbornly continuing to try to make them change their views is quite likely to be a waste of time and energy. Chances are that person will not change, and those efforts could instead be used to get other people to become aware and change. Therefore, it is much more reasonable and effective to do the latter. If someone does not change, instead of insisting, let's turn to other people.

Finally, it is important to bear in mind something that has already been said above. Although we can achieve positive results by convincing people around us, these will be far less than those we can achieve by targeting a wider audience, as organizations working against speciesism do. In fact, in order to have a massive impact, it seems that such work is necessary, otherwise, just through simple communication from person to person, there will be many people who will not be reached. Moreover, without public communication directed at society as a whole, people will tend to think that the defense of animals is a minor cause. This is because most people think that important causes do not remain solely in the realm of private communication, but have public visibility. This is completely wrong, but unfortunately this is what is commonly thought. For this reason, if concern for animals is to be taken seriously, it must be given the highest visibility outside the sphere of private conversations. This can be done through campaigns or projects aimed at reaching the general public, or through initiatives that target people from specific fields (e.g., people from academia and education, politics and the law, science, etc.). These fields are particularly influential, so changes achieved in them have a large effect on the rest of society.

Changes at the structural level

What we have just seen is also relevant because, if we reject speciesism, our goal isn't simply for ourselves personally to stop harming animals and to start helping them. Nor will we be satisfied for other people acting individually, to do the same. We will also want our society, as such, to stop harming animals, and to move on to providing them with the help and protection they need. So, as animal advocacy advances, more and more people will stand up for them and demand that they be protected. As a result, there will be increasing pressure at the political level to introduce public policies in their favor. This, in turn, may be very important, in that structural changes can also foster important changes in the attitudes of the public. When some practice is considered illegal on the basis of the harm it causes to someone, people are more likely to end up considering it wrong. Similarly, when public policies helping some group of individuals are routinely implemented, people are more likely to consider that it is wrong to leave those individuals unaided. Of course, what can be achieved institutionally can often be quite limited. Due to this, we should be careful in choosing our opportunities, since it would be a waste of time to invest our efforts in institutional changes that will be irrelevant in practice and will not help to increase future concern for sentient beings.

The changes in question that can make an important difference may have a direct bearing on practices affecting animals, both negatively and positively. In addition, there can also be changes in the way that disregard for animals is reproduced in our society. They may involve, for instance, the following:

- The end of institutional ways of supporting animal exploitation (for example, when subsidies to animal farming are rescinded).
- The cessation of institutional practices that harm animals (for example, when the compulsory use of animals in certain places, such as some live science departments, is put to an end).
- Institutional opposition to certain ways of harming animals (for example, when the use of animals for certain purposes, such as entertainment, is no longer legally permitted).
- Institutional support for helping animals (for example, when rescue protocols in cases of natural disasters affecting animals—including those in the wild—are approved).
- The creation of institutions that protect animals from some of the harms humans do to them (for example, when public officers are appointed or official bodies are created to act as attorneys for animals, or when animal law centers are established).
- The creation of institutions that actively help animals (for example, wild animal hospitals, orphanages, and rescue centers).
- Measures promoting the social visibility of concern for nonhuman animals (for example, those leading to the inclusion of the topic in primary and secondary education curricula).
- Measures increasing the social prestige for the moral consideration of animals (for example, the establishment of university courses and academic institutes focused on this topic).

All the points above are just a few examples of what can be done. Note that, in addition to legal and policy changes, institutional action benefiting animals and driving people to have a different attitude toward them is also possible in a wide range of other areas. These include the economic, educational, scientific, and cultural spheres. Among them, structural changes that deserve being mentioned are those resulting from learning new things and applying them in ways that are beneficial in potentially massive ways for animals. Two types can be distinguished that are particularly promising: first, those that make it easier to stop exploiting animals; and second, those that make it possible to help them in ways that were not possible before.

An example of the first type can be found in the development of foods whose taste and texture will at some point become practically indistinguishable from those resulting from animal exploitation. This will mean that the difference between consuming these products and those of animal origin will be much reduced, and this will make it much easier to stop using animals. And the easier it is to do so, the more people will do it. This is important not only because it will reduce the use of animal products but also because it will make it easier for people to respect animals more, since this will no longer be in such strong conflict with their behavioral habits.[21] This seems likely if we remember the survey data we saw in the introduction to this book. Many people seem to be sympathetic to the cause of animals, and would join in if it were not for the fact that they do not want to stop enjoying the products that come from their exploitation.

In addition, we can find very clear examples of the second type of progress in the case of the development of new ways to help animals in the wild. We have already seen above that there are different ways in which it is possible to help these animals. One concrete example we examined was that of vaccination against disease. We can make further progress in that direction by developing new treatments and vaccines that will save many animals. And we can make further progress in other ways of providing relief to them (for example, in caring for injured or orphaned animals, or in providing shelter from the weather or natural disasters), or by developing new ways of providing them with assistance in addition to those already in place. These can be tested and refined through adequately monitored pilot programs, which can allow us to assess their impact. The simplest way to proceed may be to start implementing these programs in industrial, agricultural, urban, and suburban areas, where many non-domesticated animals live.

The work that can be done in this area by researchers in biology and veterinary science is particularly important. Their potential to understand the situation of animals and to develop better ways of helping them is very significant. This is why it is crucial that more people in these fields have an attitude of respect toward animals.

Changes in these areas are different from those that involve raising awareness. Still, it is also true that the degree to which they can be successful will tend to be proportional to the degree to which those who can promote them (people researching these issues) are interested in promoting what is best for animals. If, however, at some point, work on them gains sufficient attention and is considered scientifically, socially, or economically relevant, many more people will be interested in joining those who research them.

The pursuit of legal rights for all sentient beings

One type of institutional advocacy work for nonhuman animals in the relatively long term consists in the pursuit to give them legal rights. To understand what this means, let's look at exactly how the law grants someone rights. Legal rights can be of different kinds. Some are rights not to be harmed. Others are rights to have some help or service provided to you. Rights considered to be "human rights," include rights not to be harmed, such as the right to life. But they also include rights to have things done for us, such as the right to health care. If animals of other species had rights enshrined in law, the exploitation they suffer today would not be permitted. Nor would the other harms and abuses they suffer. Instead, they would be guaranteed help and assistance in many cases where nothing is done for them today.

This does not happen today because of the type of society we live in. Animals are not considered as subjects with legal rights, but as things. Therefore, even when there are laws that protect them, this protection is minimal, and does not deter almost anyone from harming animals.

Some may think that nonhuman animals cannot be protected with legal rights because they cannot have responsibilities, nor respect the rights of others. It is sometimes said that "having rights implies having obligations." According to this, the reason for respecting other human beings is that they have the capacity to respect us in turn. But that is simply wrong. Babies and intellectually diverse human beings, for example, have rights even if they cannot respect others, and this is how it should be. To respect only those who can respect us is unfair to those who do not have the capacity to do so. In any case, there is a more basic reason to oppose this argument. It is the one we saw in the previous chapter with the example of the speciesist doctor. It is one thing to be able to respect and another to need respect. They are very different things that should not be confused.

For these reasons, we must demand that the law also defend nonhuman animals.[22] The legal protection that they receive at present is weak, and is not granted by the recognition of rights. But this may change in the future.

What we can do

Making progress toward the changes indicated in the previous sections is fully feasible, but only if people like us get involved. Fortunately, there are many ways in which we can act individually or, better yet, collaborate with others to spread the rejection of speciesism. When it comes to doing this work, some people are in a better position than others. This is because there are places where concern for animals is greater than in others. However, we must bear in mind that in places where the level of awareness is lower, we could have a greater impact. And, in any case, there is always something we can do, to the extent of our possibilities. Each person, depending on their work, their situation, their experience, etc., can contribute to the defense of animals in one way or another. We can help make a difference by carrying out some tasks such as the following:

- Disseminating information wherever we can do it effectively, both in person and online. The latter can be done on social networks and through any other channels such as Wikipedia, blogs, comments to news, and other spaces.
- Helping to organize events, talks, and other activities.
- Doing research, writing, revising and translating texts, and helping to distribute information in other ways.
- Participating in events or mobilizations that can raise awareness about speciesism or demand institutional change.
- Doing work to address the moral consideration of sentient animals in different professional areas, depending on our situation (examples include education and research, the media, politics, administration, and the law, among others).

As indicated above, tasks like these can have a greater impact if done in collaboration with others or with animal advocacy organizations. Those who have limited time to help can contribute by volunteering and doing those things they are skilled at. For instance, among those who can be very helpful people, there are those who have knowledge in fields such as graphic design, web design, photo and video footage and editing, communication and social media, journalism and working with the mass media, the political arena, the legal arena, administration, research, science and academia, applying new technologies to animal advocacy, or other similarly specialized tasks. Some people can volunteer just a little time every month, but their contribution can still be helpful. Others can spend more hours of their time doing advocacy work and thus have a higher impact.

Furthermore, we can also increase our effectiveness by spending some of our time reading and learning more about speciesism and how we can best defend its victims. In this way, we can be better prepared to make the best use of our time, and be able to help animals more cost-effectively.

Finally, there's another very important way to help. Even if we cannot engage in activism in our free time by doing volunteer work, we can make a very big contribution in other ways, by supporting those doing animal advocacy. We can become members or donate to antispeciesist organizations that work effectively for animals. We often spend money on things we don't really need and can do without: if we save that money and use it instead to spread antispeciesism and to defend animals, we will achieve results that will be much more important than those trivial things we can spare. We can also help by organizing fundraising events. Economic support can be crucial for the success of many initiatives and projects. The lack of resources is one of the main obstacles to the advancement of animal advocacy. For many organizations, this is the only thing that prevents them from achieving greater results, as they otherwise have clear objectives and people who are willing to work for them. Our help can break this barrier.

As in the case of veganism, the effort involved in helping animals in need is much less significant than the harm we can prevent by doing that. And it is important to remember that the advances we can make are not so difficult to attain. They are achieved every time new people join us in defending nonhuman animals.

Effectiveness and longtermism

What we have just seen shows us the importance of considering how we can help animals. But there's a lot more to this than can be mentioned here.

To begin with, throughout this book, we have seen that there are certain forms of exploitation that sometimes seem rather outrageous, such as bull-fighting, but in reality are no worse than others. Also, there are sometimes cases of animal exploitation that concern some people more because they happen close to where they live. Or because they affect animals that arouse more sympathy. But, again, this makes no difference from the point of view of the animals. There is no reason to discriminate against animals, either because of their species, because we find them more beautiful, or because they live in one place instead of another.

This means that, when deciding how best to defend animals, we shouldn't be asking ourselves 'which form of exploitation do I personally dislike the most?' or 'which animals would I most like to help?' Instead, we should be asking 'in what way are we going to have the greatest impact?' In other words, how can we help animals in the most important ways? This is a reason to consider helping animals killed on farms and in slaughterhouses, even though many people support the consumption of animals.[23] And it is also a reason to defend animals in the wild, even though many people do not know the reasons why they need help. Limiting advocacy work to defending some nonhuman animals (such as victims of the fur industry or circuses) may be easier. But this will leave the vast majority of those who need our help to their fate.

Furthermore, if we want to be as effective as possible in defending animals, we should not only be concerned with those who are living today. This may seem surprising. But in fact, it's apparent that animals will not be suffering and dying only today. On the contrary, they'll continue to be harmed as long as speciesism exists. And it is very important to realize that in the future, enormous numbers of sentient beings will continue to be born, having lives full of suffering and dying very young. Overall, the total number of beings that will suffer that fate is many times greater than the number of animals currently living or who will be born in the near future. And our actions in the present can make a big difference to the situation they will find themselves in, for better or for worse. We may be able to make things better. But it may also turn out that what humans are doing today means that the future will be terrible, much worse even than the present.

There is in fact a risk of scenarios of large amounts of suffering occurring in the future. Looking back, we can see that in the past, as well as in the present, these situations have arisen when the following three factors have coincided:

1   a certain technology has the potential to do great harm to a large number of individuals;
2   that technology may benefit a minority;
3   the individuals who benefit don't mind harming other individuals, or they see it as justified.[24]

This is what has happened in the case of animal exploitation today, particularly with the emergence of the technology that has made factory farming of birds, mammals, and aquatic animals possible. It had happened before with other forms of animal exploitation, for example, through the development of different fishing methods. And there is no reason to think that we have already seen all the forms of harm that can be done to animals. In fact, the development of new forms of profit at the expense of animals continues at present. A current example is the creation of invertebrate farms, both marine and terrestrial, which we saw in Chapter 3. Other forms of suffering may take place in the future, when the means for it to happen appear.[25] This is something that receives very little attention, despite being a very important issue. That is why it is essential to spread the word about the reasons for respecting those with the capacity to feel and suffer, not only because of what is happening to animals today but also because of what may happen to all the sentient beings who will exist in the future.

We may think that, since we do not know what will happen tomorrow, it is more important to focus on what happens today. But if we are realistic, we know that tomorrow animals will still need our help. That is therefore a very important reason to spread respect for all sentient beings. What is at stake is not only the suffering and the lives of trillions of animals today. What is also at stake is the fate of all sentient beings in the future, when we are no longer here.

This is sometimes not well understood because it is difficult to properly conceive of very large quantities. It is therefore difficult for us to get a clear idea of what is at stake when there are many animals involved. This is due to a cognitive bias, a mental attitude that, although common, is actually irrational. This bias or mistake leads us not to appreciate the difference between, for example, a billion and a trillion, even though the second figure is immensely greater than the first.[26] Something similar can happen to us if we think of the animals that need our help, since there are so many of them. This can cause us not to properly appreciate what is at stake when we decide between focusing only on the animals that are living now or defending all sentient beings, present and future. This bias distorts our priorities. We must know how to deal with it to know how to make the best decisions.

There are other cognitive biases that also lead us to make bad choices. One of them causes us to endorse the opinions of the majority without reflecting much about them.[27] This happens in the case of speciesism. Many people feel pushed to accept speciesist views simply because other people do too. But we shouldn't allow ourselves to be pulled along by what the majority happens to think, as this bias leads us to do. Rather, we should think for ourselves and make our own decisions.

There's another bias which causes us to fail to pay sufficient attention to new arguments or evidence rebutting the opinions we previously held. We can very well be influenced by this bias when we are first told the reasons for respecting all sentient beings.[28] However, if we keep an open mind and consider things in a reasoned way, and take into account all the evidence at our disposal, we will not let ourselves be carried away by this attitude either.

Similarly, we also have a tendency to make our decisions on the basis of what we are familiar with, leaving other important things aside. That is, we give disproportionate attention to the information that is available to us. But there are many other things that we may not be familiar with that may be much more important.[29] This bias is very noticeable in the case of speciesism. Most people are unaware of the reality of animal exploitation or the situation of animals in the wild. When they think of animals, what comes to their mind are the ones they more often see, like dogs and cats, or animals in TV documentaries. As a result, they have completely unrepresentative ideas of what the real situation of animals is. This also happens, even if to a lesser degree, with animal advocates, especially when they think of animals in the wild. In addition, this bias is also important in that it distorts our appreciation of the importance of the future. We of course do not have any experience of what will happen in the future. But we also are not familiar with discussions of its importance and of the risks that very bad outcomes end up occurring. As a result, we tend to think it's an irrelevant issue.

Finally, another bias leads us to consider problems as less important if their effects are difficult to calculate, or to think that the actions we can take are more of a priority if it is easier to foresee their effects.[30] This is not correct. It may well be that a certain problem is much more important than another one even if it is harder us to calculate precisely how best to address it.

This bias is very noticeable in the case of our attitudes toward the future. The long-term effects of our actions—especially the very long-term ones—are very difficult to estimate. It is easier to estimate the immediate or short-term effects of what we do. This leads us to consider the latter more important. But this need not be the case at all.[31] When we reach that conclusion only on the basis of what is easier to estimate, we are victims of the cognitive bias we are considering here. As mentioned above, even if we don't know what the future is going to be like, we can make informed estimates about how it may be if things go one way or another, and about how we can influence it for better or worse to a greater or lesser extent. And this is what is really relevant.

Unfortunately, these and other biases also confuse us when deciding on concrete ways to help others in need. Nevertheless, we can be aware of them and make an effort to minimize their impact.[32] It is possible to reflect on and improve our ways of doing advocacy work. As we have seen above, this is what should lead us to defend all sentient animals, and not just a few. And it is also what shows us that we can act better if, instead of doing activism on our own, we get involved with other organizations, encourage others to get involved in advocacy, research how to improve our effectiveness, or contribute financially to make other people's advocacy better. In this way, by becoming better informed and by thinking about both the ends we seek and the means to achieve them, we can accomplish the best results for the animals, which can make a huge difference.

Not giving up in addressing the moral consideration of animals

One of the main risks for the animals that need our help is us becoming discouraged and demoralized, especially if this leads to us giving up. It is important to bear this in mind. If those who are aware of what speciesism means do nothing about it, the situation of those it harms is unlikely to change.

But it's also possible that we don't give up totally, yet end up doing much less for animals than we could. We may be convinced that we must fight against speciesism, and yet our hopelessness may lead us to pursue only unnecessarily modest goals. For example, we may resign ourselves to trying to help only a few animals instead of all of them. Although everything we do for animals will be commendable and positive for them, there is no reason to help them just a little when we could do so much more. In fact, to help them less than we could doesn't seem the right thing to do.

In other cases, people do not want animals to be harmed but believe that it will be difficult to convince the rest of society to stop such harms out of a concern for animals themselves. An example of this may occur when people promote plant-based foods without mentioning that using these products avoids harming animals (instead arguing only, for example, that such food is healthier). It can certainly be convenient to remind people that veganism is healthy, and there is also no problem in pointing out that it can help to prevent certain diseases. In fact, as we have already seen, someone who doesn't consume animals may be in a better position to reject speciesism. This is why it can be so important to provide the means for people to live more easily without exploiting animals. In addition, there are specific cases in which arguing in this way, when addressing not a wide audience but just a small group of decision makers, can work to bring about small-scale change on the part of some institution (for example, to include a vegan option on a school menu). In these cases, if the arguments used to convince those decision makers are only addressed to them, and not to a wider audience, it is of little relevance whether they are the ones that work best to achieve a change in the public's attitude toward nonhuman animals. However, when we are trying to get a message across to a wide audience, there are other things at stake than the specific behavioral change that is being sought. Choosing to spread one message instead of another has other effects as well, as it helps certain ideas to spread in society, which can make a better future for sentient beings possible.

Something to be careful about is that health-based arguments against consuming animals can have counterproductive effects.[33] There is a widespread perception in our societies that certain animal products are less healthy than others. For example, it is often said that eating the meat obtained from animals such as pigs or cows is worse for your health than eating a chicken or a fish. From the animals' point of view, we would say instead that all animals can feel and suffer. But if we convey the idea that the consumption of certain animal products is harmful to one's health, some people may end up giving up the consumption of large animals such as pigs and cows, and increasing their consumption of chickens and fish, which are smaller. Given the different sizes of these animals, this change in diet would mean many more animals being exploited and killed. Not that this will necessarily happen, there will be many cases where this reaction will not occur. But there will also be other cases where it does, so we are in a risky situation here. Moreover, the consumption of insects has also been promoted as an alternative to vertebrate products.[34] This may have disastrous effects in terms of the number of individual animals that would be killed.

Apart from this, there is another factor here that is even more important. Speciesist attitudes are not only manifested in the different forms of animal exploitation but they also have other very negative consequences we have already seen above. These include a lack of willingness to act in favor of nonhuman animals and a disregard for the situation of animals in the wild and the risks of new situations of mass suffering occurring in the future. Changing all this requires going beyond reducing animal exploitation, and increasing concern for all sentient beings. Not eating animals makes it easier to have an attitude of respect toward them, but it doesn't cause it automatically. At least one more thing is needed. It is something very simple: that there is some reason that moves us to question our speciesist attitudes. And the rejection of speciesism will only spread in our society if there are people who speak out against it. Again, this is not to hide the fact that vegan eating can be beneficial to one's health. But neither should it make us forget the need to advocate the rejection of speciesism and to promote concern for all sentient beings. If those who oppose speciesism do not say anything against it, no one will. And the result is that it will take a lot longer for society to reject speciesism.

We shouldn't be deterred by the fear of failing in this task. We need to look at the progress made for animals and put it in perspective. It is only a few decades since the word "speciesism" began to be used. And there are now millions of people around the world who defend animals. The number of vegans, which was very small until the 1970s, has multiplied dramatically since then. Likewise, the idea that we should help animals in need in the wild would have been received with surprise by many people until a few years ago. But today, more and more people see that it makes perfect sense as the proper ethical response to the suffering of animals in the wild. So, we can conclude that we have made enormous progress, although it is necessary to see this in perspective. Major change rarely happens overnight. If we consider the discrimination and injustices suffered by humans, we can see that these are questioned and eroded only over long periods of time. It's a slow process, with many ups and downs, in which there are steps forward as well as setbacks. In the case of speciesism, however, we are seeing very rapid progress. So we have reasons not to give up, but to keep working to attain further progress in the future.

Let's achieve a different future for all sentient beings

In this chapter we have seen that animals need our help. This is true both for those exploited by humans and for those living in the wild. There is much we can do for them. If they were human beings, we would surely do so without hesitation. That is why the arguments against helping other animals only hold if we accept speciesism.

We have seen that this means taking action and getting involved in this cause to the best of our abilities. A change is needed not only on an individual level by each of us but also on a social level. And it is important that in achieving this we think not only of those who need our help today but of all those who will live in the future, who also depend on the progress we make today.

Speciesism, with all its terrible consequences, is not something untouchable and unassailable. On the contrary, it is something against which it is possible to build a better alternative. We can do so by putting aside our biases and simply thinking about how to act in the best way for animals.[35]

Notes

1　This is, for example, claimed in Carruthers, *The animal issue*, where it is argued that it is entirely acceptable that not to spend any of our free time helping others, and, at the same time, those who help animals are criticized for doing that instead of helping human beings.

2　The argument that as long as nonhuman animals are morally considerable even speciesists should reject their current use as resources has been made in Francione, *Introduction to animal rights* and Engel Jr., M. (2001) "The mere considerability of animals", *Acta Analytica*, 16, 89–107.

3　See for instance Jamieson, D. (1990) "Rights, justice, and duties to provide assistance: A critique of Regan's theory of rights", *Ethics*, 100, 349–362 and Hadley, J. (2006) "The duty to aid nonhuman animals in dire need", *Journal of Applied Philosophy*, 23, 445–451.

4　This page includes many examples of cases of helping wild animals in need of aid: Animal Ethics (2019 [2016]) "Helping animals in the wild", *Wild animal suffering, Animal Ethics*, http://animal-ethics.org/helping-animals-in-the-wild. More information can be found in Kirkwood, J. K. & Sainsbury, A. W. (1996) "Ethics of interventions for the welfare of free-living wild animals", *Animal Welfare*, 5, 235–243; Bovenkerk, B.; Stafleu, F.; Tramper, R.; Vorstenbosch, J. & Brom, F. W. A. (2003) "To act or not to act? Sheltering animals from the wild: A pluralistic account of a conflict between animal and environmental ethics", *Ethics, Place and Environment*, 6, 13–26; Anderson, A. & Anderson, L. (2006) *Rescued: Saving animals from disaster*, New World Library: Novato; Delahay, R. J.; Smith, G. C. & Hutchings, M. R. (2009) *Management of disease in wild mammals*, Dordrecht: Springer and ONE News (2015) "Beached whale swims off into the sunset after six hours beached in Auckland", *OneNewsNow*, August 26, http://tvnz.co.nz/one-news/new-zealand/beached-whale-swims-off-into-the-sunset-after-six-hours-in-auckland-q07559.html. Some rescue centers for wild animals have been created for conservationist purposes, not out of a concern for animals as sentient beings, but others have been established out of concern for animals themselves, regardless of their species.

5　See Goodall, J. (1986) *The chimpanzees of Gombe: Patterns of behavior*, Cambridge: Harvard University Press. On this, see also Mowat, F. (1987) *Woman in the mists: The story of Dian Fossey and the mountain gorillas of Africa*, London: Macdonald.

6　For a discussion of this issue, see Gruen, L.; Fultz, A. & Pruetz, J. (2013) "Ethical issues in African great ape field studies", *ILAR journal*, 54, 24–32.

7　See for instance Blancou, J.; Pastoret, P. P.; Brochier, B.; Thomas, I. & Bögel, K. (1988) "Vaccinating wild animals against rabies", *Reviews in Science Technology*, 10005–10013; Fausther-Bovendo, H.; Mulangu, S. & Sullivan, N. J. (2012) "Ebolavirus vaccines for humans and apes", *Current Opinion in Virology*, 2, 324–329 or Garrido, J. M. et al. (2011) "Protection against tuberculosis in Eurasian wild boar vaccinated with heat-inactivated Mycobacterium bovis", *PLoS One*, 6, 1–10. The COVID-19 pandemic has increased interest in safeguarding the health of wild animals to prevent the zoonotic spread of new diseases (not just those caused by coronaviruses like SARS-CoV-2, but also many others). This may be helpful for many animals in the wild, although not for reasons focused on their own interests. This is addressed for instance in Martin, A. K. & Dürr, S. (2021) "Preventing zoonotic emerging disease outbreaks: the need to complement one health with ethical considerations", *Journal of Applied Animal Ethics Research*, 1, 1–11 and Sebo, J. (2022) *Saving animals, saving ourselves: Why animals matter for pandemics, climate change, and other catastrophes*, New York: Oxford University Press.

8 See Peterson, C. & Messmer, T. A. (2007) "Effects of winter-feeding on mule deer in northern Utah", *Journal of Wildlife Management*, 71, 1440–1445 or CVB News Service (2012) "Forest officials arranging food for wild animals in Jammu and Kashmir", *News Hour India*, YouTube, http://youtube.com/watch?v=fshd_WXDJJY.

9 This happens because of the following. Some animals reproduce by having one or a few offspring. They have relatively high survival rates. But these are a really small minority in the wild. The overwhelming majority of animals reproduce by having huge numbers of offspring. Some rodents can have over a hundred offspring, and there are reptiles, amphibians, and invertebrates that can lay hundreds or thousands of eggs. Some fish can lay millions of eggs in each clutch. However, in populations that remain relatively stable, only one animal on average survives for each mother or father. The rest of them die, in many cases not long after coming into existence. And they often die very painful deaths (from lack of food, for example). This means that a large proportion of animals have no or almost no possibility of enjoying anything in their lives. But they do suffer the pain that normally accompanies their deaths. This is why their lives often have more suffering than happiness. Usually, this is not appreciated because when we think of animals in nature, large adult vertebrates (especially mammals) come to mind. But these are not really representative: the vast majority of animals that live in the wild are invertebrates or small fish that are very young. See Tomasik, B. (2015 [2009]) "The importance of wild-animal suffering", *Relations: Beyond Anthropocentrism*, 3, 133–152; Faria, C. (2016) *Animal ethics goes wild: The problem of wild animal suffering and intervention in nature*, PhD thesis, Pompeu Fabra University; Horta, O, (2017) "Animal suffering in nature: The case for intervention", *Environmental Ethics*, 39, 261–279; Hecht, L. (2021) "The importance of considering age when quantifying wild animals' welfare", *Biological Reviews*, 96, a. 12769 and Soryl, A. A.; Moore, A. J.; Seddon, P. J. & King, M. R. (2021) "The case for welfare biology", *Journal of Agricultural and Environmental Ethics*, 34, 1–25.

For a general introduction to this question, see in particular Animal Ethics (2020a) *Introduction to wild animal suffering: A guide to the issues*, Oakland: Animal Ethics, http://animal-ethics.org/introduction-wild-animal-suffering and (2020b) *Wild animal suffering video course, Animal Ethics*, http://animal-ethics.org/wild-animal-suffering-video-course.

Regarding some of the factors why animals suffer and die in the wild, see also Cooper J. E. (1999 [1982]) "Physical injury", in Fairbrother A.; Locke L. N. & Hoff G. L. (eds.) *Noninfectious disease of wildlife*, Ames: Iowa State University Press, 157–172; Wobeser, G. A. (2005) *Essentials of disease in wild animals*, New York: John Wiley and Sons; Zimmerman, D. (2009) "Starvation and malnutrition in wildlife", *Indiana Wildlife Disease News*, 4, 1–7; Martin, T. E. (2011) "The cost of fear", *Science*, 334, 1353–1354; Bunke, M.; Alexander, M. E.; Dick, J. T. A.; Hatcher, M. J.; Paterson, R. & Dunn, A. M. (2015) "Eaten alive: Cannibalism is enhanced by parasites", *Royal Society Open Science*, 2, 140369 and Gutiérrez, J. & de Miguel, J. (forthcoming) "Fires in nature: Review of the challenges for wild animals", *European Journal of Ecology*.

10 See Sagoff, M. (1984) "Animal liberation and environmental ethics: Bad marriage, quick divorce. *Osgoode Hall Law Journal*, 22, 297–307 and Rolston III, H. (1992) "Disvalues in nature", *The Monist*, 75, 250–278. The view that environmentalists should not agree with helping wild animals is challenged in Cunha, L. C. (2015) "If natural entities have intrinsic value, should we then abstain from helping animals who are victims of natural processes?", *Relations: Beyond Anthropocentrism*, 3, 51–63.

11 Among the different works on this issue, see Morris, M. C. & Thornhill, R. H. (2006) "Animal liberationist responses to non-anthropogenic animal suffering", *Worldviews*, 10, 355–379; Nussbaum, M. C. (2006) *Frontiers of justice: Disability, nationality, species membership*, Cambridge: Harvard University Press, ch. 6; Sözmen, B. I. (2013) "Harm in the wild: Facing non-human suffering in nature", *Ethical Theory and Moral Practice*, 16, 1075–1088; Pearce, D. (2015) "A welfare state for elephants? A case study of compassionate stewardship", *Relations: Beyond Anthropocentrism*, 3, 133–152; Faria, C. & Paez, E. (2015) "Animals in need: The problem of wild animal suffering and intervention in nature", *Relations: Beyond Anthropocentrism*, 3, 7–13; Cochrane, A. (2018) *Sentientist politics: A theory of global inter-species justice*, Oxford: Oxford University Press; Salazar, M. (2019) "Why is welfare biology important?", *Blog, Animal Charity Evaluators*, http://animalcharityevaluators.org/blog/why-is-welfare-biology-important; Johannsen, K. (2020) *Wild animal ethics: The moral and political problem of wild animal suffering*, New York: Routledge—summarized in (forthcoming) "Defending *Wild animal ethics*", *Philosophia*—and Jalagania, B. (2021) "Wild animals and duties of assistance", *Journal of Agricultural and Environmental Ethics*, 34, 1–15. See also Dorado, D. (2015) "Ethical interventions in the wild. An annotated bibliography", *Relations: Beyond Anthropocentrism*, 3, 219–238, as well as Animal Ethics, *Introduction to wild animal suffering* and *Wild animal suffering video course*.
12 Concerning helping wild animals in extreme weather events, see Kapembwa, J. & Wells, J. (2016) "Climate justice for wildlife: A rights-based account", in Garmendia da Trindade, G. & Woodhall, A. (eds.) *Intervention or protest: Acting for nonhuman animals*, Wilmington: Vernon, 359–390; Palmer, C. (2021) "Assisting wild animals vulnerable to climate change: Why ethical strategies diverge", *Journal of Applied Philosophy*, 38, 179–195; see also Sebo, *Saving animals, saving ourselves*. Concerning wild animals in urban areas, see Animal Ethics (2021) *Investigating the welfare of wild animals in urban environments*, Oakland: Animal Ethics, http://animal-ethics.org/welfare-urban-animal-ecology.
13 In fact, we should note that there could be as many as 10^{20} sentient animals in nature, many of which need our help. See Tomasik, B. (2015 [2009]) "How many wild animals are there?", *Essays on Reducing Suffering*, http://reducing-suffering.org/how-many-wild-animals-are-there.
14 See Faria, C. & Horta, O. (2019) "Welfare biology", in Fischer, B. (ed.) *Routledge handbook of animal ethics*, New York: Routledge, 455–466 and Soryl et al., "The case for welfare biology".
15 See Animal Ethics, *Introduction to wild animal suffering*.
16 On how equally sentient animals (sometimes the same animals) are considered and treated differently, see Taylor, N. & Signal, T. D. (2009) "Pet, pest, profit: Isolating differences in attitudes towards the treatment of animals", *Anthrozoös*, 22, 129–135 and O'Sullivan, S. (2011) *Animals, equality and democracy*, Basingstoke: Palgrave Macmillan; see also Safran Foer, J. (2009) *Eating animals*, London: Penguin Books, pp. 24–29; the question is also examined in this paper (although its title suggest an unrealistic optimism): Wolfensohn, S. & Honess, P. (2007) "Laboratory animal, pet animal, farm animal, wild animal: Which gets the best deal?" *Animal Welfare*, 16, 117–123. Lack of concern for animals due to their size and due to reasons related to aesthetic preference or scientific interest in them is explained in Morton, D. B. (2010 [1998]) "Sizeism", in Bekoff, M. (ed.) *Encyclopedia of animal rights and animal welfare*, Santa Barbara: Greenwood, 534–525 and in Feber, R. E.; Raebel, E. M.; D'cruze, N.; Macdonald, D. W. & Baker, S. E. (2016) "Some animals are more equal than others: Wild animal welfare in the media", *BioScience*, 67, 62–72.

17 Another example is the reintroduction of predators to areas where they had been absent (perhaps because they were extinct before). See Horta, "The ethics of the ecology of fear against the nonspeciesist paradigm". This has been done in certain areas with wolves. This measure is negative for the predators themselves, that are captured, separated from their families, and transported to a new and unknown place for them. For obvious reasons, it's also negative for the animals they prey on, that from then on live with fear of predators and the serious threat of being killed by them.

18 The idea that there is a stable ecological balance, which many people still have in mind today, is not accurate. On the contrary, different ecosystems are in a continuous process of change. Conserving an ecosystem means stopping that process of change at a certain point that we may find aesthetically or scientifically appealing. In contrast to this abstract idea, the suffering and death of animals is very real and concrete. See Shelton, "Killing animals that don't fit in"; Dorado, D. (2015) *El conflicto entre la ética animal y la ética ambiental: bibliografía analítica*, PhD thesis, Madrid: Carlos III University; Mosquera, J. (2015) "The harm they inflict when values conflict: Why diversity does not matter", *Relations: Beyond Anthropocentrism*, 3, 65–77 and Abbate, C. E. & Fischer, B. (2019) "Don't demean 'invasives': Conservation and wrongful species discrimination", *Animals*, 9, a. 871.

19 We have seen above that some films and TV series such as *Blade Runner, Artificial Intelligence, Tron, Westworld* or *Black Mirror*, among many others, show this in fiction, by presenting situations in which it would make perfect sense to worry about these entities. But the truth is that this topic is not mere idle speculation, but a very important issue in which serious scientific and philosophical work has been done for decades. On this, it may be interesting to see, in addition to the texts already cited in the notes to Chapter 2, these articles: Metzinger, T. (2015) "What if they need to suffer?", *Edge*, http://edge.org/response-detail/26091; Tomasik, B. (2015) "Why digital sentience is relevant to animal activists", *Blog, Animal Charity Evaluators*, http://animalcharityevaluators.org/blog/why-digital-sentience-is-relevant-to-animal-activists; Beckers, S. (2017) "AAAI: An argument against artificial intelligence", in Müller, V. (ed.), *Philosophy and theory of artificial intelligence*, Berlin: Springer, 235–247; Sotala, K. & Gloor, L. (2017) "Superintelligence as a cause or cure for risks of astronomical suffering", *Informatica*, 41, 501–505; Gualeni, S. (2020) "Artificial beings worthy of moral consideration in virtual environments: An analysis of ethical viability", *Journal for Virtual Worlds Research*, 13, 1–11 and Harris, J. (2021) "Prioritization questions for artificial sentience", *Blog, Sentience Institute*, http://sentienceinstitute.org/blog/prioritization-questions-for-artificial-sentience.

20 It is sometimes believed that we should accept a conservationist approach and not one focused on promoting what is best for animals because many discoveries in biology support conservationist positions. In reality, this assumption mixes the knowledge of certain facts with the moral positions that we can have. Biology is a field of knowledge that can guide us both if our goal is to preserve more or less abstract entities such as ecosystems or to help concrete sentient beings such as animals. We can apply our knowledge in biology for different purposes.

21 See Milburn, J. (2018) "Death-free dairy? The ethics of clean milk", *Journal of Agricultural and Environmental Ethics*, 31, 261–279 and Reese Anthis, J. (2018) *The end of animal farming: How scientists, entrepreneurs, and activists are building an animal-free food system*, Boston: Beacon Press.

22 See Cochrane, A. (2013) "From human rights to sentient rights", *Critical Review of International Social and Political Philosophy*, 16, 655–675. It is sometimes said that nonhuman animals cannot have rights because they are not legal persons.

Legal persons are those who, according to the law, can file a complaint, take other legal action, and ultimately have legal rights. This idea is based on the belief that only human beings can be legal persons. But this is a mistake. The word "person" has different meanings. A legal person is not the same as a human being. In fact, there are many legal persons that are not human beings. For example, companies, associations, and public bodies are legal persons. There is nothing to prevent all sentient beings from being recognized as legal persons. See for instance Bryant, T. L. (2008) "Sacrificing the sacrifice of animals: Legal personhood for animals, the status of animals as property, and the presumed primacy of humans," *Rutgers Law Journal*, 39, 247–330; Francione, *Animals as persons* and Dyschkant, A. (2015) "Legal personhood: How we are getting it wrong", *University of Illinois Law Review*, 2015, 2075–2109.

23 See on this for instance Cordeiro-Rodrigues, L. (2020) "The ethics of prioritisation and advocacy dilemmas: Bullfighting or veganism?", *South African Journal of Philosophy*, 39, 63–78.

24 This is explained in Baumann, T. (2017a) "S-risks: An introduction", *Reducing Risks of Future Suffering*, http://s-risks.org/intro and (2017b) "How can we reduce s-risks?", *Center for Reducing Suffering*, http://centerforreducingsuffering.org/how-can-we-reduce-s-risks and also in Althaus, D. & Gloor, L. (2019 [2016]) "Reducing risks of astronomical suffering: A neglected priority", *Center on Long-Term Risk*, http://longtermrisk.org/reducing-risks-of-astronomical-suffering-a-neglected-priority.

25 Another historical example of the concurrence of these three factors affecting both humans and other animals can be found in the emergence of contemporary weapon technology. A well-known account of other examples of risks of future suffering potentially affecting human and nonhuman beings in the not-so-far future is Harari, Y. N. (2017 [2015]) *Homo deus: A brief history of tomorrow*, New York: Harper. For an example of a risk of suffering further in time that has begun to be discussed recently see O'Brien, G. D. (2022) "Directed panspermia, wild animal suffering, and the ethics of world-creation", *Journal of Applied Philosophy*, 39, 87–102. In relation to the dangers of an increase in technology coming faster than an increase in moral consideration for other sentient beings, see Tomasik, B. (2015 [2013]) "Differential intellectual progress as a positive-sum project", *Center on Long-Term Risk*, https://longtermrisk.org/differential-intellectual-progress-as-a-positive-sum-project.

26 Desvouges, W. F.; Johnson, R.; Dunford, R.; Boyle, K.; Hudson, S. & Wilson, K. N. (2010 [1992]) *Measuring non-use damages using contingent valuation: An experimental evaluation of accuracy*, Research Triangle Park: Research Triangle Institute. The question of the appreciation of scale, together with neglectedness and tractability is examined in MacAskill, W. (2015) *Doing good better: How effective altruism can help you make a difference*, New York: Gotham Books.

27 Nadeau, R.; Cloutier, E. & Guay, J. H. (1993) "New evidence about the existence of a bandwagon effect in the opinion formation process", *International Political Science Review*, 14, 203–213.

28 Wrenn, *A rational approach to animal rights*, p. 69.

29 Kahneman, D. (2011) *Thinking, fast and slow*, New York: Penguin, ch. 12–13.

30 Caviola, L.; Faulmüller, N.; Everett, J. A.; Savulescu, J. & Kahane, G. (2014) The evaluability bias in charitable giving: Saving administration costs or saving lives? *Judgment and Decision Making*, 9, 303–316.

31 Baumann, T. (2020) "Longtermism and animal advocacy", *Center for Reducing Suffering*, http://centerforreducingsuffering.org/longtermism-and-animal-advocacy, see also Greaves, H. & MacAskill, W. (2021) "The case for strong longtermism", *GPI working paper*, Oxford: Global Priorities Institute and Reese

Anthis, J. & Paez, E. (2021) "Moral circle expansion: A promising strategy to impact the far future", *Futures*, 130, a. 102756.

32 Perhaps this is most needed when it comes to having an open mind and being unafraid to revise our ideas in the light of new evidence. See on this Galef, J. (2021) *The scout mindset: Why some people see things clearly and others don't*, New York: Penguin. An example of this attitude I am talking about can be found in Leenaert, T. (2017) "10 vegan things I recently changed my mind about", *The Vegan Strategist*, http://veganstrategist.org/2017/01/16/10-vegan-things-i-recently-changed-my-mind-about.

33 This is argued for in Ball, M. (2014) *The accidental activist: Stories, speeches, articles, and interviews by Vegan Outreach's cofounder*, New York: Lantern, the argument was previously presented in Messina, G. (2011), "Bad news for red meat is bad news for chickens", *The Vegan RD*, http://theveganrd.com/2011/08/bad-news-for-red-meat-is-bad-news-for-chickens.

34 This is often done by claiming that eating insects can have a smaller environmental impact than the consumption of vertebrates, although it means killing many more animals. See for instance Zaraska, M. (2016) *Meathooked: The history and science of our 2.5-million-year obsession with meat*, New York: Basic Books, p. 189.

35 To learn more about the different issues addressed in this book, a large number of references can be found in Animal Ethics (2018) *Bibliographic lists*, *Animal Ethics*, http://animal-ethics.org/bibliographical-lists.

Chapter 7

Conclusion

Making a stand for a better world

How will our ways be seen in the future?

Imagine you had the chance to talk to people from the past, to people who lived centuries ago. It would be amazing, there would be a lot of interesting things to talk about with them. But we should bear in mind that many of those people thought very differently than we do today. Many in those times supported and considered normal and fair practices that caused immense amounts of suffering to many human beings throughout the world (conquest, genocide, slavery, servitude, etc.). Suppose you could talk to some of them. What would you say to them? Many would think that, in a situation like this, they would take the opportunity to reproach them for their behavior. They would make it clear to them that today we generally consider the acts they carried out to be totally unacceptable.

This, however, raises an interesting question: How do you think these people would take it? How do you think they would react?

Most of them would probably be quite shocked to find that out. They would never have imagined that subsequent generations would find their actions so abhorrent. This is not surprising. Most of them simply believed that, in the future, we would continue to think and act as we did then. However, societies have changed a great deal in the last few centuries, and continue to do so today.

This kind of social change has started to take place in the case of attitudes toward nonhuman animals too. There are undoubtedly still many people who aren't aware of the reasons not to discriminate against them. But things are changing. Thanks to the work of those who want a change for animals, more and more people are becoming aware of the case against speciesism. In the few decades since the word "speciesism" was first used incredible progress has been made. No one could have imagined in the middle of the 20th century that today millions of people would proudly say that they support the defense of animals and the end of discrimination against them. All indications are that this trend will continue to grow. If so, there may come a time when the majority will reject speciesism.

In light of this, we can ask ourselves the following question: how will our current disregard for animals of other species look in the future? What will people think about the harm we cause them on a regular basis? Is it possible that it will be seen as something terrible?

Most people would probably be quite shocked to find that out. They would never imagine that those who will live in the future will regard the way we act toward animals of other species as abhorrent. This is not surprising. Most people simply believe that, in the future, people will continue to think and act as they do now.

But, wait a minute, doesn't all this sound familiar? Haven't we read it before? Of course, we have. It's the same story that we read some paragraphs above, merely repeated. People in the future will judge our actions today similarly as we judge the actions of our ancestors in the past. And today, we are as incapable of realizing this as were the people who lived centuries ago.

How can something like this happen? Because when there are widespread injustices, they become difficult to recognize. It is common for those who benefit from them to find them totally justified. This explains why many societies throughout history (in some cases very recently) have acted in ways that seem terrible to us today. We saw this already in Chapter 1. And we also saw something else then: that it would be an extraordinary coincidence if today's generations were the first to do things right, and not to commit grave injustices and other horrible acts. It makes sense, then, to suspect that we are probably still engaging in very objectionable behaviors, even though many people do not see it.

In light of this, there are two possible ways of thinking about what might happen in the future.

It's possible that injustice will continue to face growing opposition. Those who think this can point to what our current moral views are in contrast to those of the past as evidence. This is how change occurs throughout history. Certain ideas and behaviors previously in place are challenged, first by small groups of people and then by many more. Then there comes a time when the new ways of thinking are accepted, and the old ways rejected. Perhaps this is what is happening now, or will happen, in the case of speciesism. What would that mean? It would mean that we have the opportunity to put ourselves on the right side of history. We can do this by abandoning the attitudes resulting from the prejudices and moral myopia of our time. All of this gives us reason to doubt our speciesist attitudes, and our resistance to abandoning them.

On the other hand, we may think that this vision is too optimistic. Moral progress is not assured. It's possible that in the future things will improve, but it's also possible that they will get worse. It might also happen that, despite significant improvement in some respects, things will get much, much worse in others. As we have seen in the previous chapter, there are non-negligible risks that the future may bring about very negative scenarios of massive suffering. We might be able to put an end to the current ways in which animals are exploited while new ways of harming defenseless sentient beings emerge. This gives us even stronger reasons to oppose speciesism, because as long as speciesism continues to exist, there will be a very real probability that such scenarios will occur.

Thus, we find that whether we maintain a more hopeful attitude toward the future or a more cautious one, we reach a similar conclusion: we need to promote respect for all sentient beings right away.

The arguments in favor of changing attitudes that this implies may be striking at first. But in reality, they are based on some very simple ideas with which most of us agree. We can look at them again, considering what we have been examining up to this point.

What this book has been about

The central idea put forward in the previous chapters is that we have good reason to start respecting animals and to stop discriminating against them. We have seen that there is no characteristic that distinguishes every human being without exception from all other animals. If only those with a certain level of intelligence were to be taken into account, for example, there would be human beings whom we would not have to respect. Few people would accept such a conclusion, and rightly so, for what matters for being respected is only that we can suffer and enjoy ourselves.

In addition to this, we have seen that those who harm and discriminate against animals would never want to be treated in the same way. If we were in the situation of animals of other species, we would be totally opposed to speciesism. It is therefore unfair to act toward them as we do today. But, besides this, there is another reason to respect those who can feel and suffer, which is actually the most important of all. That reason is, simply, that suffering is bad, and that being able to live without being harmed is good. And this is so regardless of the species of those who can suffer or enjoy.

This is a new idea. However, new ideas invite us to rethink things, due to which, we tend to reject them, even if we don't really know how to argue why. We often react to new ideas like this without reflecting on them. However, there are times when we do stop to think. In doing so, we begin to understand that the subject is more complex than we had thought at first. We see that there are reasons for this idea that had been overlooked. And so, sometimes gradually, sometimes quickly, we change our minds. We realize that our initial rejection of this idea was not justified.

This is what happens when we become aware that speciesism is, in fact, arbitrary discrimination. It would make sense for us to only care about human beings if other animals were mere objects. But that is not the case. They are sentient individuals, beings that can suffer and enjoy themselves. Just as our suffering harms us, theirs harms them. The pain that a human being suffers feels just as bad as the equally intense suffering of an animal of another species. And if death is a harm to human beings, it is also a harm to other sentient beings.

Putting our biases aside thus means no longer discriminating against animals that do not belong to our species. But the reality faced by animals contrasts dramatically with this. We saw this very clearly when we looked at the situation they are in. On land farms and in slaughterhouses, they live lives of absolute misery, and they suffer terrible deaths. The number of animals that suffer this fate is so enormous that it is very difficult to conceive of. And this number pales in comparison with those that are fished and raised on fish farms, who also suffer far more than is commonly thought, and are also deprived of their lives. It is common for other exploited animals to suffer a similar fate or worse. This is becoming especially worrying in the case of invertebrates, as the numbers of them that are harmed for human use as resources are huge and increasing.

Thus, stopping harming animals means not exploiting them anymore. At first glance, this may seem very difficult. But it's easier than it seems. People who find it difficult to make the transition to a way of living without participating in animal exploitation have different options to do so. With a little bit of willpower, it's perfectly achievable. And for animals, it's a crucial step.

It is true that there are some drawbacks to not using animals, but these are trivial compared to the harms they suffer if we use them. Remember what the real price of consuming animal products is. For every brief moment that we enjoy tasting them, animals endure enormous amounts of suffering, and are deprived of their lives. This means that every bite we take when we eat animal products is actually a bite of their life. Let's also remember the example of the red button. When we press it, we get a pleasant feeling in return for causing enormous suffering and killing animals. That example is in fact real; it reflects what happens to nonhuman animals every day. But we can live without exploiting animals. This is something we must consider if we are not indifferent to the harm we are causing them.

There are some people who don't care about this. But there are many others who really don't want to harm animals, but also don't want to stop using the products of that harm. Those who are in this situation face a moral dilemma. One way to solve it is to try to find some kind of justification for animal exploitation. But we saw that none of the arguments used for this purpose succeeds. Because, in the end, the issue can be presented in a simple way. We can avoid harming and killing animals. Why continue to do so?

In addition, we also saw that to stop discriminating against animals means something else: to give them our help when we can. The suffering of animals matters in all circumstances, including when they suffer and die not because we humans have caused them harm, but for any other reasons. That is why not discriminating means not only not harming but also helping. And there are very different circumstances where it is perfectly possible to do so. This is true not only for domesticated animals but also for those living in nature. Contrary to what we might perhaps think, these animals do not live idyllic lives, but quite the opposite. And there are different ways in which we can help them. Fortunately, this is already happening, as we have also seen.

It is also clear that we can help animals in another way too: by becoming involved in doing advocacy work for them. Thousands of people around the world are already doing so. The help of every one of them, including yours, can be crucial. Because work against speciesism has only recently begun, what we do now is going to have a very important impact. Moreover, success in a cause like this is not an all-or-nothing matter. Unfortunately, it is impossible to save all animals. But we can save many. Our help can make a difference to a large number of them. Not only for those living today, but above all for those who will be able to live in the future, which will be many more. That is why the contribution each of us can make is so, so important.

Choosing to side with animals

What we have just seen is the reason why, toward the end of the introduction to this book, it was said that with every person who seriously questions speciesism, a step forward is taken. This is because each person has the power to influence and change the world in which they find themselves. The introduction also pointed out that that person could perhaps be you. At this point, you may already know if that is the case. Maybe you knew it before, or you may have discovered it now. But in fact this isn't what matters. What matters is that if you really are that person, it means that you have also become aware that you have to do something about it. You have to make a stand for animals.

Until today, there have been people who have done so but who believed that they were alone in this cause. Maybe you too have thought this at some point, or you are worried about it now. But, as we saw in the introduction, this is not the case. We are not a small group; we are many people throughout the world. If we don't know the others who are with us in this cause this is not because they don't exist, but because we live in many different places. So, if you ever think that you are alone in the fight, remember that you are not. You are actually part of something much bigger that is growing and changing the world.

Also, remember that there is someone else beside you: the animals. When you join their defense and reject speciesism, you are no longer alone. You may not see them all the time, but you know the animals are there. Suffering, dying... needing your help. That's why, even if they don't know it, the animals will always be with you.

Sometimes we may wonder if it is really worth getting involved in this cause instead of just going on with our lives. In those moments, it can be useful to remember that many other people have also been in your situation, and have taken the step. But it is also important above all to remember what the animals we can help are going through. We can think of the calves that at this very moment are crying in the compartments where they are confined. Or of the pigs being boiled alive. Or of some of the other animals dying of hunger and cold that we could have helped. Or of any of the animals whose situation shocked you when you learned what their lives and deaths are like. We can think about what they are facing, and ask ourselves if we really want to look the other way and fail them.

Fighting for what's worth fighting for

Being the kind of person we would like to be

Many people like to identify with characters from the movies they see or the books they read. This often happens when such characters have attitudes that we appreciate, for example, when they fight to defend those who need their help. In those cases they often face great challenges and hardships. And often they also face the contempt of other people appearing in those movies or books. But few people think those characters we like act foolishly and naively for not giving up their struggle. We don't believe that what they should do is simply resign themselves and behave like the rest. On the contrary, we think they are doing the right thing. And we think that the characters who don't care about the suffering of others act wrongly.

The question, then, is: if so many people think this when they see a movie or read a novel, how come they don't have that same attitude in real life as well?

Many people imagine that if they were in the situation of the characters they identify with, they'd act as those characters do. They think they just never have the chance to. However, in light of what we have seen, we may conclude that this is not really so. The struggle for the victims of speciesism gives us that possibility. We can do the right thing by defending nonhuman animals. Doing so does not mean being an idealistic or naive person. Rather, when we do so, we take control of our life and use it to defend those who need our help.

Each of us is the main character in a story: the story of our life. The question is: What will that story be like? We have the possibility of writing it in many different ways, each of which means that we will leave a different legacy. That legacy will still be here, long after we are gone. It's worth thinking about this and considering what we're going to do for those who need us to take a stand for them.

It's in our hands to leave as our legacy a better world for all sentient beings, both for those who live now and for those who will exist in the future. There's a lot we can do for them. We can start today.

Index

Note: Page number followed by "n" refer to end notes.